Determining Value

PEARSON
Education

We work with leading authors to develop the strongest educational materials in business and finance, bringing cutting-edge thinking and best learning practice to a global market.

Under a range of well-known imprints, including Financial Times Prentice Hall, we craft high-quality print and electronic publications which help readers to understand and apply their content, whether studying or at work.

To find out more about the complete range of our publishing, please visit us on the World Wide Web at: www.pearsoned.co.uk

Determining Value
Valuation Models and Financial Statements

Richard Barker

Judge Institute of Management
University of Cambridge

Prentice Hall
FINANCIAL TIMES

An imprint of **Pearson Education**
Harlow, England • London • New York • Boston • San Francisco • Toronto • Sydney • Singapore • Hong Kong
Tokyo • Seoul • Taipei • New Delhi • Cape Town • Madrid • Mexico City • Amsterdam • Munich • Paris • Milan

Pearson Education Limited
Edinburgh Gate
Harlow
Essex CM20 2JE
England

and Associated Companies throughout the world

Visit us on the World Wide Web at:
www.pearsoned.co.uk

First published 2001

ISBN-10: 0-273-63979-X
ISBN-13: 978-0-273-63979-4

British Library Cataloguing-in-Publication Data
A catalogue record for this book is available from the British Library

Library of Congress Cataloguing-in-Publication Data
Barker, Richard, 1968–
    Determining value : valuation models and financial statements / Richard Barker.
       p. cm.
    Includes bibliographical references and index.
    ISBN 0-273-63979-X
    1. Securities—Prices. 2. Dividends. I. Title.
  HG4028.V3 B198 2001
    332.63'2—dc21   2001021531

10 9 8 7 6 5
07 06

Typeset in 9.5/12.5pt stone serif by 35
Printed by Bell & Bain Ltd., Glasgow

Contents

Contents

Author's acknowledgements

My interest in the subject of valuation models and financial statements was inspired, directly or indirectly, by a number of people. I was introduced to the notion of shareholder value by Alan Spall at ICI, who recommended Alfred Rappaport's excellent book on the subject. My interest was extended further by reading Bill Beaver's book on financial reporting, which opened up some of the complexities of linking financial statement data to share prices. Meanwhile, David Damant, David Tweedie and others provided valuable insight and access to stock market practice. Above all, a succession of conversations with Geoff Whittington, taking place over a number of years, has deepened my understanding of the subject matter of this book. I am also extremely grateful that he took the time and trouble to read the entire manuscript carefully, giving (as ever) insightful and supportive feedback.

Additional help with this book has come from a range of people. I am particularly grateful to the following, each of whom provided valuable feedback: Allan Barton, Hal Bierman, Steve Cooper, Alan Gregory, Clive Lennox, Maureen McNichols, Dag Michalsen, Greg Milano, Tom Musto, David Myddelton, John Pointon, Andy Stark, Mathias Strohfeldt and Martin Walker. Needless to say, any remaining errors are my own.

Much of the work on this book was completed while I was a Visiting Scholar at Stanford University's Graduate School of Business. This was an excellent environment in which to work. I am indebted to many people at Stanford, but none more so than Bill Beaver, who kindly hosted my visit and was generous with his time. Beyond the campus, all four generations of the Keesling family made my time in California extremely enjoyable and worthwhile.

My other home in writing this book has been Cambridge. I would like to acknowledge my immediate colleagues in finance and accounting, Robin Chatterjee, Gishan Dissanaike, Bart Lambrecht and Geoff Meeks. I am also grateful for the support and encouragement of senior colleagues at the Judge Institute of Management, namely Sandra Dawson and Michael Dempster, who have been enthusiastic about this project despite it taking me away from Cambridge for a significant period of time. Thanks are due also to our MBA and MPhil students, who have had a considerable positive influence on these pages.

No book is complete without the editorial and marketing skills of the publishers. I am delighted that this book is in the hands of the global market leader in educational publishing, Pearson Education. In particular, I am grateful to the acquisitions editor, Jacqueline Senior, the desk editor, Louise Lakey, and the sales team, including Steve McGill.

Finally, there are two personal acknowledgements I would like to make. The first is to my parents, to whom I am grateful always. The second is to my wife Carol. Thank you for everything, this book is dedicated to you.

Publisher's acknowledgements

The publisher's would like to thank the following for permission to reproduce copyright material:

Figure 2.1 from *Irrational Exuberance*, published by Princeton University Press (Shiller, R.J. 2000); Figure 4.1 and Table 4.5 from *Financial Analysts Journal*, March–April, copyright, 1953, Association for Investment Management and Research, reproduced and republished from *Financial Analysts Journal* with permission from the Association for Investment Management and Research, all rights reserved (Molodovsky, N. 1953); Figure 4.2 from *Financial Analysts Journal*, May–June, copyright, 1998, Association for Investment Management and Research, reproduced and republished from *Financial Analysts Journal* with permission from the Association for Investment Management and Research, all rights reserved (Danielson, M. 1998); Figure 4.4 from *Financial Analysts Journal*, March–April, copyright, 1994, Association for Investment Management and Research, reproduced and republished from *Financial Analysts Journal* with permission from the Association for Investment Management and Research, all rights reserved (Leibowitz, M. and Kogelman, S. 1994); Table 4.8 from *Financial Analysts Journal*, July–August, copyright, 1978, Association for Investment Management and Research, reproduced and republished from *Financial Analysts Journal* with permission from the Association for Investment Management and Research, all rights reserved (Beaver, W.H. and Morse, D. 1978); Table 5.14 from *Financial Shenanigans: How to Detect Accounting Gimmicks and Fraud in Financial Reports*, published by and reproduced with permission of The McGraw-Hill Companies (Schilit, H.M. 1993); Tables 5.15, 5.16, 5.17 from *2000 Illustrative Financial Statements*, published by KPMG International, www.kpmg.co.uk (2000); Table 7.4 from FASB Special Report, *Reporting Financial Performance: Current Developments and Future Directions*, is copyrighted by the Financial Accounting Standards Board, 401 Merritt 7, P.O. Box 5116, Norwalk, Connecticut 06856-5116, USA, this table is reprinted with permission, complete copies of this document are available from the FASB (Johnson, L.T. and Lennard, A. 1998); Table 7.5 from *Accounting Horizons* Vol. 12 No. 3, American Accounting Association (Johnson, L.T. and Petrone, K.R. 1998); Figure 10.1 and Table 10.5 reprinted with the permission of The Free Press, a Division of Simon & Schuster, Inc., from *Creating Shareholder Value: A Guide for Managers and Investors*, revised and expanded edition by Alfred Rappaport, copyright © 1986, 1998 by Alfred Rappaport (Rappaport, A. 1998); Tables 10.7, 10.8, 10.9 and 10.10 from *CFROI Valuation: A Total System Approach to Valuing the Firm*, reprinted by permission of Butterworth Heinemann Publishers, a division of Reed Educational & Professional Publishing Ltd (Madden, B.J. 1999); Extract from the *Financial Times*, 8 April 2000 © Robert J. Shiller.

We are grateful to the *Financial Times Limited* for permission to reprint extracts from the following issues:

29 March 2000; 8 April 2000; 12 April 2000; 28 April 2000; 2 May 2000; 11 May 2000; 16 May 2000; 23 May 2000; 26 May 2000; 31 May 2000; 6 June 2000; 23 June 2000; 24 June 2000; 12 July 2000; 14 July 2000 (3 extracts); 18 July 2000 (2 extracts); 20 July 2000; 27 July 2000; 28 July 2000 (2 extracts); 31 July 2000; 2 August 2000; 4 August 2000 (2 extracts); 7 August 2000; 8 August 2000 (2 extracts); 15 August 2000 (2 extracts); 18 August 2000; 25 August 2000; 15 September 2000; 25 October 1999; 18 October 2000; 19 October 1996; 5 November 2000; 18 November 1999 © *Financial Times*.

Whilst every effort has been made to trace the owners of copyright material, in a few cases this has proved impossible and we take this opportunity to offer our apologies to any copyright holders whose rights we may have unwittingly infringed.

1 Introduction

This book addresses a primary concern of financial markets, namely the methods used to value companies. Valuation methods such as the price–earnings ratio, dividend yield and EVA® (economic value added) are found frequently in stockbrokers' reports and in the financial press.[1] There has also been an explosion of interest in 'shareholder value' in recent years, with a corresponding need to understand how value is created and measured.

While stock market participants can benefit greatly from a good understanding of valuation methods, it is remarkably difficult to find an informed and comprehensive analysis of the subject. If an investor or a student wants to understand the theory and practice of valuation, then it is very difficult to know where to start.

A good understanding of valuation methods requires two things, both of which are addressed in this book. The first is an analytical review of valuation models, identifying the relationships between them and exposing the assumptions that each of them makes. The second is an evaluation of the data that are available for use in valuation models. Variation in the type and quality of data is the key determinant of the usefulness of any given valuation model. There is therefore an important relationship between the choice of valuation model and the available data, and this book will explore this relationship in some detail.

As an illustration, consider the price–earnings (PE) ratio, which is used widely across financial markets. The PE ratio is a valuation model, because it is a formal relationship between the share price of a company and an underlying determinant of that share price.[2] Given an understanding of the assumptions and parameters of the model, the user can go directly from a forecast of earnings to an estimation of the share price. Alternative valuation models could, of course, be used to estimate the price of the same share. If the models are used properly, with their underlying assumptions understood by the user, then it would not actually matter which model is used, because each should give the same answer. One reason for favouring the PE ratio might be that earnings are considered to be an effective summary measure of the financial performance of a company. The PE ratio is therefore a simple valuation model that makes use of data that are readily available and directly relevant. Any other valuation model might produce the same answer, but in a less convenient way. The usefulness of any given

---

[1] EVA® is a registered trade mark of Stern Stewart and Co. (see Chapter 9).
[2] The PE ratio is discussed at length in Chapter 4.

valuation model depends, therefore, upon the data that are available to users. This book will analyse the extent to which earnings are, in fact, a good measure of financial performance and thereby whether the PE ratio is, in fact, a useful valuation model. This raises the issue of 'earnings quality', and highlights the need to understand data issues, in addition to understanding the methodology of valuation. In short, the analysis of the PE ratio in this book will address questions such as the following:

- Under what set of conditions is there a direct relationship between a company's share price and its earnings?
- How can the PE ratio be reconciled to other valuation models, such as the dividend yield, shareholder value model or economic value added?
- What causes variation in PE ratios across time and between companies?
- Can the manipulation of earnings by management compromise the usefulness of the PE ratio?
- What is the purpose, definition and derivation of 'normalized' earnings?
- Should the PE ratio be calculated using normalized earnings and, if so, how should the normalized PE ratio be interpreted?

The analysis therefore embraces both the theory behind the PE ratio valuation model, and also the practical issue of deriving an appropriate measure of earnings.

1.1 Unique features of the book

In spite of the obvious importance of valuation methods to the stock market, it has always been difficult to find a satisfactory analysis of the subject. Certainly, there is limited help available from analysts, financial journalists, consultants and other investment professionals. An analyst with a good understanding of valuation is better off using this understanding rather than spending time sharing it. A consultant, meanwhile, is likely to be 'selling' a specific methodology, and will thereby focus only on its strengths, and on the weaknesses of other approaches. For example, an EVA consultant will offer a conflicting story to that of a CFROI (cash flow return on investment) consultant, and neither is likely to offer a reconciliation of their respective methodologies.[3]

As discussed above, this book has two aims. The first is to present a synthesized review of valuation models, and the second is to ground this review in a practical analysis of the quality and availability of financial data. There are, of course, other books that deal with valuation, but none of these embraces these two complementary, comprehensive aims.

At the risk of generalization, it is possible to group existing books under three headings, which are finance, accounting and valuation models. The first of these groups is characterized by a focus on finance theory, for example on the

---

[3] See Chapter 10 for an analysis of CFROI.

methodology of discounting cash flows and on the use of the capital asset pricing model (CAPM) in the measurement of portfolio risk and return. There are excellent examples of books of this type, such as *Principles of Corporate Finance* (Brealey and Myers, 2000), *Valuation* (Copeland, Koller and Murrin, 2000) and *Damodaran on Valuation* (1994). Typically, these books are wide-ranging, with valuation models not being an explicit focus. Moreover, they very rarely tackle the problem of measuring economic performance in the financial statements. This is vitally important, because it limits their scope and practical use. In practice, investors receive financial information about companies in the form of profits, balance sheet values and the like. They must use such information in understanding how well a company has performed in the past and, thereby, in forecasting how well it is likely to perform in the future. These forecasts are the basis of share prices.

It is well known, however, that financial performance cannot be measured objectively. The amount of profit a company makes is open to subjective measurement, as is very well described in books with an accounting focus, such as *New Creative Accounting* (Griffiths, 1995), *Accounting for Growth* (Smith, 1996) and *Financial Shenanigans* (Schilit, 1993). In view of this subjectivity, the relationships between financial statements, forecasts of financial performance and share prices are far from straightforward.

It might be hoped that books with a focus on accounting could be used, together with finance texts, to resolve the difficulty of using financial statement data in valuation. Accounting books are generally geared towards the accounting profession, however, and they therefore tend to emphasize the *preparation* of accounts rather than the *use* of the resulting information. These two emphases are fundamentally different, and the accountant's training is generally not oriented towards issues of valuation. Accounting books tend, therefore, to restrict the use of accounts to a narrow focus on financial ratios, with little interpretation of the usefulness of these ratios to investors. There are some exceptions, and some excellent financial statement analysis texts have appeared in recent years, such as *Financial Analysis* (Rees, 1995), *The Analysis and Use of Financial Statements* (White, Sondhi and Fried, 1997), *Business Analysis and Valuation* (Palepu, Bernard and Healy, 1996), *Interpreting Company Reports and Accounts* (Holmes and Sugden, 1999) and *Financial Statement Analysis and Security Valuation* (Penman, 2001). In general, however, these books maintain a focus on the interpretation of financial statement data, as opposed to an understanding of the methodology of valuation.

Finally, it is possible to find texts that focus on specific valuation models. The main examples are *Creating Shareholder Value* (Rappaport, 1998), *The Quest for Value* (Stewart, 1991) and *CFROI Valuation* (Madden, 1999). These books have been very influential. They have a 'consultancy' bias, however, meaning that they are uncritical of their own approach and they do not attempt to introduce the reader to alternative approaches, citing the strengths and weaknesses of each approach as they go.

The present book is something of a combination of the three types just described. It aims to take a valuation framework from the finance literature and an understanding of financial statements from the accounting literature, and it then applies these in attempting to explain, reconcile and evaluate a range of valuation models. This approach is believed to be unique. It is also believed to be of the greatest direct relevance and usefulness to financial markets participants.

1.2 Who should read this book?

This book is aimed at two broad categories of reader. The first is financial markets participants. This includes the professional and private investment community, in the form of stockbrokers, fund managers, corporate financiers, venture capitalists, bankers, private investors and so on. It also includes managers in public companies, especially those working in investor relations, finance and accounting and other departments with a shareholder value focus. And of course it also includes consultants, whose role is to advise professional investors and corporations on value creation, investor communications and the like.

The second broad category includes advanced students of finance and accounting. The book is of particular relevance to professional examinations, such as those of the Association for Investment Management and Research (AIMR) and the UK Society of Investment Professionals (UKSIP). It will also be particularly helpful to MBA students, and also to final year undergraduates and first year postgraduates in accounting, finance and economics. The book should be of particular interest to students preparing themselves for interviews and careers with investment banks and consulting firms.

1.3 Structure and content of chapters

The book is structured as follows. Chapter 2 introduces the methodology of valuation, reviewing briefly the meaning of fundamental terms such as discounted cash flow (DCF), net present value (NPV) and the cost of capital. It is demonstrated that a company's share price can be expressed formally by means of the dividend discount model (DDM). The DDM is argued to be the fundamental valuation model, meaning that all other valid valuation models must be reconcilable to it. It is also shown in Chapter 2 that the dividend growth model can be derived as a simplified form of the DDM. This identifies the dividend yield as a useful valuation metric. A multi-stage dividend valuation model is also introduced, which combines the best features of the DDM and the dividend yield.

Dividend-based valuation models share a common problem, however, which is that they are 'silent' on the source of dividend payments. While it is true that the shareholder value of a company depends upon the dividends that the company is able to pay, these dividends depend in turn upon the profits that the company is able to generate in the first place. Chapter 3 therefore addresses the sources of dividend growth, and it is shown that these are the return on equity (ROE) that the company is able to achieve, along with the rate at which profits are re-invested in the expansion of the company. More fundamentally, it is shown that the company is 'creating value' for shareholders whenever the ROE on re-invested profits is expected to exceed the company's cost of capital.

This difference between the ROE and the cost of capital, known as the rate of return spread, is of central importance to valuation.

The ROE is more easily analysed by focusing on profits (earnings) rather than on dividends, and this can be done by using the PE ratio. Chapter 4 assesses the PE ratio in some detail. The relationship between the dividend yield and the PE ratio is established, and then a range of possible interpretations of the PE ratio is explored. In particular, the chapter focuses on explaining variation in the PE ratio, whether this occurs over time or between companies.

In turn, the analysis of the PE ratio highlights the importance of being able to measure financial performance. Chapter 5 therefore introduces financial accounting, and it outlines strengths and weaknesses in the structure of the financial statements. Chapter 5 also identifies key financial statement performance measures, such as NOPAT (net operating profit after tax) and EBITDA (earnings before interest, taxation, depreciation and amortization). This is followed in subsequent chapters by a more detailed analysis of the relationships between corporate valuation and the financial statements. Chapter 6 examines the balance sheet, highlighting both theoretical and practical difficulties in assigning economic meaning to net asset values. Chapter 7 then switches the focus to the income statement. It is shown that the earnings measure reported in the financial statements is not an unambiguous measure of economic performance, and that a series of adjustments to reported earnings can enhance their usefulness to investors.

Chapter 8 combines earlier chapters by examining practical issues in the measurement of the return on investment, including both the ROE and the return on capital employed (ROCE). Some fundamental relationships are demonstrated between the measure of return that is available in the financial statements and the 'true' economic return made by the company. Chapter 9 then introduces the abnormal earnings valuation model, including the special case of EVA. This model is shown to be a useful generalization of the relationships between financial statement data and share prices, although it is also shown to retain some of the analytical difficulties raised in earlier chapters. One of the strengths of the abnormal earnings model is its explicit link to an underlying cash-flow-based valuation framework. It is therefore contrasted directly with other cash flow models in Chapter 10. These include the shareholder value model, CFROI and real options. Finally, Chapter 11 concludes the book with a review and a summary.

1.4 A focus on fundamental value

The perspective taken in this book is that of *fundamental* value, meaning the value of an equity investment that is held over the long term, as opposed to the value that can be realized by short-term, speculative trading. This distinction between fundamental and speculative value is a very important one. As will be seen in Chapter 2, valuation theory is grounded on the assumption that investors are rational, wealth-maximizing individuals, and that stock market prices reflect fundamental value. This is a sensible foundation, and it would be difficult to construct a robust theory of valuation in any other way.

At any given point in time, however, there is no guarantee that stock market prices do actually reflect fundamental values. Indeed, there is good reason to suppose that they might not. Stock market behaviour is driven by investor sentiment as well as by clear-thinking rationality, and speculative activity can drive market values away from fundamentals, and thereby away from the 'theoretically correct' estimation given by a valuation model. Moreover, it can be perfectly rational for professional investors to trade on the basis of market sentiment rather than fundamental value.

Perhaps the best-known and most insightful analysis of the speculative determination of stock market prices can be found in Keynes' *General Theory* (Keynes, 1936, Chapter 12). Keynes identifies two features of the stock market that lead to speculative behaviour. The first of these is the uncertainty of the future:

> Our knowledge of the factors which will govern the yield of an investment some years hence is usually very slight and often negligible. If we speak frankly, we have to admit that our basis of knowledge for estimating the yield ten years hence of a railway, a copper mine, a textile factory, the goodwill of a patent medicine, an Atlantic liner, a building in the City of London amounts to little and sometimes to nothing.

With the exception of patents and London property prices, Keynes' examples are strikingly dated to the eyes of the modern reader. And yet the railways, mines and factories of the early part of the twentieth century are analogous to the mobile phone networks, information technologies and financial services of today. This reinforces the uncertainty of future developments and the importance of unexpected change.

In addition to uncertainty, Keynes identifies liquidity as the second feature of stock markets that induces speculation.

> In the absence of security markets, there is no object in frequently attempting to revalue an investment to which we are committed. But the Stock Exchange revalues many investments every day and the revaluations give a frequent opportunity to the individual (though not to the community as a whole) to revise his commitments. It is as though a farmer, having tapped his barometer after breakfast, could decide to remove his capital from the farming business between 10 and 11 in the morning and reconsider whether he should return to it later in the week.

In Keynes' analysis, the two factors uncertainty and liquidity combine to generate speculative bubbles. The importance of the first factor, uncertainty, lies in its influence on investors' perceptions of current stock market valuations. Investors develop what Keynes calls 'conventions', meaning commonly accepted beliefs about the uncertain future. For example, the conventions for an investor at the turn of the millennium might have been that inflation would remain under control for the foreseeable future, that stock markets would be more likely to go up than down, that equities would be likely to generate superior long-term returns, that the US government would not default on its debt, and that property would be a relatively stable investment. Similarly, a convention for any given company or sector might be an expectation of trading within a given range of the PE ratio, such that the occurrence of a ratio that was high by historic standards would raise concerns of over-valuation. In effect, of course, these conventions are myths, because we cannot have certain knowledge about the future. For all we know, the US government might well default on its debt in the future, although for the time being it is generally accepted that it will not.

All of this would not matter greatly if it were not for liquidity. If the farmer from the earlier example could not buy and sell his investment at will, but was instead committed for the long term, then he would be concerned only with the underlying, fundamental value of his business. If, however, he could liquidate his investments, then his view of the market's conventions would become important:

> Investment becomes reasonably 'safe' for the individual investor over short periods, and hence over a succession of short periods however many, if he can fairly rely on there being no breakdown in the convention and on his therefore having an opportunity to revise his judgement and change his investment, before there has been time for much to happen. Investments which are 'fixed' for the community are thus made 'liquid' for the individual . . . But it is not surprising that a convention, in an absolute view of things so arbitrary, should have its weak points . . . [Professional investors] are, in fact, largely concerned, not with making superior long-term forecasts of the probable yield of an investment over its whole life, but with foreseeing changes in the conventional basis of valuation a short time ahead [of others] . . . [this] is an inevitable result of an investment market organised along the lines just described. For it is not sensible to pay 25 for an investment of which you believe the prospective yield to justify a value of 30, if you also believe that the market will value it at 20 three months hence.

If, therefore, an individual believes that the market is fundamentally overvalued but that, nevertheless, he or she believes that the consensus is that the market will rise, then he or she should buy and not sell. This is, of course, a shortterm, speculative strategy. It is important, however, because it raises the possibility of bluff and double-bluff, whereby investors can trade on what they believe the market believes, rather than on what they believe the fundamentals to be.

The relevance of Keynes' analysis can be illustrated very clearly by the internet stock boom of the late 1990s. As the market valuations of dot.com and other technology stocks began to rise at unprecedented rates, so novel rationalizations of these valuations began to emerge. These changes in conventions reinforced the higher valuations, which in turn brought forth further new conventions. For example, the internet was argued to have dramatic potential for opening global markets, including unprecedented opportunities for cross-selling, for bringing down the barriers to entry across industries and for rationalizing supply chain costs. Business models were created that offered low marginal costs, very high returns on capital and huge growth potential, fuelled by network effects, the value of options to enter new markets and the high values attributable to intangible, knowledge-based assets. In general, it became accepted that a 'new economy' was emerging. In a similar fashion to the Industrial Revolution, the economy appeared to have experienced a step-change in the rate of sustainable economic growth. And, in the light of growing consumer and investor confidence, the stock market became comfortable assuming that the future would bring uninterrupted strong economic growth, coupled with low inflation and modest interest rates. Meanwhile, stock market gains in themselves encouraged the growth of share options and shareholder value targets, completing a virtuous circle and encouraging the self-belief of all concerned. In this context, the previously unthinkable became the norm, and companies without profits were attributed huge valuations. 'Traditional' valuation measures such as the PE ratio were abandoned in favour of metrics such as the price–sales revenue ratio or, even less demanding, non-financial metrics such as the rate of customer growth. In summary, there was a dramatic shift in the market's conventions.

As the year 2000 progressed, however, investors were increasingly looking over their shoulders to see whether or not other investors' were losing faith in the new conventions. This was acknowledged as follows by the leading Wall Street internet analyst Henry Blodget:

> Henry Blodget, the closely watched internet analyst at Merrill Lynch, issued the latest in a string of cautious research reports on the dot.com sector and downgraded several stocks . . . [he] said the internet sector was moving from a period of 'hyper growth' to 'long-term' growth. This means investors need to use more traditional methods of assigning value to a company's shares, he said.
>
> That view is in contrast to the attitude that prevailed among Wall Street internet analysts a year ago, which held that new economy stocks could not be fairly judged by traditional methods . . . 'Analytical and valuation discipline have again become critical for successful stock picking,' Mr Blodget wrote in the report.
>
> Source: *Financial Times*, Christopher Grines, 8 August 2000

In effect, Henry Blodget was announcing the shift from speculative to fundamental valuation. This is particularly important since, as the leading analyst in the industry, his view was itself part of the accepted conventions behind lofty valuations. Indeed, there seemed to be the curious phenomenon that most investors individually agreed that current valuations were too high, but that collectively they continued to invest, no doubt in the belief that the 'momentum' remained upwards, and that exit would be possible before prices started to fall. In this context it is worth noting Keynes' suggestion that speculative behaviour is self-reinforcing, because 'worldly wisdom teaches that it is better for reputation to fail conventionally than to succeed unconventionally'. If an investor traded on the basis of fundamental values alone, then he or she might well have missed the extraordinary bull run in the US and other markets, and would no doubt be castigated for failing to go with the crowd. Alternatively, if everyone rises with a bubble and then falls with it also, no individual reputation is exposed. This is particularly the case in a world where fund managers are rewarded on the basis of performance *relative* to other funds, rather than performance in absolute terms. The risk of adverse performance arises by deviating from the consensus portfolio allocation, in a fashion similar to the risk that an analyst runs if his or her earnings forecast stands out from the crowd.

This discussion is reinforced by Philip Coggan, writing in the *Financial Times* back in October 1996. At that time, the US stock market had been growing so rapidly that many investors were getting nervous about a possible crash (though, in the event, the bull run had hardly got under way).

> Nine years ago, on October 19 1987, shares fell 22 per cent on Wall Street and began a global chain reaction that quickly became known as Black Monday. Then, as now, markets had regularly been reaching all-time highs. Only a prescient few were warning that shares were overvalued. Now, as then, bears are limited in number and subject to

ridicule. Will history repeat itself? . . . Much depends upon which measure is used. Shares in the US do not look that expensive in relation to corporate earnings . . . The real problems come when the US market is valued in terms of assets or dividends . . . [yet] it is not unknown for the importance of valuation measures to change over time . . . Nevertheless, it is wise to be sceptical about arguments that 'things are different this time'. Enthusiasts for Japan late in the 1980s argued that Western valuation measures did not apply to the Tokyo market, where shares offered little in the way of yield and traded in PE ratios in the high double-digits. Eventually the stock market rise was revealed to be a bubble.

Source: *Financial Times*, Philip Coggan, 19 October 1996

As events turned out, the consensus became one that reinforced further growth, and valuations shifted dramatically upwards. The possibility that this further rise represented a speculative bubble is outlined in depth by Robert Shiller in a recent book on the subject (Shiller, 2000). Writing in the *Financial Times*, he summarizes as follows:

If one looks at a long historical plot of US stock prices, the abrupt increase after 1995 is so striking that one wonders if there is some error in these data. But there is no error: the market has taken off like a rocket. Importantly, this price rise is not matched by a similarly spectacular increase in the rate at which corporations earn profits . . . [yet] the internet is not the only precipitating factor behind the stock market boom. Much that affects the psychology of the market has changed. For example . . . a change in attitude towards business . . . new compensation schemes, such as share options . . . the declining cost of trading shares has encouraged investment . . . [and] the news media have responded by expanding dramatically their coverage of financial markets . . . Even so, these and other factors do not seem enough to explain a doubling or tripling in the value of stock markets in five years. We also need an 'amplification mechanism' that translates such changes in opinions into something much bigger in market prices. Fortunately, such an amplification mechanism is well known: the familiar story of the irrational exuberance that comes with a speculative bubble.

Source: *Financial Times*, Robert Shiller, 8 April 2000

While it is important to acknowledge the effect on stock market prices of speculative behaviour, the focus of this book will be on fundamental value. In part, this is simply because the determinants of speculative behaviour are grounded in individual and collective psychology, rather than in theories of finance and accounting. More significantly, though, it is because fundamental values are of greater intrinsic importance. Speculative activity is a zero-sum game, meaning that the gains made by the sellers of over-priced shares are equal and opposite to the losses of the buyers. For the economy as a whole, there is no net effect, at least after allowing for transactions costs and for possible influences on corporate investment. Additionally, there is no net effect on long-term investors, whose overall return is governed by fundamentals alone. This is especially important for institutional investors, who are increasingly dominant in stock markets and whose shareholdings are often so large as to effectively enforce longer-term investment. Finally, it is unrealistic to suppose that speculative trading is in some sense independent of fundamental values. While stock markets might occasionally be prone to speculative bubbles, and while certain sectors might come in and out of 'fashion', the price that investors are willing to pay for equity investments must ultimately be grounded in underlying fundamentals. The primary aim of investors should therefore be to have an understanding of the theory and practice of fundamental valuation; and this is the aim to which this book is addressed.

References

Brealey, R. and S. Myers (2000). *Principles of Corporate Finance* (6th edn). Auckland: McGraw-Hill International.

Copeland, T., T. Koller and J. Murrin (2000). *Valuation: Measuring and Managing the Value of Companies* (3rd edn). New York: Wiley.

Damodaran, A. (1994). *Damodaran on Valuation: Security Analysis for Investment and Corporate Finance*. New York: Wiley.

Griffiths, I. (1995). *New Creative Accounting: How to Make Your Profits What You Want Them to Be*. London: Macmillan.

Holmes, G. and A. Sugden (1999). *Interpreting Company Reports and Accounts* (7th edn). London: Financial Times–Prentice Hall.

Keynes, J.M. (1936). *The General Theory of Employment, Interest and Money*. London: Macmillan.

Madden, B.J. (1999). *CFROI Valuation: A Total System Approach to Valuing the Firm*. Oxford: Butterworth-Heinemann.

Palepu, K.G., V.L. Bernard and P.M. Healy (1996). *Business Analysis and Valuation*. Cincinnati: South-Western College Pub.

Penman, S.H. (2001). *Financial Statement Analysis and Security Valuation*. New York: McGraw-Hill.

Rappaport, A. (1998). *Creating Shareholder Value: A Guide for Managers and Investors* (2nd edn). New York: Free Press.

Rees, W.P. (1995). *Financial Analysis* (2nd edn). London: Prentice Hall.

Schilit, H.M. (1993). *Financial Shenanigans: How to Detect Accounting Gimmicks and Fraud in Financial Reports*. New York: McGraw-Hill.

Shiller, R.J. (2000). *Irrational Exuberance*. Princeton, NJ: Princeton University Press.

Smith, Terry (1996). *Accounting for Growth: Stripping the Camouflage from Company Accounts* (2nd edn). London: Century Business.

Stewart, G.B. (1991). *The Quest for Value*. New York: HarperBusiness.

White, G.I., A.C. Sondhi and D. Fried (1997). *The Analysis and Use of Financial Statements* (2nd edn). Chichester, NY: Wiley.

2 Stock market valuation

Overview
- Investment, value and the stock market
- Valuation theory
- Introduction to the dividend discount model (DDM)
- Using the DDM to value shares
- The dividend yield and the dividend growth model (DGM)
- Relative and prospective (forward) valuation using the dividend yield
- Multi-stage dividend discount models
- Problems with dividend-based valuation

This chapter will lay the foundations for the book with an introduction to stock market valuation. The discussion will include the meaning and purpose of investment, the role of the stock market, the difference between the value of a share and its price and the theory of valuation. The remainder of the book will then build on this foundation and will focus in detail on the valuation of equity investments.

Readers who have completed a finance course are likely to find the material in this chapter familiar and straightforward, and they are therefore encouraged to skip through these pages.

2.1 Investment and value

Individuals make investments because they want to enjoy the benefits of wealth in the future rather than at the present. A particularly important example is pensions. People choose not to spend all of their income as soon as they receive it. Instead they invest a portion of it now, with a view to spending in retirement. Investments therefore represent a trade-off. Consumption is foregone now in order that it can take place in the future.

The value of an investment must therefore be equal in some way to the value of consumption. If consumption in retirement is valued more highly than current consumption, then there is an incentive to increase the level of investment, and thereby reduce current consumption. This incentive will continue until the point at which the benefit of investment is judged to be about the same as the benefit of current consumption. In a sense, therefore, the value of an investment is a highly personal and subjective assessment. What matters is how a given individual chooses to define the trade-off between current and future consumption. In turn, this depends upon such factors as the individual's future earning capacity, and his or her view of the future.

The aggregation of all individuals' trade-off decisions will determine the market rate of interest, and the prices of individual assets must themselves be determined relative to this overall market rate of interest.[1] Suppose, for example, that there are two government bonds available. An investment in either bond costs $1 000. The first bond guarantees to pay back $1 200, while the second will only pay back $1 100. Clearly, there will be few takers for the second bond. If an investor has $1 000 to invest, then he or she will look for the highest return available. In so doing, an implicit *relative* valuation is taking place, and the value of all investments is being assessed relative to all others. This would be true for any form of investment, whether it is an oil painting, an antique or a piece of land, but it is especially true for financial assets. This is because financial assets all offer a return in exactly the same form, cash, and nothing besides. As investments, they are very obviously and directly comparable.[2]

The value of any financial asset therefore depends upon the value of all other financial assets. Valuation is a *relative* concept, and nothing can be valued in isolation. This is of central importance, and it forms the basis of valuation theory.

2.2 The stock market

The stock market exists as a medium for investment. Individuals are able to invest directly in companies, using the stock market as a point of trade. When a company issues shares, individuals give up money in exchange for an implicit promise of a greater amount of money at some point in the future. They become holders of shares, which represent their legal ownership of a portion of the company and, thereby, their right to receive the uncertain future cash return. The actual receipt of this cash return comes in two forms. The first is income, which is paid by the company as dividends, and the second is capital, which is typically realized by means of a transfer of share ownership, with the company itself playing no direct part.[3]

---

[1] The rate at which individuals are willing to trade-off current against future consumption is termed the marginal rate of substitution. The rate at which the economy is able to convert current investment into future consumption is termed the marginal rate of transformation. The rate of interest is determined at the point where these two marginal rates are equal, since this point represents the optimal trade-off between current and future consumption (see Copeland and Weston (1988, Chapter 1) for a fuller discussion).

[2] Financial assets are likely to be very easily traded, with low associated transactions costs and (typically) high trading volume. This allows their prices to respond quickly to reflect relative changes in expected returns. This strengthens further the direct comparability of financial assets.

[3] The company retains direct involvement to the extent that it engages in share buy-backs or in merger and acquisition activity involving changes in share ownership.

The initial transaction, where the individual invests cash in the company, is termed a primary market transaction. Any subsequent dealing between shareholders is said to take place on the secondary market. In this way, it is the secondary market that continually updates the share price as shares change hands. Most share investment decisions take place on the secondary market. Institutional investors manage large share portfolios on the secondary market, and they are continually updating their views on the value of their investments. Stockbrokers are also conducting an ongoing analysis of the value of shares as they are traded. And for individuals themselves, the trade-off between consumption and investment uses the secondary market share price as a guide, with other individuals being trading partners. In short, while the primary market is the means by which cash is actually invested in companies, and while it is the return that the companies make that determines the value of the investment, it is the secondary market that is of the greatest practical importance.

It is essential to recognize that the share price determined on the (secondary) stock market is only an estimate at best. It represents the market's 'best guess' about the future cash returns that the company will generate. The share price will change as the market receives new information and revises its expectations of the future.

It is also worth noting that there is no necessary relationship between what is expected to happen in the future and what actually will happen. For example, the price of a share can be bid up simply by investors buying and selling to one another at ever higher prices. An increase in the value of the stock market does not necessarily mean that investors are growing collectively wealthier, but only that they are increasing their expectations of the future cash returns to be generated by companies. Only time can tell whether or not the investors' expectation of the future is justified by companies' actual performance.

Share prices and stock market investment

The availability of cash for new investment has been hugely helpful to the UK stock market . . . Net retail sales of mutual funds, though no longer at the giddy heights of March and April, were still running above £1bn a month in May and June. Most companies were still throwing off surplus cash, and are more likely to be increasing share repurchases than embarking on a new wave of rights issues. And although the new issues pipeline is still full . . . [and] the steady flow of cash acquisitions is showing signs of drying up . . . the balance of supply and demand still seems set to favour the market.

Source: Financial Times, Lex Column, 7 August 2000

Even though a central function of the stock market is to provide equity capital for corporate investment, secondary market trading is essentially independent of investment by companies. If the supply of shares remains fixed (i.e. in the absence of new equity issues, rights issues, etc.), then the buying pressure from individuals forces up prices, as individuals exchange cash for share ownership. If companies themselves generate cash surpluses that are paid back to shareholders, either as dividends or share repurchases, then the demand–supply imbalance is exaggerated further. Hence, cash flow can 'favour the market' even if the underlying fundamentals of corporate wealth creation are unchanged.

| 2.3 | **Valuation theory** |

This discussion can be formalized within a valuation framework. Since investments are made with a view to generating a return, the *price* of any investment (such as a share in a company or a government bond) will be determined by the rate of return that can be earned. More precisely, and as will now be demonstrated, the price of an investment will be set such that its expected, risk-adjusted return is the same as that for all other investments.

In equilibrium, the price of any financial asset will depend upon two things, expected return and risk. The return on the asset is itself comprised of three factors. These are: first, the amount of money that the asset is expected to generate; second, the point in time when the money flows are expected to occur; and, third, the effect of inflation. In turn, risk is a measure of the estimated range within which future returns are likely to fall.[4] Taken together, return and risk differentiate one financial asset from another and therefore form the basis of the individual's choice between alternative investments.

The precise relationships between price, return and risk can be introduced with the aid of a simple example, see Table 2.1.

Table 2.1 The value of an investment: price, return and risk

	Cash flows ($)			Probability of cash in-flow	Rate of inflation
	Year 0	Year 1	Year 2		
Scenario 1	−100	110		100%	0%
Scenario 2	−100		121	100%	0%
Scenario 3	−100	115.5		100%	5%
Scenario 4	−100	100		50%	0%
		120		50%	0%

Table 2.1 illustrates four scenarios. In each one, an investor makes an investment of $100 on the first day of the year. It is conventional to describe this first day as 'year 0', and then to describe the final day of the year as 'year 1' (and the final day of the subsequent year as 'year 2'). In effect, this makes an assumption that all investments and all returns take place on either the first or the last day of the year, which simplifies the calculations.

As Table 2.1 shows, the scenarios differ in terms of the size, timing and riskiness of the return that is available to investors for their $100 investment. Scenario 1 illustrates the most straightforward of the determinants of value, which is the amount of money that the asset is expected to generate. The investor pays out $100 in year 0 (1 January), and then receives $110 in year 1 (31 December). The

---

[4] More formally, risk measures the dispersion of estimated future returns around their mean (expected) value.

probability that $110 will be received is 100%, and there is therefore no risk. There is also no inflation. The return that the investor makes is $10, or 10% of the original investment. Alternatively stated, if the risk-free rate of return for the economy is *not* 10%, then $100 is the 'wrong' price for this investment. Suppose, for example, that the risk-free rate of return is 5%. In this case, the correct price for a risk-free return of $110 should be the amount that, when multiplied by 105%, equals $110. This turns out to be $104.76, as follows

$$\$104.76 \times 105\% = \$110$$

Or, alternatively stated

$$\$104.76 = \frac{\$110}{(1 + 0.05)}$$

If, then, the investor only paid $100 for this investment, then he or she is better off than would otherwise have been possible. The expected return at the end of the year is $110, rather than $105. This difference of $5 one year from now is equivalent to $4.76 now, because the $4.76 invested at a return of 5% is equal to $5. In other words, if the current price of the investment increases from $100 to $104.76, then the rate of return that is expected is 5%, and the asset becomes priced correctly relative to all other assets. In the process, the investor has become wealthier by $4.76.

A more formal way to consider the relationship between price and expected return is in terms of a simple formula. If the expected rate of return is denoted as k, the price of the financial asset as P and the amount of the cash flow return as C, then the following relationship holds[5]

$$P_0 = \frac{C_1}{(1 + k)}$$

This simple formula is fundamental to the theory of valuation. It is a means of expressing future returns in terms of how much investors would be willing to pay for them now. The process of dividing a future cash flow by (one plus) the expected return is called *discounting* or, more generally, *discounted cash flow analysis* (*DCF*). A cash flow of $110 in year 1 has to be discounted at a rate of 5% in order to convert it into its equivalent value of $104.76 in year 0. In other words, the process of discounting expresses future returns in terms of their *present value*, which is the current price that investors are willing to pay for an investment, given the rate of return achievable elsewhere. The present value can therefore be compared directly with an asset's actual cost (i.e. its market price). If the present value exceeds the cost, then the investment is wealth-creating (or 'value-creating'). The difference between present value and cost is termed *net present value* (*NPV*). In the example just given, the investment cost was $100, the present value was $104.76 and the NPV was therefore $4.76.

---

[5] The numerical subscript refers to the time period, such that (for example) P_0 is the share price at the beginning of year 1, and P_1 is the share price at the end of year 1. Strictly, the formula should be written in such a way that expectations of variables are differentiated from actual realizations of those variables. This is not done in order to keep the exposition as simple as possible.

While the investor did actually pay $100 for the investment, the price that he or she would have been willing to pay actually depends, therefore, upon the returns available elsewhere. These returns are referred to as the investor's *opportunity cost*, because they are the returns foregone by investing in scenario 1 rather than in an alternative investment. An investment is a good one if its return exceeds its opportunity cost or, in other words, if it has positive NPV.

The requirement that an investment should have a positive NPV is actually quite demanding, because it requires that the investment offers a *better* return than comparable investments. If the competitive rate of return is (say) 15%, then an investment is fairly priced if it, too, offers a 15% return. In general, it is all too common to see NPV analysis mis-used. For example, it is generally the case that investment decision-makers across different companies consistently forecast positive NPV, treating it as the norm. This has to be wrong. Not every investment can expect a return higher than that achievable in comparable investments. In particular, an NPV equal to zero is to be expected for financial assets such as shares and bonds, because prices change rapidly to reflect new information. If a valuation gives an NPV different from zero, then this stands in need of justification.

Returning to Table 2.1, scenario 2 illustrates that the return on an investment comprises both the amount *and* the timing of the cash inflow. The timing is important because a given sum of money received today is worth more than the same sum of money received at some point in the future. This is termed the 'time value of money'. The sooner an investment return is realized, the sooner it can be re-invested to generate a further return. For example, $110 in year 1 was shown to be worth $104.76 in year 0. In comparing scenarios 1 and 2, therefore, the issue at stake is whether $121 in year 2 is worth more or less than $110 in year 1. In essence, this is the same question that has already been addressed above. If the opportunity cost in year 2 is 10%, then the two amounts have the same present value (since $110 invested at 10% equals $121).

Taking the time value of money into account requires that the rate of return is *compounded* over the number of years in question. Over a two-year investment, the price will therefore be determined according to the following equation

$$P_0 = \frac{C_1}{(1 + k)} + \frac{C_2}{(1 + k)^2}$$

In the general case, where future cash flows can occur in any period of time, the DCF valuation formula for the price of an investment is as follows[6]

$$P_0 = \frac{C_1}{(1 + k)} + \frac{C_2}{(1 + k)^2} + \ldots + \frac{C_\infty}{(1 + k)^\infty}$$

An important issue in using this model is the effect of inflation. If prices change over time, then they cease to be directly comparable. They become different from one another in much the same way that currencies differ, and they require the use of an inflation rate to make them comparable, just as exchange rates

---

[6] Cash flows need not, of course, extend infinitely, and the general model applies to any finite period.

convert currencies. If, for example, the rate of inflation is 5%, then $105 in year 1 is equivalent to $100 in year 0. In other words, $1 in year 0 'currency' is worth $1.05 in year 1 'currency'.

Market rates of interest are typically 'nominal', meaning that they are based upon inflated money amounts. They can be adjusted to 'real' rates as follows:

$$(1 + \textit{nominal rate of interest}) = (1 + \textit{real rate of interest}) \times (1 + \textit{rate of inflation})$$

So, for example, if the rate of inflation is expected to be 5%, and the real rate of interest is 10%, then the nominal rate of interest will be 15.5%. These, in fact, are the values assumed in scenario 3. The correct price in year 0 is $100 if the real cost of capital is 10% and the inflation rate is 5%.

If the DCF model is calculated using inflated cash flows, then the use of the nominal rate of interest will give the correct present value, as above. If the cash flows are not inflated, then the present value will be too low. As an alternative to estimating inflated cash flows, it is equally valid to adjust the cost of capital from its nominal to its real value. These two methods will give the same result, and they both require the same input data. The important message is that cash flows and discount rates should be consistent with one another, taking into account the effect of inflation. So, from scenario 3, the real return in year 1 is $110 and the real cost of capital is 10%. This gives the correct price of $100. Combining a real return of $110 with a nominal cost of capital of 15.5% would give an incorrectly low price of $95.24.

The discussion so far has illustrated the relationship between the price of an investment and its expected return. The price will also depend, however, on the riskiness of the return. It has so far been assumed that the return that investors expect to receive is, in fact, the return that they do receive. In practice, of course, investments are uncertain and, with the possible exception of some government-issued securities, the actual return will turn out to be higher or lower than originally expected. Risk is a measure of the expected variation in possible returns. Low risk implies that returns are not expected to deviate greatly from their most likely level.

Most investors are risk-averse, meaning that they prefer a return that is guaranteed to one that is uncertain. This causes risky investments to be worth less, for a given return, than less risky investments. This is illustrated in scenario 4. If the investor has an equal chance of earning either $100 or $120 in year 1, then the expected return is no different from the $110 return in scenario 1. The price of the investment will be lower for scenario 4, however, because of the greater variation in the expected actual outcome. The effect of the risk is to increase the investors' cost of capital. The extent to which the cost of capital increases will depend upon the extent of investors' risk aversion.[7]

---

[7] The effect of inflation combines the factors of return and risk. It affects the return because it is concerned with a change in the value of the monetary unit. Additionally, uncertainty about the level of future inflation adds to the riskiness of any given investment. Other things being equal, an investment in a country with a long-term record of stable inflation is therefore more valuable than an investment in a more volatile environment.

It should be noted that this book does not address directly the measurement of risk. There is an extensive, very well-established and accessible literature on this subject (e.g. Copeland and Weston, 1988 and Brealey and Myers, 2000), and the wheel need not be re-invented here. The simplifying assumption of a constant cost of capital will often be made. This will keep the spotlight on valuation models and financial statements, which are the primary focus of the book.

2.4 The dividend discount model (DDM)

This general analysis of valuation can now be applied to the specific case of equity valuation. In particular, the theory above can be used to derive the dividend discount model (DDM), which may be regarded as the 'fundamental' equity valuation model. Indeed, it is difficult to overstate the central importance of the DDM in any discussion of equity valuation. Any theoretical valuation model must be reconcilable with the DDM, or else it is conceptually flawed.[8] In other words, if any variable such as earnings, book values or cash flows is used in a valuation model, then, unless this is done in a manner consistent with the DDM, the model is formulated wrongly. This is a point that will be returned to on many occasions, and each valuation model analysed in this book will take the DDM as its reference point.

To see why the DDM is of such central importance, it will be necessary to build the model from first principles. This is straightforward, and starts by recognizing that a share is valued in much the same way as any other investment – by comparing, after adjusting for the time value of money, the cash outflow (i.e. the share price at purchase) with the cash inflow (i.e. dividends received plus the share price at sale).

Suppose that a share is purchased on the first day of the year and then sold on the last day, and also that dividends are paid just before the share is sold. The total return for the year will be the sum of the dividend received and the capital gain, divided by the initial purchase price. For example, if an equity investment of $1 000 is made on 1 January, with the expectation of a dividend of $50 before the share is sold, ex-dividend on 31 December, for $1 100. The total return for the year would be 15%

$$total\ return = \frac{dividend + capital\ gain}{initial\ investment}$$

i.e.
$$15\% = \frac{50 + (1\ 100 - 1\ 000)}{1\ 000}$$

---

[8] This statement is not without its assumptions. For example, shares in sports clubs such as Manchester United plc may be held without reference to future dividends, because ownership conveys other, non-financial 'rewards'. Likewise, investors may hold so-called 'ethical' investments because of their contribution to society as a whole, and not just because of their dividend payments to shareholders. Finally, and perhaps most importantly, shares may be held for speculative reasons, as discussed in the Introduction.

This can be expressed as follows

$$k = \frac{D_1 + (P_1 - P_0)}{P_0}$$

where k denotes the expected rate of return on the equity investment, D is dividends and P is share price.

The current price (P_0) reflects an expectation that the total return over the next year will be 15%. By the end of the year, the investment may or may not have achieved 15%, depending upon whether or not the dividend turns out to be 50 and the price to be 1 100. The current share price is determined such that the rate of return that shareholders require is equal to that which they expect to receive. In other words, the price that an investor is willing to pay for a share is equal to the discounted value of the total resulting cash inflows (dividends and proceeds from selling the share), as follows

$$P_0 = \frac{D_1 + P_1}{(1 + k)}$$

This expression is, however, incomplete as a model of the share price. The current price (P_0) is shown to depend upon the future price (P_1), which itself can be expressed as follows

$$P_1 = \frac{D_2 + P_2}{(1 + k)}$$

A revised expression for the current share price is therefore as follows[9]

$$P_0 = \frac{D_1 + P_1}{(1 + k)} = \frac{D_1 + \frac{(D_2 + P_2)}{(1 + k)}}{(1 + k)} = \frac{D_1}{(1 + k)} + \frac{D_2}{(1 + k)^2} + \frac{P_2}{(1 + k)^2}$$

This expression is still incomplete, however, because although P_0 is now expressed independently of P_1, a further need now arises for an expression for P_2. And if an expression for P_0 is derived that avoids the need for P_2, then the need will arise to derive P_3. And so the process continues. In the end, an expression for the current price that does not rely upon the future price is possible only if dividends are continued indefinitely, as follows

$$P_0 = \frac{D_1}{(1 + k)} + \frac{D_2}{(1 + k)^2} + \frac{D_3}{(1 + k)^3} + \ldots + \frac{D_\infty}{(1 + k)^\infty}$$

This is the dividend discount model (DDM) and can be stated more neatly in the following form

$$P_0 = \sum_{t=1}^{\infty} \frac{D_t}{(1 + k)^t}$$

The DDM is the most uncontroversial and generally accepted statement about how much a share is *theoretically* worth. It has long been central to finance theory, and is generally credited to Williams (1938). The DDM states that the

---

[9] The implicit assumption is made here that the cost of capital, k, itself does not change over time.

current share price depends upon future discounted dividends only, and not upon any future share price. If a share is sold in order to realize a capital gain, then one shareholder is buying from another the capitalized value of future dividends from the company. While this is a cash flow between the two shareholders, it is not a cash flow from the company to either shareholder. It is therefore not relevant to the underlying value of the share.

2.5	**Using the dividend discount model**

Given the fundamental importance of the DDM, it is important to reflect on how the model works, and on what is implied by use of the model.

A first observation is that dividends in the model are necessarily defined to include *all* cash flows between the company and its shareholders. This is a broader definition than would normally be applied to dividends. It is required because the underlying valuation framework is based upon cash outflows and inflows for the shareholders. Dividends therefore include share buy-backs and special dividends, and they are net of new injections of equity capital by shareholders.[10]

Second, the focus on dividends implies valuation of only the equity-financed part of a company, and not the whole. In other words, the DDM concerns shareholder value and not enterprise value, where the latter includes the value of the company's assets belonging to other providers of finance. The value of equity given by the model can be expressed either in terms of dividends per share (and therefore share price) or dividends in total (and therefore market capitalization). Either model can be converted swiftly into the other by means of multiplying or dividing by the number of shares in issue.[11]

Third, the model is valid if the company is unable to pay dividends in one or more periods of its life. This might well be the case for a start-up company, for example, which requires heavy investment in its early years in exchange for the prospect of high dividends in future years. In such a case, the values of D_1, D_2 and D_3 (for example) might be zero in the DDM. This poses no complications, either conceptually or computationally. Indeed, as a general statement, the model will allow dividends to take any value at all in any period of the company's life (the value could even be negative if new equity is issued). It is, however, essential that the company is expected to pay dividends at some stage in the future. A company may have a policy of not paying dividends, but it remains valuable to shareholders if, eventually, the value of the company's assets will be returned to shareholders. Any given shareholder need not actually receive a dividend from the company during the period of his or her shareholding,

---

[10] An additional issue, of course, is that of taxation, which is not dealt with explicitly in this book. In practice, shareholders will evaluate their returns net of tax, which will (amongst other things) introduce distortions in valuing earnings that are retained as opposed to those that are paid out as dividends.

[11] Such an approach makes the implicit assumption that the most recent price at which shares were exchanged (i.e. the current market price) is representative of all shares. This is unlikely to be the case in a thinly traded, illiquid market. Moreover, it makes no allowance for the premium that is typically paid when a controlling stake is acquired in a company.

but this shareholding is nevertheless valuable because it conveys legal (and tradable) ownership and control of the company's assets.

Fourth, the DDM is forward-looking. In forecasting performance, there is a need for an estimation of both dividends and the cost of capital. If the dividends forecast is uncertain, then the cost of capital will be high. Once performance is realized and dividends are actually paid, however, then there is no longer any uncertainty. And while the volatility of historic performance will no doubt affect any assessment of the uncertainty of future performance (and therefore the cost of capital), the historic record itself consists of dividends alone. Related to this, it cannot be observed directly whether a share price change is caused by revised expectations of dividends or of the cost of capital, or both. While investors might have estimates of these two variables, both for the original and for the revised share prices, they can never be certain that their estimates are consistent with the consensus of the market.

Finally, it is important to observe that the model makes no direct statement about what happens within a company in terms of investment performance, re-investment of profits and so on. The DDM is concerned only with the cash flows that the company returns to its shareholders. In practice, of course, some assessment of the company's investment performance is needed in order to forecast dividends, but the DDM itself is silent on these matters. It is simply a formal expression for the shareholder value of the company, with the future dividend performance taken as given.

In summary, Table 2.2 illustrates how, in principle, the DDM can be used to understand the effect on share prices of various types of economic event. It should

Table 2.2 Using the DDM to interpret economic news

Economic news event	Implication using the DDM	Effect on share price
High profit reported	Increases the expected level of future dividends.	Increase
Fall in interest rates	Fall in the cost of capital, increasing the value today of cash inflows received in the future.	Increase
Dividend cut	Reduces the expectations of future dividends. A dividend cut might also adversely affect the cost of capital because of an increased perception of risk.[a]	Decrease
Increase in inflation	Impact on future dividends will depend upon the relative exposure of income and expenditure to inflation. Nominal cost of capital increases.	Depends upon strength of opposing effects

Note: [a] This assumes a relationship between current dividend policy and future dividend growth. Additionally, the effect on the cost of capital relies on a presumption that the dividend is used by management to signal expected business performance to investors. If the dividend is reduced, then this is likely to reduce the managers' credibility in sending signals to the market. In turn, this increases investors' perceived investment risk, manifested in a higher cost of capital. See below for further discussion.

be noted that, at any given point in time, the share price given by the DDM is based upon currently available information. For an economic event to change the DDM-determined share price, it must constitute a change in the available information. In other words, it must be a genuine 'news' story that causes a change in the market's expectations of future discounted dividends. If, for example, interest rates fell, but the fall had already been anticipated by the market, then share prices would not change. Also, while the DDM is a theoretically valid framework for estimating how much prices 'should' change, in practice the change might not be as predicted. For example, unexpectedly good corporate performance would, in theory, cause the share price to rise. In practice, though, it might (for example) cause a large institutional investor to sell a block of shares, either to take profits or to prevent its holding from becoming too large in a portfolio. This sale might temporarily depress the share price, depending upon the volume of other trades taking place on that day.

In short, the role of the DDM as a valuation model is to act as a framework for the systematic interpretation of the share price effects of news items. The model is entirely general. In principle, any item of news whatsoever can be filtered through the DDM into the share price.

2.6 The dividend yield and the dividend growth model (DGM)

While it is true to say that the theoretical value of a share is given correctly by the DDM, it is unfortunately not true that the model should therefore be used to the exclusion of any other valuation method. If reliable information existed on both dividends and the cost of capital in perpetuity, then the DDM would be used exclusively. The reality, of course, is different. The inherent uncertainty of the future makes the information demands of the DDM simply too great.[12] In turn, this opens up a whole realm of different possibilities for valuing shares. The issue is not what the 'correct' valuation model is, but rather what model will work best, given the limitations of available information. This point is fundamental to all valuation models.

In addressing this need for a feasible valuation model, a starting point is to review the dividend yield model, which is a highly simplified form of the DDM. The dividend yield model has two major benefits. First, it is theoretically consistent with the DDM, although with the qualification that it makes some strong assumptions. Second, it is easy to use and does not make onerous and unrealistic data demands. These benefits have their flip-side, of course, which is that the model may, in practice, be unrealistically simple.

---

[12] Though note that, even with the DDM, the theroretical need to forecast dividends to infinity is illusory. In practice, the effect of discounting will make dividends in the distant future immaterial. For example, a dividend of $50 received five years from now at a cost of capital of 15% is worth $24.86 today. In contrast, the same dividend 15 and 50 years from now has a present value of, respectively, only $6.14 and $0.05.

In its most basic form, the dividend yield model makes two assumptions. The first is that dividends will neither increase nor fall, such that their current level will be maintained in perpetuity. The second is that the cost of capital will also remain constant. These two strong assumptions allow a dramatic simplification of the DDM, such that the share price is given by current dividends divided by the cost of capital, as follows (the proof of this simplification is given in the Appendix at the end of this chapter)

$$P_0 = \frac{D_1}{k}$$

Or, alternatively stated, the cost of capital is equal to the dividend yield (where the dividend yield is defined as dividends divided by the share price)

$$k = \frac{D_1}{P_0}$$

Suppose, as an illustration, that the cost of capital is fixed at 20% and the dividend expected at the end of the year (and thereafter every year) is $200. Then the share price given by the model would be $1 000.

This model has a straightforward interpretation. The price of a share at any time is the market's best estimate of the underlying value of the share. If both the rate of return that shareholders expect and the level of dividends are fixed, then the determination of the share price becomes very simple. If the share price is set such that the income yield from dividends equals the shareholders' required return, then the share price itself will also remain constant. There would be no capital gains (i.e. no changes in the price), because the future expectations would always (by assumption) be the same. It would not matter whether the share was bought now or at any time in the future. Its price would be the same and its dividend yield (and thereby its rate of return) would be the same also.[13]

Of the two strong assumptions made to derive this model, the most restrictive is that current dividends will remain constant. This assumption can, however, be lifted easily, and replaced with the less onerous (though still strong) assumption that the current dividend grows at a constant rate in perpetuity. This gives the following, more commonly used, version of the dividend yield model, the dividend growth model (DGM), where the growth rate of dividends is denoted by g (again, the proof is given in the Appendix)

$$P_0 = \frac{D_1}{k - g}$$

---

[13] Strictly, only the ex-dividend share price is constant, and the share price between dividend payments will include the accrued value of the expected dividend. A similar analysis applies to fixed interest government bonds, especially perpetuities with no maturity date.

Or, alternatively stated, the cost of capital is equal to the dividend yield plus the constant growth rate of dividends

$$k = \frac{D_1}{P_0} + g$$

As an illustration of the DGM,[14] suppose that a company pays a dividend of $80 at the end of the current year, and that this dividend is expected to grow at a rate of 12% in perpetuity. If this company has a cost of capital of 20%, then its share price will be $1 000. This is, of course, the same price that was given above for the no-growth model. The difference between the two illustrations is that the dividend yield is only 8% in the dividend growth case, whereas it is 20% in the no-growth model. The difference (12%) is the rate at which dividends are expected to grow. This expected growth is reflected in the current share price, such that the dividend yield will always be less than the cost of capital if dividends are expected to grow.

The DGM is simple yet useful. It is derived from the DDM, and therefore theoretically valid. It provides a straightforward basis from which to value shares, using only current dividends, the cost of capital and an estimated dividend growth rate.

Of course, the model also has important limitations. For example, it is unable to deal with a company that pays zero dividends at the end of the first year.[15] This makes it more appropriate in valuing relatively stable, established companies than either start-ups or companies in distress. A similar restriction is that the growth rate of dividends cannot exceed the cost of capital. If it did, there would be no solution for the share price. Try, for example, a cost of capital of 10% and a dividend growth rate of 12% in the model above. This combination does not work because it assumes that the discounted dividend stream continues to grow indefinitely, giving it an infinite value. This implies that the company grows forever at a rate faster than the economy in which it is based, which cannot be possible.

In general, the model is extremely sensitive to small changes in the parameters. This is because, unlike the DDM, each variable is assumed to be relevant over the entire lifetime of the company, such that a small change in the current dividend growth rate (for example) will have a very significant effect on the share price. In the example above, an increase in the dividend growth rate to either 13% or 15% would increase the share price to $1 143 or $1 600, respectively.

---

[14] An alternative, fairly common, name is the Gordon Growth Model (Gordon, 1962), after the researcher most closely associated with the development and early empirical testing of the model. The term dividend growth model is preferred here because it is more descriptive and emphasizes the connection with the DDM.

[15] A simple solution to this would be to calculate the share price from the time that dividends are first paid, and then to discount this price back to present value. A more intractable problem is when a company pays dividends intermittently.

Dividend growth model and the US economy

Warren Buffett has long grumbled about an overpriced stock market . . . Surveys show that most US investors expect annual nominal returns of 12 per cent over the next decade. Mr Buffett thinks 6 per cent is more likely, composed of 3 per cent economic growth, 2 per cent inflation and a bit of dividend yield.

Source: *Financial Times*, Lex Column, 2 May 2000

This is a straightforward application of the dividend growth model. Based upon a 1% dividend yield and an estimated 3% real growth rate (5% nominal), Warren Buffet concludes that investors should expect a real return of 4% (6% nominal). In contrast to this, the survey evidence suggests an over-optimistic expectation of a 12% return. If – for the sake of argument – Warren Buffet and 'most US investors' are agreed on the expected inflation rate and on the (observable) dividend yield, then they differ by 6% in their expectation of real returns. This is a huge difference – for example, the value of a $1 000 investment growing at 3% would be $1 344 after ten years, whilst it would be $2 367 at 9% growth. If stock market prices currently incorporate an expectation of 9% growth, and if Warren Buffet is right, then the failure of companies to meet over-optimistic expectations of earnings will lead to a fall in prices, coupled with a loss of investor confidence.

2.7 The dividend yield in practice: a relative measure

While the dividend yield was derived above as an expression for *determining* the *value* of a share, it is actually best viewed as a starting point in *understanding* the *price* of a share. This may seem like a minor distinction, but it is a very important one in analysing why and how the dividend yield can be useful in practice. This is because, first, investment decisions always take the form of a *choice* between alternative investments and, second, there are limitations in the availability of quantitative data for valuations. These two reasons are worth exploring in some detail.

First, the stock market is not a place where individual investments are valued in isolation from one another, but where investors are looking for shares that are either under-priced or over-priced *relative* to one another. Finding such shares is not easy, of course, because everyone is looking for them – a process which itself causes pricing errors to be minimized.[16] In order to attempt to detect relative valuation differences, as opposed to absolute valuation errors, investors need a relative measure. The DDM does not serve this purpose well, because it is a relatively complex model focused on determining the value of an individual share. The dividend yield, by contrast, can be a useful benchmark for comparing investments.

---

[16] This is the concept of the efficient market, where the economic incentives of market participants cause them to trade until the share price is updated with all available information.

In the first place, the dividend yield is easy to use. If one share has a dividend yield of 10% and another of 8%, then it can be stated simply that the former has a yield premium of 25% – or, alternatively, that the latter has a yield discount of 20%. Likewise, the yield for an individual share can be expressed relative to the market as a whole or (probably more helpfully) relative to its sector. This simple measure gives us an obvious starting point for analysing the share. In the example just given, the yield premium of 25% must exist because, for one company relative to the other, either investors' cost of capital is higher or else lower dividend growth is expected. This gives a basis for examining whether the difference implicit in the share price is really justified. To illustrate, suppose that company A is expected to pay a dividend of $120, with a growth rate of 9% and a cost of capital of 15%. This gives a share price of $2 000 and a dividend yield of 6%. If company B has a current share price of $1 200 and is expected to pay a dividend of $90, then its cost of capital and dividend growth rate might be given by one of the three options shown in Table 2.3 (these three being illustrative, of course, and not exhaustive).

Table 2.3 Explaining a dividend yield premium

	Company A	Company B		
		Option 1	Option 2	Option 3
Dividend (D_1)	120	90	90	90
Dividend growth rate (g)	9%	12.5%	9%	7.5%
Cost of capital (k)	15%	20%	16.5%	15%
Share price (P_0)	2 000	1 200	1 200	1 200
Dividend yield	6%	7.5%	7.5%	7.5%
Yield premium (B vs. A)		25%	25%	25%

It is evident from the share price and the dividend forecast that company B has a dividend yield premium of 25% over company A. This implies that company A has either relatively higher risk or lower dividend growth. As Table 2.3 illustrates, however, the actual cost of capital and dividend growth rate are indeterminate, and it remains for the investor to use the yield premium as a basis for relative valuation. It might be, for example, that the investor considers both companies to have the same level of risk. It would follow that company B's dividend growth rate, as implied by the share price, is 7.5% (option 3). This then gives the investor a benchmark from which to conduct some fundamental analysis of the investment decision between company A and company B. The issue is simply whether or not the 1.5% growth differential is realistic. This is a much more straightforward question to answer than the determination of the 'correct' share price. All the investor needs to know in order (for example) to prefer company B to company A, is that the differential is less than 1.5%. The investor does not need to know what the actual growth rate will be. For example, company B will be the better investment whether its dividend growth rate is 8% or 10%, or (indeed) any other value above 7.5%.

In general, the dividend yield has a simple, yet powerful, economic interpretation. The use of yields, returns and growth rates is independent of company size, enabling a direct comparison between any two companies. Moreover, the dividend yield can be used not just to compare one equity investment with another, but also to compare equities with fixed interest investments. In this way, a *yield ratio* can be derived, which can be used to examine whether, at a macro level, an investor's assumptions about the value of equities are consistent with the market's valuation of bonds. And once this macro evaluation has been made, then the investor can use precisely the same dividend yield measure to disaggregate to a micro level and to evaluate individual equities.

The second reason for using the dividend yield to understand rather than to determine the share price is closely related to the arguments just presented. In practice, there is considerable uncertainty in the information that is available to value any given share. There are, however, two very different respects in which the future is uncertain. On the one hand, the investor cannot quantify future outcomes beyond the very near future. The investor might, for example, be able to estimate profit for the next year or so, but he or she would be guessing beyond that. On the other hand, however, the investor might have a qualitative understanding that extends beyond the ability to quantify. So, for example, he or she might not be able to put a number on profits five years from now, but will nevertheless have a lot of loosely related information that is relevant to this future profit. This might include a feeling about how well the company is run, about the outlook for its product development, about economic growth and political risk in the markets it serves, and so on. In other words, while the investor might feel reluctant to quantify future profits and dividends, he or she might nevertheless feel able to judge whether or not the assumptions implicit in the share price are correct. And this judgement does not need to be precise. It is sufficient to be able to say that growth will be either higher or lower than the market expects, rather than by how much higher or lower. After all, what matters is picking the investments that will out-perform, rather than 'knowing' what the actual investment performance will turn out to be. In practice, investors cannot ask for more than this.

This discussion has attempted to show why the dividend yield can be useful as a valuation metric, in spite of its simplicity, and in spite also of its apparently naive assumptions when viewed as a model of share price determination. This is because it is not, in fact, best seen as a method of determining the true underlying value of a share, but rather as a theoretically sound basis for examining relative share price differences.

It is also interesting to examine changes in the dividend yield over time, rather than just between companies at a point in time. This is illustrated in Figure 2.1.

Figure 2.1 plots the long-run real dividend yield in the United States, using data from Shiller (2000). The dividend yield has fluctuated around a fairly stable long-run trend of 5%, although of particular interest is the rapid decline in recent years. This decline is due to a sharp increase in share prices, rather than to a steep fall in dividends. One interpretation of this is that the market is over-valued. An alternative explanation is that there has been a decline in the cost of capital, or an increase in the expected dividend growth rate, or both. Lending support to the over-valuation argument is the observation that the 1929 crash came at the point when dividend yields had declined steeply. Notice also that the very poor growth prospects during the Great Depression were associated with high dividend yields.

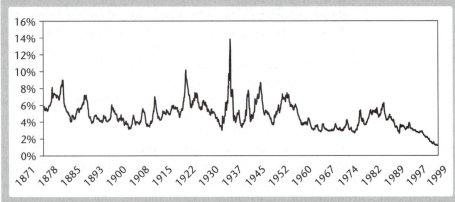

Figure 2.1 Long-run real dividend yield in the United States
Source: Shiller (2000)

2.8 Prospective (forward) dividend yields

A natural extension of the discussion above is to consider dividend forecasts beyond those for the current year. Analysts' forecasts are typically available for at least two years, and sometimes more. In practice, it is common to find analysts' reports comparing the share price with future dividend forecasts, rather than just with the forecast for the current year. In this way, a number of different measures of the dividend yield are possible, each of which is referred to as a prospective (or forward) dividend yield. This is illustrated in Table 2.4, where one-year (i.e. D_1/P_0), two-year (D_2/P_0) and three-year (D_3/P_0) prospective dividend yields are calculated for two different companies.

It can be seen that both companies have the same share price but a different dividend profile. A simple comparison of the prospective dividend yields reveals the underlying differences between the companies. The difference in growth rate can be seen when looking at the dividend yield for the two companies in the current year. Looking ahead to the dividend forecasts, it can be seen that this difference in yields diminishes quickly. While company A maintains a fairly stable prospective dividend yield, company B experiences rapid growth.

This is 'rule of thumb' evidence that the relative pricing of the two companies appears reasonable. It is important, however, not to place too much emphasis on evaluating prospective dividend yields beyond the current year. As was seen above,

Table 2.4 Prospective dividend yields

	Year 1	Year 2	Year 3	Year 4	
Company A					
Dividend	12	14	16	18	
Share price at end of year 4					265
Present value (20% cost of capital)	10	10	9	9	128
Current share price	165				
Prospective dividend yield	7.3%	8.5%	9.7%	10.9%	
Company B					
Dividend	2	8	12	20	
Share price at end of year 4					294
Present value (20% cost of capital)	2	6	7	10	142
Current share price	165				
Prospective dividend yield	1.2%	4.8%	7.2%	12.1%	

the one-year model is readily reconcilable to the DDM. This is because it is possible to show that the share price depends upon specific assumptions about the cost of capital and growth in *current* dividends. The two-year prospective dividend yield (for example) does not have such a straightforward economic interpretation.

2.9 Multi-stage dividend discount models

This chapter has so far explored two dividend-based valuation models: the DDM and the dividend yield model (including the DGM). These are, in fact, two ends of a spectrum of possible models and, instead of choosing one or the other, a hybrid model can be used that combines the best features of both. The flexibility of the DDM can be used for those years where there is sufficiently reliable data, and then the DGM can be used thereafter.

In its simplest form, a hybrid model is called a two-stage DDM. If, by way of example, dividend forecasts are available for the next five years, then the model would be as follows

$$P_0 = \frac{D_1}{(1+k)} + \frac{D_2}{(1+k)^2} + \frac{D_3}{(1+k)^3} + \frac{D_4}{(1+k)^4} + \frac{P_4}{(1+k)^4}$$

where

$$P_4 = \frac{D_5}{k-g}$$

It can be seen that this model uses the DDM for years 1–4 (stage 1 of the model), but then reverts to the DGM for an estimation of the share price at the end of year 4/beginning of year 5 (stage 2). This estimated share price represents the value of dividends in perpetuity from year 5, and because it is a price at the end of year 4, it must itself be discounted back to its present value at year 0.[17]

---

[17] It might be perceived to be easier to forecast the 'exit' (year 4) price directly, rather than through the DGM, though this would, in effect, amount to the same approach.

The two-stage model is particularly appropriate for a company that is growing at a rate that is temporarily either above or below its long-run average. This is because abnormally high or low growth cannot be sustained, and it is therefore inconsistent with the constant growth rate assumed by the DGM. Indeed, since it is unlikely that any company would actually grow at a constant rate, it is clearly sensible for investors to use their own forecasts of dividends for as many years as possible (five in the example above). Once forecasting becomes unrealistic, however, then investors can fall back on a constant growth rate assumption, guided perhaps by the expected growth rate in the economy as a whole. This does not imply that the investor actually believes that growth will be constant, but only that he or she has no reason to believe otherwise. In contrast to the explicit forecast for the forthcoming five years, the investor is 'admitting' that performance beyond year 5 is an unknown but that, nevertheless, some value must be put on it.

A dividend model need not, of course, comprise only two stages. There could, for example, be a first stage consisting of dividend forecasts (as above), followed by a second stage where a high level of growth is assumed, a third stage of slower growth and a fourth stage of zero growth. Such a model is conceptually no different from a two-stage model. It is just another of a wide range of possible hybrid models on the spectrum from the DDM to the dividend yield.[18] It has the benefit, however, of allowing the user to structure the available information about a company, making clear the implications for valuation.

As an example of this, suppose that the forecasts and assumptions as shown in Table 2.5 are made for a start-up company. The company pays no dividends for the first two years, but once established it is expected to grow rapidly. Beyond the first few years, competition is expected to erode the rate of growth, until eventually dividend payments are maintained at a constant level.

Table 2.5 Multi-stage dividend discount model

Year	Dividends	Cost of capital	Value
1	0	12%	0
2	0	12%	0
3	10	12%	7
4	10	12%	6
5–8	Growth rate 15%	12%	27
9–18	Growth rate 5%	12%	50
19 onward	No further growth	12%	31
	Current share price		121

---

[18] A popular variant is the H model (Fuller and Hsia, 1984), which assumes a linear decline in the growth rate during stage 1 of a two-stage model. This avoids the abrupt change in dividends arising if constant rates are chosen in both stages.

These assumptions give a current share price of $121. They also make full use of the information that investors have about the company, and they model the investors' understanding of how the company is expected to develop.

Notice that a straightforward DGM could not be used in this example, because there are no dividends paid at the end of the first year. The simplest model to use would be one where a constant growth rate is applied to year 3 dividends to give a price at the beginning of year 2. This price could then be discounted to give a current price. If this is done, the resulting growth rate for a share price of $121 would be 5.6%. It can be seen that estimating this growth rate without the benefit of the multi-stage model would be extremely difficult. In effect, the multi-stage model provides a helpful analytical structure, making explicit the hidden assumptions behind the valuation.

2.10   Problems with dividend-based valuation

Before leaving dividend-based valuation, it is important to discuss some theoretical and practical problems. These apply particularly to the dividend growth model, with its implicit assumption that there is an informative relationship between current dividends and all future dividends (and thereby between current dividends and the share price). In practice, there is likely to be such a relationship, but in theory there need not be.

The most important criticism of dividend-based valuation comes from Miller and Modigliani (1961), whose work is frequently quoted in support of the idea that dividend policy is irrelevant to valuation. Consider, for example, that there might be investment using retained earnings without any dividends being paid, or there might alternatively be the same level of investment achieved by a combination of a new equity issue and a dividend payment.[19] Either way, the value of the company is unaffected. This being the case, as long as a company maintains its investment plans it can pay whatever it likes in dividends at the end of the year, without affecting the underlying value of the company. In turn, this suggests that there is no reason to expect some sort of direct relationship between current dividends and future dividends, implying that (even though the DDM remains valid) current dividend-based valuation is without foundation. In short, we are left with what Penman (1992) has termed the 'dividend conundrum', whereby 'price is based upon future dividends but observed dividends do not tell us anything about price'.

Fortunately, this conundrum is less problematic than it appears at first. The argument that current dividends *need* not be relevant to future dividends does not mean that that they *are* not. In practice, the level of the current dividend is often consciously decided by management with a view to the company's ability to sustain or to grow the dividend in the future. In effect, company managers themselves often have a DGM implicit in their dividend decisions, and

---

[19] The equivalence of these two financing methods requires that shares are priced efficiently by the stock market and that there are no transactions costs or taxes associated with raising equity and paying dividends.

changes in the level of dividends are used as a signal of managers' own expectations of future dividend performance.[20]

The Miller and Modigliani critique does, however, highlight the importance of understanding the relationship between current dividends and future dividends. In so doing, it suggests significant problems. For example, dividend growth models do not necessarily 'travel' well. In a world of cross-border investment, it is vitally important to have comparable cross-border measures. Countries vary, however, in their patterns of dividend payments. This is partly due to legal and taxation differences but, more fundamentally, it is due to varying decision-making processes. As is highlighted by Miller and Modigliani, there is no reason why countries should not use dividend payments in very different ways, thereby compromising the usefulness of the dividend yield in assessing valuation differences. Even within a single country, or within a single market sector, the differences can be great. For example, the role of the dividend has been reduced in recent years because of the growing importance of share buy-backs and special dividends, both of which make the current dividend less useful as an indicator of future dividends.

Perhaps the most fundamental problem of all, however, is that dividend-based valuation models do not address the determinants of dividend growth. In other words, they do not help in explaining the relationship between current dividends and future dividends. For any company, the ability to achieve growth in dividends rests ultimately on the rate of return that can be achieved on the company's investments. This is particularly evident for companies that do not currently pay dividends. While it remains true for these companies that value depends upon future dividends, there is no dividend-based information at all on which analysts can ground their valuations.

The next chapter will start to address these issues by examining the underlying determinants of dividend growth.

Dividend policy and market reaction

The best that can be said about yesterday's dividend cut from British Energy is that it has taken some of the uncertainty out of its share price. Sadly, even the resulting 22 per cent drop to 132p is unlikely to assuage investors' doubts about the direction of the electricity market. The decision to halve the dividend so soon after buying back £82m of shares has scarcely boosted confidence in the management's ability to assess the value of the company's own shares . . . What matters for now is sentiment. Investors surprised by the dividend cut will remain sceptical of the management's statement that it is 'rebasing' its dividend to a new and sustainable level.

Source: Financial Times, Lex Column, 11 May 2000

The amount of dividend that a company pays in any given year is determined by management, and is therefore discretionary. Over time, however, the rate at which dividends grow is constrained by the company's underlying earnings growth

---

[20] The signalling behaviour of dividends was explored as long ago as in Lintner (1956). For recent evidence regarding UK companies, analysts and fund managers, see Barker (1999).

rate, such that aggregate, long-run dividend payments are not discretionary. Since it is likely that managers have better information than financial markets concerning the company's prospects for earnings growth, they can effectively use their discretion over dividend policy to convey – via the dividend growth model – their expectations concerning growth and value. Specifically, current dividend policy affects both the yield and the achieved dividend growth rate, and an increase in the rate of dividend growth is a positive signal to the market. In the example above, however, the managers of British Energy had set themselves a dividend growth rate that the company was unable to sustain, and a dividend cut became necessary. This had two negative effects. First, the share price dropped to reflect the managers' reduced expectations of future earnings performance. Second, the credibility of the managers was damaged, and investors became sceptical even of the revised dividend policy. Moreover, the company had sent a conflicting signal by buying back shares. In effect, a buy-back is a large, one-off dividend, and it can be a signal from managers that they believe the company's shares to be under-valued.

A similar story emerges from the following article:

Dividend policy is sometimes viewed as a more reliable signal of a management's judgement of its company's financial position than its general statements about prospects. But a dividend cut today from M&S, whose troubles have been clear for months, would have little value as a signalling device. The central question, for M&S as for any other company, is whether the business can reinvest any surplus cash more profitably than its shareholders could.

Source: Financial Times, Lex Column, 23 May 2000

While acknowledging the importance of the dividend as a signalling mechanism, this article responds to the Miller and Modigliani critique, making it clear that dividend growth and shareholder value depend ultimately on the return on corporate investment, and not on dividend policy. This will be the subject of Chapter 3.

Summary

The main points from this chapter may be summarized as follows:

- The *dividend discount model (DDM)* is the fundamental valuation model. It is the only valuation model that is entirely consistent with valuation theory without the need to make any constraining assumptions. All valuation models must be reconcilable to the DDM.

- The DDM states that the *value* of a share is equal to the discounted value of all future dividends (or, alternatively, that the share *price* equals *expected* value).

- According to the DDM, any change in the share price must be due to either a change in the market's expectations of future dividends or to a change in the cost of capital at which those dividends are discounted. There are no other possibilities.

- The DDM is correct in theory but unworkable in practice, because its demands for data about the future are unrealistic. In practice, alternative valuation models must be used.

- The DDM can be simplified by imposing assumptions. By assuming constant dividends and constant cost of capital, the *dividend yield model* is derived, where the cost of capital equals the ratio of current dividends to the share price. Alternatively, if dividends are assumed to grow at a constant rate, then the *dividend growth model* (DGM) is derived, where the cost of capital equals the dividend yield plus the dividend growth rate.

- The DGM allows currently available information to be used to determine the share price. It therefore differs from the DDM because it imposes assumptions about what will happen in the future, rather than requiring the future be 'known'.

- The assumptions of the DGM are strong, however, making it difficult to use in *determining* the *value* of shares. The DGM therefore can be more effectively used to *understand* the share *price*. An important application is in understanding *relative pricing differences*, as reflected in *yield premiums* or *yield discounts*. This role is well suited to decisions between alternative investments, and it enables the use of 'soft' data that would, in practice, be difficult to quantify within a dividend discount model.

- Multi-stage dividend discount models combine the best features of the DDM and the DGM, using dividend forecasts wherever possible and making simplifying assumptions only when there is no better alternative.

- Dividend-based valuation can be problematic, and Miller and Modigliani highlight the difficulties in using current dividends to predict future dividends. This suggests a need to understand and to model the underlying determinants of dividend growth, which is the subject of Chapter 3.

References

Barker, R.G. (1999). 'The Role of Dividends in Valuation Models Used by Analysts and Fund Managers', *European Accounting Review*, 8(2), 195–218.

Brealey, R. and S. Myers (2000). *Principles of Corporate Finance* (6th edn). Auckland: McGraw-Hill International.

Copeland, T.E. and J.F. Weston (1988). *Financial Theory and Corporate Policy*. London: Addison-Wesley.

Fuller, R.J. and C-C. Hsia (1984). 'A Simplified Common Stock Valuation Model', *Financial Analysts Journal*, Sept.–Oct., 49–56.

Gordon, M. (1962). *Investment, Financing, and Valuation of the Corporation*. Homewood, IL: Irwin.

Lintner, J. (1956). 'Distribution of Incomes of Corporations Among Dividends, Retained Earnings, and Taxes', *American Economic Review*, May, 97–113.

Miller, M. and F. Modigliani (1961). 'Dividend Policy, Growth, and the Valuation of Shares', *Journal of Business*, 34(4), 411–33.

Penman, S. (1992). 'Return to Fundamentals', *Journal of Accounting, Auditing and Finance*, 7, 465–83.

Shiller, R.J. (2000). *Irrational Exuberance*. Princeton, NJ: Princeton University Press.

Williams, J.B. (1938). *The Theory of Investment Value*. Cambridge, MA: Harvard University Press.

Special cases of the dividend discount model

The DDM can be simplified greatly by means of imposing assumptions about the time-series behaviour of dividends. Specifically, the assumption of constant dividends gives the dividend yield model, and the assumption of constant dividend growth gives the dividend growth model.

Dividend yield model

If dividends are constant, then the DDM can be written as follows

$$P_0 = \frac{D_1}{(1 + k)} + \frac{D_1}{(1 + k)^2} + \frac{D_1}{(1 + k)^3} + \ldots + \frac{D_1}{(1 + k)^\infty}$$

Multiplying through by $(1 + k)$ gives

$$P_0(1 + k) = D_1 + \frac{D_1}{(1 + k)} + \frac{D_1}{(1 + k)^2} + \ldots + \frac{D_1}{(1 + k)^{\infty-1}}$$

If the first equation is subtracted from the second, then most terms cancel

$$P_0 k = D_1 - \frac{D_1}{(1 + k)^\infty}$$

The final term in this equation is in the limit equal to zero, and the dividend yield model is therefore given by

$$k = \frac{D_1}{P_0}$$

Dividend growth model

Following a similar procedure to the above, the assumption of a constant rate of dividend growth allows the DDM to be written as follows

$$P_0 = \frac{D_1}{(1 + k)} + \frac{D_1(1 + g)}{(1 + k)^2} + \frac{D_1(1 + g)^2}{(1 + k)^3} + \ldots + \frac{D_1(1 + g)^{\infty-1}}{(1 + k)^\infty}$$

Multiplying through by $(1 + g)$ and dividing through by $(1 + k)$ gives

$$\frac{P_0(1 + g)}{(1 + k)} = \frac{D_1(1 + g)}{(1 + k)^2} + \frac{D_1(1 + g)^2}{(1 + k)^3} + \ldots + \frac{D_1(1 + g)^\infty}{(1 + k)^{\infty+1}}$$

If $k > g$, then the final term in this equation is in the limit equal to zero. Subtracting the second expression from the first therefore gives

$$P_0 - \frac{P_0(1 + g)}{(1 + k)} = \frac{D_1}{(1 + k)}$$

Rearranging

$$P_0(1 + k) - P_0(1 + g) = D_1$$

$$P_0 = \frac{D_1}{k - g}$$

3 Growth in dividends and share prices

Overview
- What causes dividends to grow?
- The rate of dividend growth
- Links between dividend growth and valuation
- The rate of return spread: cost of capital vs. return on equity
- Income vs. growth stocks
- The need to look beyond dividends

The previous chapter showed that the price of a share depends upon expected future dividends, and that the rate of growth of current dividends is therefore of central importance to equity valuation. This chapter will now explore the importance of dividend growth further, identifying the sources of growth as a means of providing insight into valuation models. In so doing, the chapter will introduce the role of financial statements in valuation, including the parts played by profit, book value and return on capital.

3.1 What causes dividends to grow?

One way for dividends to grow is for shareholders to continuously invest more capital in the company, through new equity issues, rights issues and so on. Growth arises simply because a larger amount of capital is likely to generate a larger income stream. Importantly, however, growth in dividends *per share* requires that the rate of return on new equity capital exceeds that on existing capital. Consider, for example, a company that has shareholders' capital of $1 000, which generates an ongoing cash flow of $100 (10% return), all of which is paid as dividends. If invested capital increases by $400 to $1 400, and if the incremental return on new investment is only 5%, then dividends will increase by 20% to $120. Suppose, however, that there is one share for every $1 of invested capital. Then dividends *per share* were initially 10 cents, but they became 8.6 cents after the increase in capital. In other words, while total shareholder value increases with the injection of new capital, the value of individual shares falls.[1]

---

[1] If the DDM is applied to the aggregate dividend stream of the company, then aggregate dividend growth would be shown to lead to an increase in shareholder value. If, however, the model is applied to the price of the shares held by the original investors in the company, then the annual dividend

Dividends per share can also increase via a second, equivalent route. Whenever a company earns a positive return on capital, it has a choice between either paying the profit back to its shareholders (in the form of dividends) or re-investing it in the company. In effect, any re-investment increases the capital value of each share and, with a positive rate of return, this enables sustainable growth in dividends per share.[2] This dividend growth through retained profits increases the value of existing shares, which contrasts with growth through new equity issues, where shareholder value is spread across both new and existing shares. In other words, retentions are associated with fewer shares at higher prices, while new equity issues lead to more shares at lower prices. Total shareholder value is the same for a given investment through either route, however, and there is no substantive difference between these two cases.[3] Indeed, even though dividends per share are more likely to increase when there are retentions rather than new issues, dividends per dollar of invested capital will be the same in both cases. Either way, the investment of new capital will lead to a higher overall return per dollar of capital if the rate of return on new investment exceeds that on existing investment, and vice versa.[4]

The equivalence of these two sources is made more obvious by recognizing that both depend, ultimately, on a positive return on capital. It is clear from the case of retentions that the existence of a positive return enables the re-investment that, in turn, enables growth. Less directly, but based upon similar reasoning, a continuous supply of new capital can only be possible if the economy is growing, by means of generating positive returns. While ongoing new investment is a necessary precondition of sustainable dividend growth, it is therefore the existence of a positive return on capital that is the key prerequisite of growth.

It is possible, of course, for the return on capital itself to increase, leading to an increase in dividend growth without an associated increase in invested capital. Shareholders therefore get something for nothing, because their (unchanged) investment generates a higher dividend stream.[5] Increases in the return on capital cannot, however, be a sustainable source of dividend growth, because there is necessarily a limit to the rate of return that can be achieved. In any given year, a company's return on equity is likely to either rise or fall,

would fall from 10 cents to 7.5 cents. The rising shareholder value and the declining share price are reconcilable through the change in the number of shares in issue.

[2] In any given year, an increase in the ratio of profit that is paid back rather than retained (i.e. increasing the payout ratio) will increase dividend growth. This is simply another way of saying that the company has decided to increase the dividend. Such increases cannot, however, be sustained. This is partly because growth in the payout ratio is constrained by the requirement that dividends are paid out of profits. More fundamentally, though, higher levels of dividend payout imply lower levels of re-investment of profits. In turn, this means that there will be fewer profits in future with which to pay future dividends. In other words, increasing the slice of the profit cake that is paid as dividends in the current year leads to a smaller cake in future years.

[3] Strictly, the effect is the same only under the assumptions of Miller and Modigliani (1961), as discussed in Chapter 2.

[4] More formally, if the marginal return on equity exceeds the average return on equity, then the average return will rise with new investment, and vice versa.

[5] This assumes, of course, no change in the cost of capital.

due to changes in demand, or productivity or input costs. Over time, though, fluctuations within a company's rate of return on equity are likely to fall within fairly tight parameters. Sustainable dividend growth cannot therefore come from an ever-increasing return on capital, but is instead dependent upon ongoing new capital investment.

In summary, sustainable dividend growth requires both that a company earns a positive rate of return on shareholders' capital and also that shareholders' capital is enabled to grow, either through new investment or through the retention of profits. Both of these requirements lead to the common-sense conclusion that the rate of return on equity is the fundamental determinant of dividend growth.

3.2   The rate of dividend growth

The relationships between dividend growth, invested capital, return on capital and valuation can now be explored in more depth. In doing this, it is worth recalling that dividends are defined here to include all cash flows between the company and its shareholders. This definition embraces both of the forms of capital investment discussed above (i.e. both new issues and retentions). So, for example, if a company pays $80 in dividends out of profits of $100 while, at the same time, raising new equity of $130, then dividends as defined here would be $(50). This definition ensures consistency with the cash-flow-based valuation theory outlined in Chapter 2.[6]

On the basis of this definition of dividends, a fundamental relationship exists between the key variables in the financial statements. Specifically, if the variable B is defined as the value of shareholders' invested capital that is recorded in the accounts (i.e. 'book value' of shareholders' capital) and if the variable E is defined to be the earnings achieved during a given year (i.e. the profits attributable to shareholders), then the following relationship holds

$$B_0 + E_1 - D_1 = B_1$$

In words, the change in invested capital over the year (the difference between B_0 and B_1) is equal to the earnings generated during the year (E_1) less the net amount paid out to shareholders (D_1).

The relationship between E and D can be summarized in the form of an earnings retention ratio, defined as b. Since earnings must either be retained or paid out, the sum of the proportions retained and paid out must be equal to one (i.e. $b + (1 - b) = 1$). The amount that is retained is given by bE, while payouts are given by $(1 - b)E$. The variable $(1 - b)$ is therefore defined as the dividend payout ratio, and the above expression can be simplified as follows

$$B_0 + b_1E_1 = B_1$$

---

[6] The intuition behind this definition of dividends is clearer if an emphasis is placed on aggregate dividends (and shareholder value), rather than on dividends per share (and share price). This is because new issues and retentions have the same effect on shareholder value, while their differential effect on dividends per share can be misleading (as discussed earlier).

Finally, there is also a relationship between the book value of shareholders' capital and earnings, since earnings are the product of the invested capital and the rate of return on capital (commonly referred to as the return on equity, ROE). While earnings are the *amount* of the return on invested capital, the ROE is the *rate* of return. Specifically, if the ROE is defined as R, then $E_1 = B_0 R_1$, and the expression above becomes

$$B_0(1 + b_1 R_1) = B_1$$

This expression has a straightforward interpretation. The growth in invested capital is determined jointly by the return on equity and the proportion of the return that is retained rather than paid out. This relationship holds true regardless of the assumptions that are made regarding the ROE or the payout ratio. In other words, it is entirely general and involves no underlying assumptions.

It can be shown that if the extra assumptions are imposed that both R and b are constant over time, then the growth term, bR, applies also to both earnings and dividends. The proof of this relationship is given in the Appendix. It is, however, an intuitive result. Dividend growth must come from earnings growth which must, in turn, come from growth in invested capital, arising from the re-investment of prior year earnings.[7]

If, however, either the retention ratio or the return on equity do not remain constant, then the rate of dividend growth will change also. This implies that the constant growth assumption of the dividend growth model is itself necessarily based on the assumptions of a constant retention ratio and a constant return on equity and, thereby, on constant, equal rates of growth in invested capital, earnings and dividends. More formally, dividends *must* grow at the rate bR if the dividend growth model is to be valid.

This discussion can be illustrated by taking the example of a simple company, in which all of shareholders' invested capital is used to acquire a single financial asset (such as a bond). This asset generates an annual cash return. To keep the example simple, it can be assumed that there are no costs incurred by the company, such that the cash return from the asset is equal to the company's annual earnings (or profit). The rate of return on the asset can vary each year (e.g. a variable-rate bond). Also, the company can decide whether to retain the annual earnings and re-invest them in the financial asset (e.g. purchasing additional bonds), or else return them to shareholders.

This example has two benefits for the purposes of this chapter. First, it represents the simplest case of a 'real' company. In contrast to the discussion in Chapter 2, where the valuation of dividends was analysed but the source of the dividends was not addressed, the present example introduces shareholders' capital, corporate assets and annual profits. This allows some insight into the role of the financial statements in valuation models. This insight is limited, of

---

[7] Alternatively, the company might pay dividends and simultaneously raise new equity capital. This possibility arises from the earlier discussion of the two methods of new investment. If there is to be a constant rate of dividend growth, however, then there cannot be occasional issues of new capital, because these would lead to step changes in the rate of growth.

course, because there are no operating assets or operating cash flows, but for the time being it is sufficient to have just a single asset as the only source of profit. The second benefit is that the example assumes that the company's cash flows are always equal to its earnings and that, likewise, shareholders' invested capital is expressed in terms of a value that is realizable for cash. This ensures consistency with the underlying valuation framework introduced in Chapter 2, which used cash flow data exclusively. In later chapters the differences between cash flow data and financial statement data will be explored, including (for example) the implications of a company's earnings differing from its cash flow. For the time being, these differences are assumed not to exist, which will allow a clearer demonstration of the key characteristics of valuation models.

The change in the dividend growth rate caused by changes in the retention ratio and the return on equity can be demonstrated with a numerical example. Table 3.1 reports on a company with an initial value of invested capital (B_0) of $1 000, a return on this capital (ROE) of 20% and a retention ratio (b) of 60% (i.e. the dividend payout ratio ($1 - b$) must therefore be 40%). In the first three years, the variables R and b are held constant, with the effect that invested capital, earnings and dividends all grow at the same rate. This growth rate is 12%, which is the product of R and b (20% × 60% = 12%).

Table 3.1 Dividend growth: the effect of a change in the rate of capital investment

	Year 1	Year 2	Year 3	Year 4	Year 5	Year 6
Initial capital investment (B_t)	1 000.00	1 120.00	1 254.40	1 404.93	1 581.95	1 781.27
Return on equity (R_{t+1})	20%	20%	20%	20%	20%	20%
Earnings (E_{t+1})	200.00	224.00	250.88	280.99	316.39	356.25
Retention ratio (b_{t+1})	60%	60%	60%	63%	63%	63%
Dividends (D_{t+1})	80.00	89.60	100.35	103.96	117.06	131.81
End of year invested capital (B_{t+1})	1 120.00	1 254.40	1 404.93	1 581.95	1 781.27	2 005.72
Invested capital growth	12.0%	12.0%	12.0%	12.6%	12.6%	12.6%
Earnings growth		12.0%	12.0%	12.0%	12.6%	12.6%
Dividend growth		12.0%	12.0%	3.6%	12.6%	12.6%

During the fourth year, earnings continue to grow at 12%, but at the end of the year the retention ratio has increased to 63%. In other words, an extra 3% of earnings ($8.43) is retained relative to the previous year. This has three effects. First, dividend growth in the fourth year has slowed from 12% to 3.6% (with the difference, 8.4%, given by the ratio of $8.43 to $100.35, the year 3 dividend). Second, the growth in invested capital has increased from 12% to 12.6% (with, again, the 0.6% difference being given by the ratio of $8.43 to $1 404.93, the value of opening invested capital). Third, the effect of this increase on invested capital, together with a constant return on equity, was to increase the future growth rate of dividends to 12.6% (which equals bR, or 63% of 20%). If, conversely, there had been a one-off decrease in the retention ratio, then this would have raised dividend growth in the current year but lowered the sustainable dividend growth rate, because the earnings paid out would not be re-invested to generate future growth.

This example of a change in the retention ratio may be contrasted with the effect of a change in the return on equity. Specifically, Table 3.2 shows the effect of a permanent increase in the return on equity in year 4.

Table 3.2 Dividend growth: the effect of a change in the return on equity

	Year 1	Year 2	Year 3	Year 4	Year 5	Year 6
Initial capital investment (B_t)	1 000.00	1 120.00	1 254.40	1 404.93	1 615.67	1 858.02
Return on equity (R_{t+1})	20%	20%	20%	25%	25%	25%
Earnings (E_{t+1})	200.00	224.00	250.88	351.23	403.92	464.50
Retention ratio (b_{t+1})	60%	60%	60%	60%	60%	60%
Dividends (D_{t+1})	80.00	89.60	100.35	140.49	161.57	185.80
End of year invested capital (B_{t+1})	1 120.00	1 254.40	1 404.93	1 615.67	1 858.02	2 136.72
Invested capital growth	12.0%	12.0%	12.0%	15.0%	15.0%	15.0%
Earnings growth		12.0%	12.0%	40.0%	15.0%	15.0%
Dividend growth		12.0%	12.0%	40.0%	15.0%	15.0%

A permanent increase in the return on equity serves first to increase the rate of growth in earnings in the fourth year. In turn, and because the retention ratio remains unchanged, this causes the same rate of growth in dividends. The actual growth rate achieved is 40%. Also, the increase in retained earnings generates a permanent increase in the rate of growth of invested capital to 15%, where the increase is simply the retention ratio multiplied by the increase in the rate of return (i.e. $bR_4 - bR_3 = 15\% - 12\% = 3\%$). From year 4 onwards, b and R are constant, and invested capital, earnings and dividends therefore all grow at the constant rate 15% (= bR).[8]

It will be helpful to present one final example, where the growth rate of dividends is affected by a simultaneous, permanent change in both b and R. It is assumed that R increases to 23% in year 4, at which time b falls to 52%, as shown in Table 3.3.

This example is constructed such that both R and b change in a way that maintains long-run dividend growth beyond year 4 at approximately 12%. In other words, the effect of the increase in R is offset by the effect of the reduction in b. In year 4, the increased R causes earnings to increase, but the reduced b causes the amount of retained earnings to stay approximately the same. In other words, dividends grow in year 4 to a level where retained earnings allow the growth in invested capital to equal (but not exceed) 12%. The absolute level of earnings and dividends generated in future will always exceed that which was

---

[8] The current share price will reflect all these future gains. The gains themselves will occur gradually over time, but the *expectation* of them causes them all to be recognized in the current share price. Note also that the level of invested capital, I, is not directly relevant to the share price. All that matters is the earnings that the investment generates.

Table 3.3 Dividend growth: the effect of a change in both the rate of investment and the return on equity

	Year 1	Year 2	Year 3	Year 4	Year 5	Year 6
Initial capital investment (B_t)	1 000.00	1 120.00	1 254.40	1 404.93	1 572.96	1 761.08
Return on equity (R_{t+1})	20%	20%	20%	23%	23%	23%
Earnings (E_{t+1})	200.00	224.00	250.88	323.13	361.78	405.05
Retention ratio (b_{t+1})	60%	60%	60%	52%	52%	52%
Dividends (D_{t+1})	80.00	89.60	100.35	155.10	173.65	194.42
End of year invested capital (B_{t+1})	1 120.00	1 254.40	1 404.93	1 572.96	1 761.08	1 971.71
Invested capital growth	12.00%	12.00%	12.00%	11.96%	11.96%	11.96%
Earnings growth		12.00%	12.00%	28.80%	11.96%	11.96%
Dividend growth		12.00%	12.00%	54.56%	11.96%	11.96%

possible before the increase in R, but the increased payout ratio ensures that a greater percentage is distributed to shareholders to maintain the same constant growth rate as before. In effect, the shareholders are investing in the company at the same annual rate as before, but their annual return has increased.[9]

These examples demonstrate the impact on dividend growth of simple changes in the retention ratio and the return on equity. Whenever there are changes of this type, the constant growth rate bR is no longer valid. In the Appendix, a general expression is derived for dividend growth, which includes the constant rate bR as a special case. This illustrates the demanding nature of the underlying assumptions of constant dividend growth, although it also reinforces the conclusion that dividend growth depends exclusively upon the return on equity and the rate of new investment. For the time being, it is worth noting simply that the DGM makes very strong implicit assumptions.

3.3 Links between dividend growth and valuation

The above discussion can now be combined with the analysis in Chapter 2 of the relationship between the share price and dividend growth. In particular, since it has been demonstrated that dividend growth depends upon the return on equity and the rate of new investment, it must follow that the share price itself depends upon these two variables.

Consider first the DGM, which is reproduced below. It should be remembered that this model assumes constant dividend growth and a constant cost of capital

$$P_0 = \frac{D_1}{k - g}$$

---

[9] In practice, an increase in the expected ROE is actually likely to have the opposite effect to that described here, namely that the rate of re-investment would increase in view of the higher expected return. It might also be expected the ROE on new investment would itself decline as the level of investment grows.

It has just been shown that the 'hidden' assumptions of constant growth in the DGM are that the rate of return on equity (R) and the retention ratio (b) are both constant, implying a rate of dividend growth equal to bR. With these assumptions in place, and also noting that dividends can be expressed in terms of earnings and the payout ratio (i.e. $D = (1 - b)E$), the dividend growth model can be re-stated as follows

$$P_0 = \frac{(1 - b)E_1}{k - bR}$$

This expression shows clearly that an increase in the return on equity will always lead to an increase in the share price. This happens in two ways. First, an increase in the return on equity will lead to an increase in earnings and, second, it will reduce the difference between the cost of capital (k) and the dividend growth rate (bR). The first effect increases the numerator on the right-hand side of the equation, while the second effect causes the denominator to fall. Both changes serve to increase the share price. This result is intuitive. The more that a company is able to earn on a given sum of invested capital, the more the company must be worth.

Share prices and the return on capital

Just as equity analysts around the world were settling comfortably into the idea that the markets were journeying towards more 'sensible' valuations of glamour stocks, there was a lurch in the other direction . . . The week started with a fall of 9.4 per cent in the Nasdaq index, heavily weighted with US high-tech stocks . . . But on Thursday the Nasdaq jumped 2%, and moved up further in early trading yesterday . . . Are these valuations crazy? Estimates by Goldman Sachs, the bank, suggest that at current share prices, investors are expecting technology, media and telecommunications companies (TMT) to deliver a 21 per cent a year return on investment for the next ten years, compared with a historical return on capital of 14%.

Source: Financial Times, Editorial, 8 April 2000

The high valuations of TMT stocks are based necessarily upon expectations of high cash flow returns on shareholders' capital (i.e. high future dividends). On the basis of current share prices, Goldman Sachs has estimated the demanding implicit expectation of a 21% return on capital over a ten year period.

The effect on value of a change in the retention ratio is less obvious. The simplest case arises when the retention ratio is equal to 0 and all earnings are paid as dividends. The DGM then reduces very simply to

$$P_0 = \frac{E}{k} = \frac{D}{k}$$

This is the no-growth dividend yield model. When dividends and earnings are one and the same, there are no earnings re-invested in the company and the growth in dividends is necessarily 0. This requires, of course, making the simplifying assumption that R is constant. In effect, it is assumed that E is constant, perpetuity earnings generated by a fixed investment (B) and a fixed rate of return (R). Under these no-growth conditions the share price will remain unchanged in perpetuity.

If the retention ratio is not equal to 0, implying dividend growth, then the share price effect of a change in the retention ratio will depend upon the relationship between the cost of capital and the return on equity. In the special case where the two are equal, the DGM can be expressed as follows

$$P_0 = \frac{(1-b)E}{k-bR} = \frac{(1-b)E}{(1-b)k} = \frac{E}{k}$$

Here, again, the share price equals discounted perpetuity earnings. In this case, although there is dividend growth through retentions, shareholders are *indifferent* between receiving dividends and re-investing profits in the company. This is illustrated in Table 3.4. The data from the example above are used to present three separate scenarios, with the retention ratio given values in year 4 of 0.4, 0.6 and 0.8, respectively. In each scenario the cost of capital, retention ratio and return on equity are fixed, and the share price is therefore determined using the DGM (e.g. the share price at the beginning of year 4 is $1 405, which, for $b = 0.6$, equals dividends of 112.4 divided by an excess of cost of capital over dividend growth rate of 8%).

Table 3.4 The effect of a different rate of new investment when the cost of capital equals the return on equity

(Return on equity = cost of capital = 20%)		Retention ratio = 0.4		Retention ratio = 0.6		Retention ratio = 0.8	
		Year 4	Year 5	Year 4	Year 5	Year 4	Year 5
Investment in shares	Opening price (P_t)	1 405	1 517	1 405	1 574	1 405	1 630
	Dividends (D_{t+1})	169	182	112	126	56	65
	Closing price (P_{t+1})	1 517	1 638	1 574	1 762	1 630	1 890
	Return from income (D_{t+1}/P_t)	12%	12%	8%	8%	4%	4%
	Return from growth (P_{t+1}/P_t)	8%	8%	12%	12%	16%	16%
	Total return	20%	20%	20%	20%	20%	20%
External investment	Opening investment		169		112		56
	Return (Opening × k)		34		23		11
	New investment	169	182	112	126	56	65
	Closing investment	169	385	112	261	56	132
Total investment value		1 686	2 023	1 686	2 023	1 686	2 023

Since k is defined to be the opportunity cost of investing in the company (and it therefore has the same risk characteristics as the equity investment), and because $k = R$, then the shareholder is indifferent between dividends and retentions. The current share price and the total investment value remain unchanged whatever the retention ratio. For example, the value at the end of year 2 is $2 023. For a retention ratio of 40%, this value is comprised of a share price of $1 638 and an investment outside the company of $385, whereas for a 60% retention ratio the split is $1 762 and $261, respectively. In other words, a higher retention ratio is associated with a greater proportion of value retained within the company, implying a higher share price over time. In turn, this changes the balance of investment return inside the company in favour of growth over income. For example, when the retention ratio is 40%, the return from dividend income is 12% and from dividend growth is 8%, whereas for a retention ratio of 60% these ratios are exactly the opposite. Notice, however, that the overall expected return remains at 20% in all cases, both inside and outside the company.

In summary of this section, there are two special cases where the share price is equal to perpetuity earnings divided by the cost of capital. These cases arise either when the retention ratio equals zero or when the cost of capital equals the return on equity. In a more realistic setting, of course, neither of these two conditions is likely to hold. It is therefore important to examine the implications of the situation where, with a retention ratio different from zero, the cost of capital differs from the return on equity.[10]

3.4 The rate of return spread: cost of capital vs. return on equity

It will be helpful at this point to step back and reconsider the definitions of the cost of capital (k) and the return on equity (R). The variable k is defined as the shareholders' expected rate of return when making or holding an equity investment. It is a risk-adjusted return that equals the expected return available from a comparably risky investment. In contrast, the variable R is the actual return that a company is able to make on the capital that has been invested. It is an earnings gain as a percentage of a capital investment. Both k and R are therefore types of investment returns from a given company. The two returns are fundamentally different, however, because the former is a return on an equity investment in the company, whereas the latter is the investment return made by the company itself.

As an example, two companies may be in the same industry and have similar risk characteristics. They will therefore have the same value of k. They might also have the same level of invested capital, B. If, however, they differ in the return on equity that each expects to achieve on this capital, then the firm with the higher return will generate higher future earnings which, when discounted, will give a higher share price. This is illustrated in Table 3.5.

Consider first company A. Shareholders have invested $1 000, which is expected to achieve a rate of return of 20%. This is the same rate as the cost of capital. The shareholders are therefore no better or worse off than they would

---

[10] The zero retention ratio can actually be viewed as a special case of the return on equity being equal to the cost of capital. This is because valuation theory implicitly assumes that shareholders are reinvesting dividends elsewhere at a return equal to the cost of capital.

Table 3.5 Share price when the return on equity exceeds the cost of capital

	Company A	Company B
Cost of capital, k	20%	20%
Earnings, E_{t+1}	200	250
Retention ratio, b	60%	60%
Dividends, D_{t+1}	80	100
Return on equity, R	20%	25%
Price, $P_t = (1 - b)E_{t+1}/(k - bR)$	1 000	2 000
Shareholders' invested capital, B_t	1 000	1 000

otherwise be, and the share price equals the amount of the invested capital. In contrast, company B is expected to achieve a return on equity of 25% on the same $1 000 investment. This translates into a doubling of the share price from $1 000 to $2 000. In effect, company B has *created value*, because it is expected to achieve more with the invested capital than shareholders could earn in a comparably risky opportunity elsewhere. In short, if the return on equity exceeds the cost of capital, then value is created, but if it falls short, value is destroyed. It could be seen, for example, that an actual return on equity of 15% in perpetuity would reduce the share price to $545.

Value creation therefore arises when markets are not fully competitive. If a company is able to generate a return in excess of its cost of capital, then it is achieving something that comparably risky investments cannot achieve. This implies some form of advantage over the competition, and the reward for this is a higher share price.

Maximizing the rate of return spread

Retailing and retail property are two different businesses. They may be mutually dependent, but it is increasingly clear that being good at one is no guarantee of being good at the other. Such was clearly the thinking at Carrefour, the French hypermarket company, which recently announced it will sell some €1.5bn (£917m) of shopping mall assets to Klépierre, the quoted French company specialising in retail assets . . . Retailing industry analysts at Credit Lyonnais estimate that while Carrefour is earning 7 per cent return on equity on its real estate business, it earns 15–20 per cent returns on its core retailing business . . . Given Carrefour's need for capital to expand its hypermarkets business, particularly in central and eastern Europe, selling its shopping malls to a property expert makes sense.

Source: Financial Times, Norma Cohen, 4 August 2000

Carrefour has a competitive advantage in retailing, but not in real estate. This is manifested in its rate of return spread being greater in the former. The company's decision to withdraw capital from real estate and to re-invest in retailing is therefore value creating. Equally, the deal creates value for Klépierre shareholders if the company's specialization in real estate enables a positive rate of return spread over its €1.5bn investment.

If a company does have a return on equity that differs from its cost of capital, then a change in the rate of new investment will change the share price. Shareholders' total wealth is affected because they are changing the split between investment inside the company and investment outside, and each investment is generating a different return. If, for example, the retention ratio increases, then the investment in the company increases. If the return on equity exceeds the cost of capital, then the shareholders' funds are more effectively employed. Value is created and the share price rises. This is illustrated in Table 3.6, which uses the same data as above, except that the retention ratio is now 70% in both companies.

Table 3.6 The effect on share price of changing the rate of new investment when the return on equity exceeds the cost of capital

	Company A	Company B
Cost of capital, k	20%	20%
Earnings, E_{t+1}	200	250
Retention ratio, b	70%	70%
Dividends, D_{t+1}	60	75
Return on equity, R	20%	25%
Price, $P_t = (1 - b)E_{t+1}/(k - bR)$	1 000	3 000
Invested capital, B_t	1 000	1 000
Return from income (yield)	6%	2.5%
Return from growth	14%	17.5%
Total return	20%	20%

The share price of company A remains unchanged, and all that happens is that a greater proportion of the return comes in the form of an expectation of future growth, rather than actual income in the current year. The reason for the absence of a price change is that the cost of capital equals the return on equity. When company B invests incremental capital at an expected rate R that exceeds k, however, its share price increases to $3 000. This dramatic increase shows the importance of the rate of return spread, and of the ability of the company to invest more effectively than the competition.

In interpreting this dramatic effect of a change in the retention ratio, it is important to recognize the very strong implicit assumptions made by the use of the dividend growth model. First, the share price is calculated on the assumption that the 5% rate of return spread is maintainable in perpetuity. In practice, competition would be expected to erode gradually a positive spread. Second, an increase in the retention ratio would be expected to reduce somewhat the overall return on equity. This is because the most attractive investment projects will be started first, and each incremental investment would be expected to achieve a somewhat lower return. Third, and finally, it is important to recall that dividends are defined here to include all cash flows between a company and its shareholders. If a company has the opportunity to earn at a rate in excess of its cost of capital, then even though it might continue to pay dividends out of earnings, it might also raise new capital. In a conventional sense, its payout ratio would fall between zero and one, but in the sense used here its payout ratio would be negative, since the net cash flow is from shareholders to the company, rather than vice versa. Indeed, the example above is unrealistic in that the retention ratio is assumed to be independent of the rate of return spread. In practice, the share price will reflect the company's expected rate of return, on the assumption that shareholders will invest in the company whenever it is in their interest to do so (i.e. whenever the expected spread is positive). The dividend growth model, by contrast, allows the retention ratio to take any value, regardless of whether this is consistent with the expected rate of return. In the example above, there was value creation through a simple change in the retention ratio, but this was possible only because the retention ratio had initially been set arbitrarily at a constant, sub-optimally low level.

The example makes it clear, however, that the relationship between the rate of new investment and the rate of return spread is an important one for the value of the company. If there is profit retention and/or new capital investment, then (with a positive rate of return on equity), dividends will grow. Unless the incremental investment can achieve a return in excess of the cost of capital, however, then surplus funds are better paid back to shareholders than re-invested.

Value-creating growth

Just as the core Gap brand has started showing growth again, the Group's Old Navy and Banana Republic formats have slipped into trouble. In July, Old Navy's same store sales, which had been growing rapidly for years, dropped 17–19% while Banana Republic's were flat. The group blames much of this on an isolated problem at Old Navy's distribution centre . . . Investors, however, were less sanguine, knocking a fifth off the stock. This is, after all, the second time in four weeks that Gap has lowered its earnings estimates and the fifth month in a row that its like-for-like revenue growth – a negative one per cent groupwide – has been below expectations . . . Meanwhile, Gap's rapid roll-out of the downmarket Old Navy chain, now nearly 40 per cent of the group's square footage, should be tempered. More broadly, Gap must convince shareholders that it can execute properly at a time when it is expanding its selling space by more than 20 per cent annually.

Source: Financial Times, Lex Column, 4 August 2000

Investors' concerns over Gap's expected earnings raise questions about the company's ability to generate a positive rate of return spread. Against this background, the plan to invest further capital is worrying. This is especially because it is the under-performing Old Navy operation that is being expanded, suggesting that the rate of return spread is not being maximized. While the investment will cause earnings (and dividends) to grow in absolute terms, Gap faces a need to 'convince shareholders' that this growth will lead to value creation.

3.5 Income vs. growth stocks

The example above can be extended to consider, for any given combination of the cost of capital and the return on equity, the effect of varying the retention ratio. This can be done by first showing the relationship between total return and its sub-components, income and growth, as given by the simple DGM

$$k = \frac{D_{t+1}}{P_t} + g$$

Recognizing that dividends are equal to earnings multiplied by the payout ratio, and that (constant) growth is equal to the retention ratio multiplied by the return on equity, it follows that

$$k = \frac{(1 - b)E_{t+1}}{P_t} + bR$$

Finally, recognizing that return on equity is itself the ratio of earnings to invested capital, the following break-down of total return is derived

$$k = \frac{(1 - b)E_{t+1}}{P_t} + \frac{bE_{t+1}}{B_t}$$

This expression shows that the split of total return between income and growth is a weighted average of earnings to price and to invested capital, with the weight given by the retention ratio. In the example in Table 3.5, using this formula shows that the 20% return achieved by company A is 8% due to income and 12% due to growth. In contrast, company B has only 5% income yield, but 15% growth. The split between income and growth for both companies is a function of the level of re-investment. In the example in Table 3.6, where the retention ratio is increased to 70%, company A has an income yield of 6% and growth of 14%.

In each of the examples given, company A and company B have the same payout ratio. The difference between them in the income/growth split arises because the higher return on equity achieved by company B will generate faster growth. In turn, the expectation of this faster growth increases the current share price and so lowers the dividend yield, making company B a growth stock rather than an income stock. Notice, however, that for both companies in both examples the total return remains at 20% and is therefore independent of either the return on equity or the cost of capital. This is because the total return that the shareholder receives is mediated by the share price. Whatever performance either company achieves, and whatever the rate of retention of earnings, as long as the two companies carry the same risk, then the share price will adjust to equalize the expected return across them both. Alternatively stated, whatever earnings either company generates, they will be discounted at the same cost of capital.

3.6 The need to look beyond dividends

This chapter has shown that the constant dividend growth assumption of the DGM is itself dependent upon two further assumptions – that both the return on equity and the rate of new investment are constant. One lesson from this is that simple valuation models should be treated with caution, and that the existence of underlying assumptions needs to be recognized. In practice, the future performance of a company is determined by an enormous range of highly uncertain variables, such as customer demand, product development, management quality, the monetary and fiscal environment, and so on. It follows that the value of the company must also rest upon each of these variables. Yet the simple DGM purports to represent the value of the company by focusing on just two simple parameters – the discount rate and the rate of dividend growth. This implies the bold assumption that these simple parameters do, in fact, represent faithfully the whole range of variables upon which value is actually based, and that a constant growth rate allows all future dividends to be projected from current dividends.

A second lesson from this chapter is the need to understand the rate of return on equity. It has been shown that the rate of return spread determines whether or not a company is able to create value for its shareholders. The retention ratio has also been shown to be important, but only when there is a positive or negative rate of return spread. The retention ratio is therefore of secondary importance. It is a management decision about how to split earnings between dividends and re-investment, and its importance rests upon those earnings being available in the first place. Indeed, the practical importance of the retention ratio is overstated by the use of the simple dividend growth model.

Above all, this chapter has shown that what matters to shareholder value is the return on equity, since this determines the rate of return spread and (through new investment) the rate of dividend growth. While it is true that the value of a company depends upon its ability to pay dividends, this ability itself rests upon the ability to generate earnings. The conclusion from this chapter, therefore, is the need to focus hereafter on the return on equity and the generation of earnings.

Summary

The main points from this chapter may be summarized as follows:

- Dividend growth requires, first, a positive rate of return on invested equity capital and, second, a continuous flow of new equity capital, either through the retention of profits or through new issues. These requirements are connected, since a positive return on equity enables new investment.

- If constant dividend growth is assumed, as in the dividend growth model, then it is also implicitly assumed that the rate of return on equity and the retention ratio are both constant. In turn, this implies that invested capital, earnings and dividends all grow at the same rate, equal to the product of the return on equity and the retention ratio.

- An increase in the return on equity leads to an increase in shareholder value.

- The effect on shareholder value of new investment (and earnings growth) depends upon the rate of return spread, which is defined as the difference between the return on equity and the cost of capital.

- If there is no new investment and if the return on equity is constant, then there is zero dividend growth. The share price equals earnings divided by the cost of capital.

- If the return on equity equals the cost of capital, then there is no expectation of value creation, and changes in expected future investment have no effect on current shareholder value. The cost of capital will again equal earnings divided by the share price, but the share price will grow over time as earnings are re-invested or other equity is invested.

- If the return on equity differs from the cost of capital, then a change in future investment plans will either create or destroy shareholder value. For example, when the expected retention ratio increases, shareholder value is created (destroyed) whenever the return on equity exceeds (falls short of) the cost of capital; and vice versa when the retention ratio decreases.

- The central importance of the return on equity highlights the need to understand the role of earnings in the valuation of companies.

Appendix | The constant rate of dividend growth

Since earnings are equal to book value multiplied by the ROE, the change in earnings from one year to the next can be expressed as follows

$$\frac{E_{t+1}}{E_t} = \frac{B_t R_{t+1}}{B_{t-1} R_t}$$

Since (as shown in Chapter 2) $B_{t-1}(1 + b_t R_t) = B_t$

$$\frac{E_{t+1}}{E_t} = \frac{B_{t-1}(1 + b_t R_t)R_{t+1}}{B_{t-1} R_t}$$

If the additional assumption is made that the return on equity (ROE) is constant over time, then this implies that $R_t = R_{t+1}$, and the above expression simplifies to

$$\text{growth in } E = b_t R = \text{growth in invested capital}$$

If, additionally, the payout ratio is assumed to remain constant, then the growth rate of earnings must be equal to that of dividends. Since $D_t = (1 - b)E_t$, this is shown as follows

$$\text{growth in } D = \text{growth in } E = \frac{(1 - b)E_{t+1}}{(1 - b)E_t} - 1$$

In summary, if both the retention ratio and the return on equity are constant, then the rate of change of dividends is equal to that of both earnings and invested capital, and it is given by the product of the return on equity and the retention ratio.

A general, one-period model for the rate of dividend growth

Since, as defined above, $D_t = B_{t-1}R_t(1 - b_t)$ and $B_t = B_{t-1}(1 + b_t R_t)$, a general model for the single-period dividend growth rate is as follows[11]

$$\frac{D_{t+1}}{D_t} = \frac{(1 + b_t R_t)R_{t+1}(1 - b_{t+1})}{R_t(1 - b_t)}$$

---

[11] This model can be 'tested' using the numerical example in Chapter 3, for example to derive the 54.56% growth rate in year 4 of the final example.

If, as would be expected in reality, both R and b are likely to change over time, then dividend growth for *each* year is given by the model above. Compounded dividend growth for all years would be given by an altogether more complicated model still, which stands in stark contrast to the extreme simplicity of the dividend growth assumptions made by the DGM.

For the benefit of clarity, this general model can be reconciled back to the constant parameter assumptions of the DGM. The first step is to assume that there is no variation in the dividend payout ratio. This allows the general model for dividend growth to simplify to the following

$$\frac{D_{t+1}}{D_t} = \frac{(1 + bR_t)R_{t+1}}{R_t}$$

If it is then assumed that R is constant also, then the model simplifies further to the constant growth rate bR.

The same exercise can be repeated by starting with the assumption that R is constant and b is variable. In this case, the general model reduces to the following

$$\frac{D_{t+1}}{D_t} = \frac{(1 + b_t R)(1 - b_{t+1})}{(1 - b_t)}$$

Again, the assumption that b is constant also allows the model to simplify further to the constant growth rate bR.

4 The price–earnings ratio

Overview ● A simple model of the price–earnings (PE) ratio
● The 'normal' PE ratio
● The PE ratio and value creation
● Interpretation of the PE ratio: business cycles, competitive advantage and growth

This chapter reviews the price–earnings (PE) ratio. First, a simple model of the PE ratio is derived from the DGM. This demonstrates the consistency of the PE ratio with dividend-based valuation, although the simple model is shown to be valid only in the restricted case where the PE ratio is expected to be constant over time. Second, the 'normal' PE ratio is introduced, which is shown to arise in a fully competitive economic environment with zero value creation. It represents a 'base case' for a more general analysis of the PE ratio. Next, the PE ratio is analysed when a company achieves a rate of return on equity different from the cost of capital, and when value is thereby created or destroyed. This analysis of value creation explores the behaviour of the PE ratio over the course of a business cycle, and also where a company has a competitive advantage over a limited time period. The relationships between earnings growth and growth in the PE ratio are then examined and, finally, the chapter concludes with some empirical evidence regarding the PE ratio.

4.1 A simple model of the price–earnings ratio

Earnings are profits attributable to shareholders. They are the main output of a company's accounting system, and they are designed to be a 'bottom-line' measure of performance. It is not surprising, therefore, that investors seek to establish a direct relationship between earnings and share prices, in the form of the PE ratio. In effect, the PE ratio summarizes in a single number the relationship between the financial performance of a company (earnings) and the stock market's valuation of expected performance (share price).

The importance of the PE ratio

The PE ratio is the most common of all valuation models, and it is ubiquitous in analysts' reports and in the financial press. Consider, for example, the following:

International power businesses such as AES of the US trade on prospective price–earnings multiples in the thirties – a far cry from National Power's 14 times.

Pfizer is paying 19 times . . . at first sight that looks high . . . but it is well below average pharmaceuticals ratings and Pfizer's own mid-30s multiple.

Source: *Financial Times*, Lex Column, 18 November 1999

Statements such as these typically assume that the reader understands the reasons why a given PE ratio multiple is high or low, or why a given PE relative can or cannot be justified. The reader is rarely, however, offered anything more than this, and the intuition behind the PE ratio is infrequently explained. The aim of this chapter is to address these issues.

In order to examine in some depth the meaning and interpretation of PE ratios, it will be best to start with the simplest PE valuation model, and to develop the analysis from there. This requires reconciling the PE ratio as a valuation model with the earlier discussion of dividend-based valuation – remembering that, in order to be a theoretically correct valuation model, the PE ratio must be consistent with the dividend discount model.

In fact, deriving a simple model of the PE ratio follows very easily from the earlier analysis of the dividend yield. A necessary assumption, however, is that the cash flow generated by a company in any given year is equal to the earnings of that year. As will be explored in Chapter 5, this is actually a very strong assumption. For the time being, though, treating cash flows and earnings as synonymous will allow a simple reconciliation of dividend-based valuation with earnings-based valuation. It will also help in exploring the basic properties of the PE ratio. The assumption will, of course, be relaxed as the analysis of the PE ratio is developed in later chapters.

The link between dividends and earnings is given by the payout ratio (i.e. $D = (1 - b)E$), and the dividend growth model can therefore be re-stated as follows

$$P_0 = \frac{(1 - b)E_1}{k - bR}$$

which, by dividing both sides by earnings, gives a PE ratio, as follows

$$\frac{P_0}{E_1} = \frac{(1 - b)}{k - bR}$$

This expression for the PE ratio is commonly found in finance texts, although it is very rarely explored in any depth. It states that the PE ratio is equal to the payout ratio, divided by the cost of capital less the dividend growth rate. Notice that earnings in the simple PE model are for the forthcoming year. These will be referred to as 'current earnings'.

A common response to this equation is, first, to be struck by the simplicity of its derivation and, second, to be unsure of quite what it means. Why, for example, should the PE ratio be a function of the payout ratio? Also, are there any 'hidden' assumptions being made, or are the relationships entirely general? More fundamentally, how can this equation help in understanding how to interpret a given PE ratio?

The equation does, in fact, require a careful interpretation, and it is important to recognize that – at this level of analysis – it does not add anything to the understanding of valuation already provided by the DGM. This should not be surprising, because the model uses the same variables and the same assumptions, including the equivalence of earnings and cash flows. The equation above is not, in fact, a *general* model of the PE ratio. Indeed, the PE ratio is only a function of *b*, *ROE* and *k* in the form above *if* all of these variables are constant in perpetuity, *and* if earnings equal cash flows in the current year. In other words, the model reflects the same relationships between variables that have already been explored for the DGM. If, for example, the cost of capital is equal to the return on equity, then a change in the retention ratio will have no effect on the share price – and also, with a given level of earnings, no effect on the PE ratio. If the cost of capital does not equal the return on equity, however, then a change in the retention ratio (i.e. in the rate of new investment) will change the share price, because of its effect on the differential between the rate of dividend growth and the cost of capital. In turn, this will change the PE ratio.

The hidden assumptions of the simple PE model are extremely important. They must be made in order that a simple relationship can be said to exist between the share price and current earnings. In general, the PE relation is far from simple, and it is complicated by two factors. The first is expected changes in the cost of capital, the return on equity and the retention ratio. The second is the difference between earnings and cash flows. The first of these factors will be reviewed in this chapter, and the second (more complex) factor will be the subject of later chapters.

4.2 The 'normal' PE ratio

The share price is the present value of all future earnings generated by a company, and the PE ratio therefore summarizes the value of future earnings relative to current earnings. It is a *multiple* that translates earnings for the year into a share price that represents the value of earnings in perpetuity. It is the rate at which earnings are said to be capitalized.

The PE ratio may be viewed as having a 'normal' level, which arises whenever the investment returns from a given company are expected to be neither better nor worse than those available from comparable companies. In other words, the normal level arises in the fully competitive economic environment where the cost of capital and the rate of return on equity are constant and equal to one another, and value is neither created nor destroyed. At this level, the PE ratio will be equal to the reciprocal of the cost of capital (i.e. $1/k$).

To illustrate this, assume that the cost of capital and the return on equity are both at the constant rate 20%, and that the retention ratio is 60%. The PE ratio will then be 5 (= 1/0.2), as shown below

$$\frac{P_0}{E_1} = \frac{(1-b)}{k-bR} = \frac{(1-0.6)}{0.2-0.6\times0.2} = 5$$

Or, in the general case where $k = R$

$$\frac{P_0}{E_1} = \frac{(1-b)}{k-bR} = \frac{(1-b)}{(1-b)k} = \frac{1}{k}$$

If, for example, current earnings are expected to be $100, then the share price would be $500. Earnings over the life of the company have a total present value five times greater than current earnings.

With the assumption that the cost of capital and the return on equity both remain equal to 20%, the PE ratio will be constant over time, because the value of future earnings will remain the same relative to that of current earnings. This is true regardless of whether there is a change in the rate at which earnings are retained. It is the same conclusion reached in Chapter 3, using the dividend growth model, where it was shown that growth through retentions does not change share-holder value when the rate of return spread is equal to zero. In other words, there will be a fixed relationship between the current share price and the given level of current earnings, regardless of whether earnings are distributed in full (the no-growth case) or only in part (the growth case). It does not matter whether or not earnings grow, because there is no scope for growth in the present value of future earnings relative to current earnings, such that the stock market puts the same price on each dollar of current earnings.

To continue the simple example just given, a retention ratio of 60% can be contrasted with one of 50%. This gives the data over a three-year period (see Table 4.1).

The rate of growth in both the share price and earnings is greater when the rate of new investment is higher. Whatever the level of investment, though, the rate of return that the company achieves is equal to the rate available to

Table 4.1 With zero rate of return spread, PE ratio is normal, constant and independent of the rate of new investment

(Return on equity = cost of capital = 20%)	Retention ratio = 60%			Retention ratio = 50%		
	Year 1	Year 2	Year 3	Year 1	Year 2	Year 3
Share price at start of year	500	560	627	500	550	605
Earnings	100	112	125	100	110	121
Earnings growth		12%	12%		10%	10%
Share price growth		12%	12%		10%	10%
PE ratio	5	5	5	5	5	5

shareholders elsewhere. Each incremental dollar invested generates the same value of earnings, such that the total value of shareholders' investment grows at the same rate as earnings, implying a constant PE ratio.

This reciprocal relationship between the PE ratio and the cost of capital will, of course, hold in all cases where the return on equity and the cost of capital are equal and constant. If, for example, both the ROE and the cost of capital are either 15% or 25%, then the PE ratio will be 6.67 (equal to 1/0.15) or 4 (equal to 1/0.25), respectively. To illustrate this, suppose that company A has a PE ratio of 6.67 and company B has a PE ratio of 4, both with share prices of $500. Company A must be less risky than company B because shareholders are willing to expect a lower rate of return. Other things being equal, this would give a higher share price at which shareholders are willing to invest in company A. On the other hand, company B is expected to generate a higher return than company A which, other things being equal, would give it the higher share price. The share price for both companies is the same, however, because the difference in expected returns on investment is exactly offset by the difference in the shareholders' required rates of return.

While the share prices are the same for both companies, the PE ratios are different. The PE ratio summarizes the relationship between the present value of the earnings stream and the amount of current earnings. While any given investment in company B will generate higher current earnings than achievable by company A, the present values of these earnings will be the same. And since it is the difference in the cost of capital that equates the present values of the current earnings, so too the cost of capital must equate the difference in the ratios between these earnings numbers and the given share price. The ratio between the PEs for the two companies (6.67/4) is equal to that between the costs of capital (25%/15%). In short, whenever the rate of return spread is constant and equal to zero, a higher expectation of earnings in the current year must imply a lower ratio between these earnings and the share price.[1]

As a final point regarding the normal PE ratio, it is worth outlining a second case where the PE ratio will necessarily be equal to one over the cost of capital. This is when the retention ratio is equal to zero. This gives a very simple relationship between the PE ratio and the dividend yield. Earnings are equal to dividends because there are no retentions. There is also no growth in either dividends or earnings, again because there are no retentions (and also no new equity capital). In other words, this is the no-growth dividend yield model, and the *earnings yield* (defined as the ratio E/P) equals the dividend yield that, in turn, equals the cost of capital. These relationships are as follows

$$Earnings\ yield = \frac{E_1}{P_0} = \frac{D_1}{P_0} = k$$

$$PE\ ratio = \frac{P_0}{E_1} = \frac{1}{k}$$

[1] If earnings are retained, then shareholder value will grow, although each dollar of capital retains the same value. If expected ROE is greater, then shareholder value growth through retained earnings is expected to be greater. This is the 'reward' to shareholders for accepting the greater risk.

It should be noted, however, that the simple conclusions of the no-growth model are independent of the rate of return on equity. It would not matter whether earnings of, say, $100 were achieved with invested capital of $100, $200 or $1 000 (an ROE of 100%, 50% and 10%, respectively). All that matters is that the ROE is constant and that no earnings are retained. In this sense, the PE ratio does not have the same interpretation as it does in the case of value-neutral growth. It is not a 'normal' PE ratio in the sense that there is a fully competitive environment, but only in the sense that earnings have been constrained to be constant in perpetuity.[2]

There is also a further difference between the growth and no-growth models, which can be illustrated by comparing the PE ratio with the dividend yield. As soon as there is growth in dividends and earnings resulting from a positive retention ratio, the earnings yield will not be equal to the dividend yield. It will instead be greater and will comprise an income component (the dividend yield) and a growth component (given by the ratio of retained earnings to share price), as follows

Earnings yield = cost of capital = dividend yield + retained earnings yield

$$\frac{E_1}{P_0} = k = \frac{D_1}{P_0} + \frac{bE_1}{P_0}$$

Whenever the PE ratio is at its normal level, the shareholders' expected rate of return for the year equals the earnings yield, which is the sum of the dividend yield and the retained earnings yield. The change in the share price from one year to the next is equal to the amount of retained earnings per dollar of share price. This is because this re-investment of earnings has the same value per dollar as existing invested capital. As will be seen below, however, if the PE ratio is not at its normal level, then this relationship breaks down. There will no longer be equality between the earnings yield and the cost of capital, because the rate of return spread is expected to change over time. This change means that there will no longer be a simple relationship between current earnings and the discounted value of future earnings.

4.3   The PE ratio and value creation

The discussion so far has shown that if either the rate of return spread or the retention ratio is equal to zero, then the PE ratio will equal the reciprocal of the cost of capital. Conversely, the PE ratio will exceed its normal level if the expected rate of return spread is positive, and vice versa. The simplest illustration of this arises when the rate of return spread is both positive and constant, and when the retention ratio is constant also. The numerical example shown in Table 4.2 demonstrates the increase in the PE ratio caused by an increase in the rate of

---

[2] This case is a theoretical possibility rather than a likely outcome. For example, it is most unlikely that a company with a very high expected ROE would neither retain any profit nor issue any new equity capital.

Table 4.2 The PE exceeds its normal level when the rate of return spread is positive

	Year 1	Year 2	Year 3	Year 4	Year 5
Initial capital investment (B_t)	1 000	1 150	1 323	1 521	1 749
Return on equity (R_{t+1})	25%	25%	25%	25%	25%
Earnings (E_{t+1})	250	288	331	380	437
Retention ratio (b)	60%	60%	60%	60%	60%
Dividends (D_{t+1})	100	115	132	152	175
Dividend growth (g)		15%	15%	15%	15%
Cost of capital (k)	20%	20%	20%	20%	20%
Opening price (= $D_{t+1}/k - g$)	2 000	2 300	2 645	3 042	3 498
PE ratio (= P_t/E_{t+1})	8.0	8.0	8.0	8.0	8.0

Table 4.3 With a positive rate of return spread, the PE changes with the rate of new investment

	Year 1	Year 2	Year 3	Year 4	Year 5
Initial capital investment (B_t)	1 000	1 175	1 381	1 622	1 906
Return on equity (R_{t+1})	25%	25%	25%	25%	25%
Earnings (E_{t+1})	250	294	345	406	477
Retention ratio (b)	70%	70%	70%	70%	70%
Dividends (D_{t+1})	75	88	104	122	143
Dividend growth (g)		17.5%	17.5%	17.5%	17.5%
Cost of capital (k)	20%	20%	20%	20%	20%
Opening price (= $D_{t+1}/k - g$)	3 000	3 525	4 142	4 867	5 718
PE ratio (= P_t/E_{t+1})	12.0	12.0	12.0	12.0	12.0

return spread. The cost of capital, the return on equity and the retention ratio are constant at 20%, 25% and 60%, respectively, and the PE ratio is constant at a value of 8.

The PE ratio exceeds 5, which is its normal level with a 20% cost of capital. This implies that the company has value-creating opportunities in the future that are not reflected in current earnings. Since, in this context, retained earnings are worth more to shareholders than dividends, a change in the retention ratio will cause a change in the share price. As shown in Table 4.3, an increase in the retention ratio from 60% to 70% increases the share price from $2 000 to $3 000 which, with a given level of current earnings, increases the PE ratio from 8 to 12.[3]

This example illustrates the effects on the share price of a change in both the rate of return spread and the retention ratio. The conclusions reached are exactly the same as those reached in Chapter 3 using the DGM. This should be

---

[3] This interpretation follows from the underlying assumptions of the DGM. As was discussed in Chapter 3, however, it is very important to recognize that the rate of return spread and the retention ratio are not, in fact, independent, and that neither are they likely to be constant.

no surprise. While the language of the PE ratio has been used rather than that of the dividend yield, the underlying model has been precisely the same. This is illustrated further in Table 4.4 which shows, for a company trading on a (randomly chosen) PE ratio of 8, a range of possible combinations of the return on equity, cost of capital and retention ratio.

Table 4.4 Rates of return on equity consistent with PE ratio = 8 in constant growth model

Retention ratio (new investment as % of earnings)	Cost of capital				
	7.5%	12.5%	17.5%	22.5%	27.5%
20%	–	12.5%	37.5%	62.5%	87.5%
40%	–	12.5%	25.0%	37.5%	50.0%
60%	4.2%	12.5%	20.8%	29.2%	37.5%
80%	6.3%	12.5%	18.8%	25.0%	31.3%

If, for example, the cost of capital is 17.5% and the retention ratio is 60%, then a PE ratio of 8 requires that the return on equity must equal 20.8%. Within the confines of constant growth assumptions, Table 4.4 therefore illustrates alternative interpretations of a given PE ratio – i.e. if a given share is trading on a PE ratio of 8, then what does this actually mean?

The most straightforward possibility is the zero rate of return spread, which is illustrated in the second column of Table 4.4. Whenever the cost of capital is 12.5%, which is the 'normal' return for a PE ratio of 8, then the return on equity must also be 12.5%, regardless of the retention ratio. In contrast, all other columns in the table represent a permanent abnormal return on equity, meaning that the company is earning persistently either more or less than its cost of capital on its invested capital. It can be seen that the 12.5% 'normal' cost of capital is critical. If the actual cost of capital is more than this level, then the return on equity must also be more. This is because, for a PE ratio of 8, a cost of capital of 12.5% is consistent with zero value creation. If, therefore, the cost of capital exceeds 12.5%, then maintaining a ratio of 8 between the share price and current earnings requires a positive rate of return spread. In other words, since future earnings will be worth less in present value terms when the cost of capital is higher, a higher return on equity is required to support a given PE ratio. If, for example, the cost of capital equals 25%, then a normal PE ratio would be 4. If the PE ratio is actually at 8, then there must be a positive rate of return spread.

The required return on equity will vary with the retention ratio. If the rate of return spread is positive, then more value will be created as more earnings are retained. If the return on equity is held constant, the share price increases as the retention ratio increases, thereby increasing the PE ratio. It follows that a lower rate of return spread is required to prevent the PE ratio from rising above 8 as the retention ratio increases. In turn this implies a lower expectation of current earnings and, with the PE ratio fixed at 8, a lower share price. As Table 4.4 confirms, an increase in the retention ratio is associated with a decline in the required return on equity. Take, for example, the cost of capital of 22.5%, which would be associated with a normal PE ratio of 4.4. Maintaining a PE ratio of 8 requires a positive abnormal return on equity. When the retention ratio is constrained to be only 20% in perpetuity, a return on equity as high as 62.5% is required for the value of the retentions to justify the premium in the PE ratio. When retentions are as high as 80%, by contrast, a positive rate of return spread of only 2.5% is required to keep the PE ratio at 8.[4]

Earnings growth and value creation

The UK third generation mobile licence auction ended with the score at £22.5bn. Nobody is cheering. Vodafone, TIW, BT Cellnet, Orange and One2One are paying between £4bn and £6bn to provide services they cannot define or value with any confidence. Putting up the networks will cost another £2bn to £5bn. No wonder investors are nervous. The mobile future is uncertain. It is impossible to prove that the licence winners have over-paid. But it is hard to see how they can earn a return on this investment that exceeds their cost of capital and creates value for shareholders.

Source: Financial Times, Lex Column, 28 April 2000

While the cost of the investment in licences is certain, the return is not. The investment will generate earnings growth simply by scaling up the investors' operations, but whether or not this is beneficial to the share price depends on whether value is created – which, as the article points out, requires a positive rate of return spread.

While these examples illustrate the general relationships between the PE ratio, the rate of return spread and the rate of new investment, it is very important to recall that the validity of the simple PE model (and therefore of this analysis) rests upon two constraining assumptions. The first of these is the equality of earnings and cash flows. The relaxation of this assumption will be dealt with at length in later chapters. The second assumption is constant growth, which itself implies the unrealistic assumption of a constant retention ratio that is independent of the rate of return spread.[5] The analysis so far has not allowed for the possibility of a *change* in the PE ratio. Whether earnings have been normal or abnormal, they have been assumed (as required by the DGM) to be either constant or else growing at a constant rate. The limitations of this assumption are vitally important. It will be recalled that the reason for exploring the PE ratio was that dividend-based valuation was argued to be limited. The source of dividend growth is the return on equity, and seeking to understand earnings gen-

---

[4] The opposite relationships to those just described also hold true. Whenever the cost of capital falls below 12.5%, a PE ratio of 8 is supported by a return on equity that is also below 12.5%. For example, when the cost of capital is 7.5%, the normal PE ratio is 13.3, and the ROE does not need to be as high as 7.5% for a PE ratio of 8. To maintain a given PE ratio, the negative rate of return spread must be reduced (i.e. the required rate of return increases) as the retention ratio increases since (all else being equal) higher retentions would imply a lower share price.

[5] Constant growth implies a constant retention ratio, irrespective of the rate of return spread. This allows a simple change in the retention ratio to have a significant effect on the share price. While this result provides some insight into the relationship between investment and value creation, it should not be taken too literally because retentions (which, in the framework above includes newly invested shareholder capital) are dependent upon (not independent of) value-creating opportunities.

eration is therefore more powerful than focusing on dividends alone. In this regard, focusing on the PE ratio has introduced the benchmark of a 'normal' return on equity, thereby grounding the analysis in economic fundamentals. By maintaining the assumptions of zero or constant growth, however, the analysis of the PE ratio has been limited to the special cases where the DGM remains valid. In order to extend the analysis, it will be necessary to relax the assumptions of constant growth, thereby abandoning the simple PE model (and the dividend growth model) and analysing the factors that cause the PE ratio to change over time. In the context of Table 4.4, this recognizes that a PE ratio equal to 8 can arise because the return on equity (for example) is not constant. Indeed, it is likely to be different in every year. Even if the long-run return on equity is approximately 12.5%, annual variations in earnings will cause the PE ratio itself to change. This being the case, an observed PE ratio of 8 should not usually lead to the conclusion that the company has a cost of capital of 12.5%. It is also possible that it has a variable PE ratio. This possibility is the most likely in practice, and it will now be examined in the remainder of this chapter.

4.4 The PE ratio and the business cycle

The normal PE ratio can be used as a benchmark against which to analyse actual variation in the PE ratio. Two examples of this will be considered in this chapter. The first is fluctuation in earnings growth, for example over the course of a business cycle, where a company's opportunities to earn abnormal returns come and go. The second is abnormal returns earned during a limited time period in which a company has a competitive advantage, such as during a period of patent protection. The first of these examples is analysed in this section of the chapter, and the second in the following section.

The normal PE ratio and a fluctuating PE ratio are contrasted with one another in Figure 4.1.[6] The terms 'normal earnings' and 'normal PE' refer to the case of constant growth and a zero rate of return spread. Earnings and the share price grow at the same rate, implying a constant PE ratio over time. The second dataset in the diagram allows the return on investment to vary each year, such that earnings, earnings growth and the PE ratio are also variable. This is shown as 'actual' earnings and 'actual PE' in the diagram. The data in the diagram are calculated in such a way that the normal data give the same share price at any point in time as the actual data.[7] The example therefore illustrates a fluctuating rate of return spread around a constant underlying trend.

---

[6] This analysis is based on Molodovsky (1953) reproduced with permission by the Association for Investment Management and Research (AIMR®). AIMR does not endorse, promote, review or warrant the accuracy of the products or services offered by Pearson Education.

[7] This actually requires the additional assumption that all earnings in excess of the underlying return on investment must be distributed as dividends and thereby not retained. In other words, the retention ratio must change slightly in each period. This is because the effect of the excess retained earnings would be to change the share price to a level slightly different from that assumed by the constant earnings growth model. This adjustment simply ensures the integrity of the comparison between the two models. It assumes that all abnormal earnings are entirely transitory, and that they do not affect the constant growth rate that is assumed.

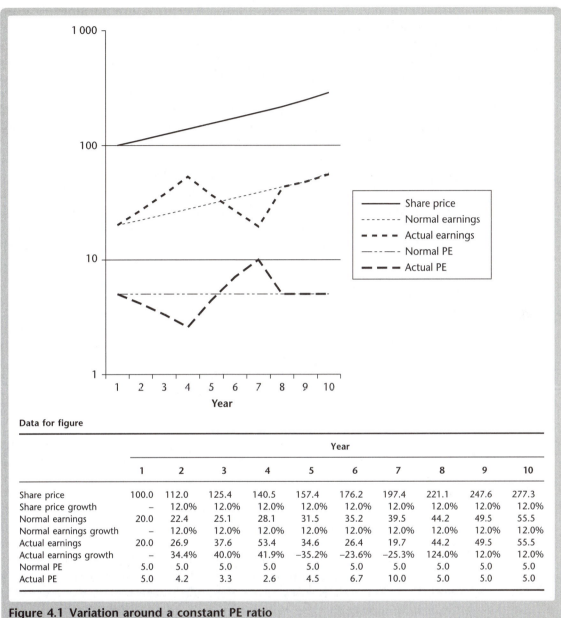

Data for figure

	Year									
	1	2	3	4	5	6	7	8	9	10
Share price	100.0	112.0	125.4	140.5	157.4	176.2	197.4	221.1	247.6	277.3
Share price growth	–	12.0%	12.0%	12.0%	12.0%	12.0%	12.0%	12.0%	12.0%	12.0%
Normal earnings	20.0	22.4	25.1	28.1	31.5	35.2	39.5	44.2	49.5	55.5
Normal earnings growth	–	12.0%	12.0%	12.0%	12.0%	12.0%	12.0%	12.0%	12.0%	12.0%
Actual earnings	20.0	26.9	37.6	53.4	34.6	26.4	19.7	44.2	49.5	55.5
Actual earnings growth	–	34.4%	40.0%	41.9%	−35.2%	−23.6%	−25.3%	124.0%	12.0%	12.0%
Normal PE	5.0	5.0	5.0	5.0	5.0	5.0	5.0	5.0	5.0	5.0
Actual PE	5.0	4.2	3.3	2.6	4.5	6.7	10.0	5.0	5.0	5.0

Figure 4.1 Variation around a constant PE ratio
Source: Molodovsky (1953)

In practice, of course, earnings growth will never be constant year on year. It will therefore be helpful to regard the actual data as the performance that the company will actually realize, and the normal data as a hypothetical benchmark. This comparison is not just of hypothetical interest, though, and it has a very practical application. To illustrate this, consider the first year of the example. The share price at this time might be estimated based upon the constant growth model. While growth is not actually expected to be constant, the underlying assumptions of the model will nevertheless give a reasonable estimate of the share price. In the example, it is estimated that the return on investment will consistently be equal to the cost of capital.[8] In some years performance will actually be better and in others it will be worse, but the zero rate of return spread is the benchmark that is the basis of the current share price. Expected performance can therefore be evaluated against this benchmark.[9]

As can be seen from Figure 4.1, the relationship between the 'normal' and the 'actual' data illustrates the dynamics of the PE ratio. Take, for example, the second year of data. Using the normal variables, both earnings and the share price grow at a rate of 12%, and the PE ratio therefore remains at 5. For the actual data, however, the share price grows at 12% but earnings grow much faster at a rate of 34.4%. The PE ratio therefore *declines* from 5 to 4.2. A similar pattern follows in years 3 and 4, where share price growth continues at 12% but earnings grow at 40.0% and 41.9%, respectively, causing a further decline in the PE ratio to 3.3 and then to 2.6. This decline in the PE ratio is reversed in year 5, when the share price continues to rise but earnings growth is negative. The PE ratio does not rise beyond its long-run equilibrium level of 5 until year 6, however, when there is a further fall in earnings. The PE ratio reaches its maximum level of 10 in year 7, when actual earnings fall to their lowest level. Thereafter, earnings converge to the level assumed by the long-run constant growth model, and the PE ratio settles at its normal level of 5.

The decline in the PE ratio corresponding to an increase in earnings growth may seem counter-intuitive at first sight. A high PE ratio is commonly regarded as an indicator of earnings growth. More accurately, though, it represents the value of all future earnings relative to earnings in the current year. If, then, high earnings growth is expected in the current year, then this just means that there is a higher starting point from which earnings are expected to grow from year 2 onwards. Other things being equal, therefore, high earnings growth in the current year is likely to imply lower future earnings growth and, therefore, a lower PE ratio. This must, in fact, be the case in the example above. The actual pattern of earnings growth has been chosen to be equivalent to a constant rate of 12%. If, then, actual growth exceeds 12% in the first year, it must also be expected to fall below 12% at some future date, and so the PE ratio must fall below its normal level.

This example has illustrated two principles. First, the normal level of the PE ratio is an important benchmark. It represents a state of equilibrium, where current earnings have a sustainable level of growth. Any departure from this state stands in need of justification. The PE ratio will be at its maximum when actual earnings are at their lowest level relative to normal earnings, and vice versa. At the peak of a business cycle, therefore, the PE ratio will be at its lowest level; and in the depth of a business cycle trough, the PE ratio will be at its maximum. If economic activity is stable rather than cyclical, then the PE ratio itself will also be stable. Second, if the rate of realized earnings growth increases relative

---

[8] It could equally well be assumed that the underlying benchmark is a rate of return spread permanently different from 0.

[9] This is very similar to the use of the DGM that was outlined in Chapter 2. While the analyst knows that dividend growth will not be constant, he or she can nevertheless use the model to understand the constant growth assumption that is, in effect, implicit in the share price. In turn, this gives a benchmark for testing the analyst's own expectations of dividend growth.

to the rate of normal earnings growth, then the PE ratio will fall. This is because any such increase in earnings must be temporary. On average, earnings must sooner or later fall to the normal level that is implied by the share price. Any 'excessive' earnings growth must be compensated for by a fall in the PE ratio, which is a reflection of an expectation of lower future earnings growth. More generally, growth in actual earnings will be in the opposite direction to growth in the actual PE ratio. If earnings fall, the PE ratio rises, and vice versa.

In concluding this discussion, it is important to remember that the share price reflects an *expectation* of future performance. The actual performance will always turn out to be different from the expectation, and the market will revise its expectations of future returns accordingly. The underlying PE valuation model remains valid, of course, but the parameters will change. An increase in earnings growth relative to trend will therefore not necessarily lead to a downgrade in the PE ratio, because the market might revise its expectations about the trend. Indeed, the realization of excess earnings is in itself a good indicator that the company is likely to do even better in the future. In effect, therefore, earnings growth might have exceeded the initially assumed trend, but might fall short of the recently revised trend, causing the PE ratio to rise. Similarly, the realization of an opportunity to earn abnormal returns might give the market confidence, leading to a downward revision of the cost of capital. This would increase the share price without there needing to be any revision in the expectation of future earnings. The interpretation of a change in the PE ratio must therefore take into account both the change in current earnings and the change in the underlying sustainable earnings rate that is implicit in the share price.

The PE ratio and sustainable earnings growth

With about €56bn ($51.9bn) being wiped off Nokia's share price in a matter of hours last Thursday, the world's number one producer of mobile telephones may be asking what it did wrong. The fall, which in absolute terms is probably the largest ever single day loss by a European company, came despite the company announcing record second-quarter profits . . . However, what the market focused on was the Finnish company's warning that third-quarter earnings per share would be lower than those of the second quarter . . . What perhaps is really worrying investors is the fear that Nokia will find it more difficult to recapture its premium margins. As its two closest rivals have found, making money even in a booming market is not that easy. Ericsson's troubled handset division recorded a loss in the second quarter, while Motorola of the US managed an operating margin of just 4 per cent in handsets.

Source: Financial Times, Nicholas George, 31 July 2000

Nokia's strong rise in earnings coincided with an even stronger decline in the share price, causing a sharp reduction in the (historic) PE ratio. This happened for two reasons, both of which lowered the market's expectations of Nokia's expected rate of return spread. First, Nokia issued a warning about earnings growth. The reported earnings were therefore deemed high relative to the sustainable trend, which is consistent with a fall in the PE ratio. Second, the investors' assessment of Nokia's peer group raised concerns about the ability of the industry as a whole to generate a positive rate of return spread. This reinforced the downgrading of Nokia's expected earnings growth.

4.5	The PE ratio and the sustainability of competitive advantage

In the example above, a pattern of variable earnings growth was contrasted with an equivalent, underlying model of constant earnings growth. This demonstrated the interpretation of the PE ratio when there are swings in profitability. Another source of variation in the rate of earnings arises when a company enjoys a temporary competitive advantage. This might happen with a patent or other intellectual property right, or it might arise if the company is the first to enter a new product market, or is maybe the first to introduce a more efficient method of operation. In such a case, rather than having variation in actual earnings around a hypothetical normal earnings benchmark, there is more likely to be a limited period during which earnings are abnormally high. As the source of the competitive advantage is eroded, however, the return on equity will fall to the level of the cost of capital, and the PE ratio will reach its normal, competitively determined level, equal to one over the cost of capital. This possibility is illustrated in Figure 4.2. It is assumed that there is a PE ratio of 14, and also a (constant) cost of capital of 15% and a retention ratio of 80%. These assumptions are chosen at random, and different numbers could equally well have been used. With these particular fixed parameters in place, the graph plots the duration of any given rate of return spread.[10]

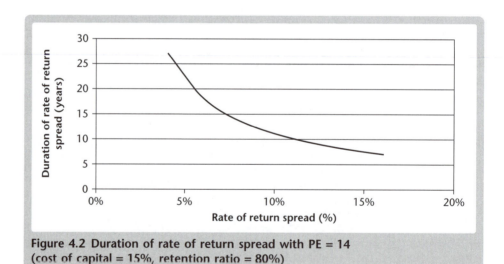

Figure 4.2 Duration of rate of return spread with PE = 14 (cost of capital = 15%, retention ratio = 80%)

Source: Based on Danielson (1998)

---

[10] An analysis similar to this can be found in Danielson (1998), reproduced with permission of AIMR® (see note 6), where a formal model is developed to include the abnormal earnings duration. An alternative model that also allows for a limited period of abnormal earnings is Gordon and Gordon (1997) which, unlike Danielson, makes the same assumptions as those in this chapter. Finally, an insightful analysis of this subject is Durand (1992).

If, for example, the company's competitive advantage is assumed to be sustainable for a period of 11 years, then a PE ratio of 14 requires that the return on investment exceeds the cost of capital by 10% over this period. Alternatively, if the company is only able to earn abnormal returns for eight years, then it must have a rate of return spread of 14% in order to justify a PE ratio of 14. Of course, the same graph could have been shown with the assumption of a different PE ratio. If the assumed PE ratio had been higher, then either or both of the duration period and the rate of return spread would also have needed to be higher.

Notice that, for a cost of capital of 15%, the PE ratio of 14 greatly exceeds the normal PE ratio of 6.67. This reflects the positive rate of return spread, which leads to earnings growth in excess of the cost of capital, implying that the share price reflects future value creation. As the period of competitive advantage erodes, however, so the PE ratio also declines. The fewer the years of abnormal earnings that remain in the future, the lower will be the present value of future earnings relative to current earnings.

To extend this example, Figure 4.3 shows the actual erosion in the PE ratio over the 11 year period when the rate of return spread is equal to 10%.

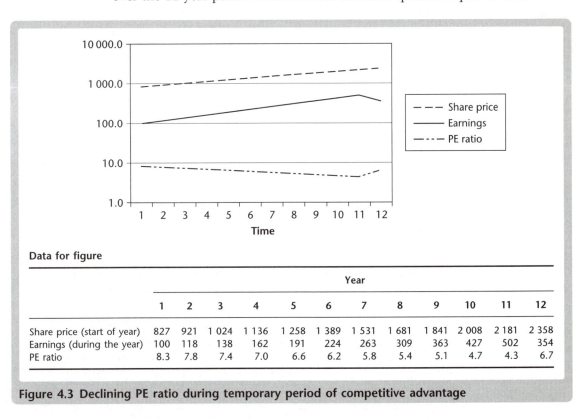

Data for figure

	Year											
	1	2	3	4	5	6	7	8	9	10	11	12
Share price (start of year)	827	921	1 024	1 136	1 258	1 389	1 531	1 681	1 841	2 008	2 181	2 358
Earnings (during the year)	100	118	138	162	191	224	263	309	363	427	502	354
PE ratio		8.3	7.8	7.4	7.0	6.6	6.2	5.8	5.4	5.1	4.7	4.3	6.7

Figure 4.3 Declining PE ratio during temporary period of competitive advantage

The PE ratio at any point in time depends upon the cost of capital, the rate of return spread and the rate of new capital investment. These variables determine jointly the present value of future earnings relative to expected current earnings. In this example, the PE ratio declines for precisely the same reasons as it did in the business cycle example. If an increase in earnings is associated with a fall in the sustainable growth level of earnings, then the PE ratio will fall. In the example, the decline in the PE ratio continues gradually during the 11 years of competitive advantage. This decline reflects the gradually diminishing number of future years in which the company enjoys its competitive advantage, and thereby the gradual decline in the value of earnings in the future relative to those currently achieved. At the end of year 11, the competitive advantage has been eroded entirely. Current earnings fall and the PE ratio rises to its normal level, equal to the reciprocal of the cost of capital. It should be noticed, however, that the share price itself rises throughout. This is because of the retention in earnings. The rate at which the share price increases is itself declining each year, however, and it will ultimately equal its sustainable rate.

It is important to keep in mind the assumptions that are implicit in an example of this type. All variables have been held constant except for a change in the rate of return on equity in year 11. The example conveys an important message about the relationship between the PE ratio and sustainable competitive advantage, but it necessarily does so by making simplifying assumptions. A whole range of different assumptions could, in practice, be made. These would allow for greater variation in the PE ratio over time, but they would also lose the simplicity of the underlying model. This trade-off between real-world complexity and simple valuation models is especially important for the PE ratio. After all, the PE ratio is attempting to summarize all aspects of valuation in just a single number.

The PE ratio and patent protection

No matter how encouraging AstraZeneca's results, for the immediate future they will be over-shadowed by prospects for anti-ulcer drug Losec (the world's best-selling drug), which is due to lose its US patent next year . . . Though AstraZeneca is trading on a discount to the global average for pharmaceuticals companies on 2001 earnings, for 2002 figures the positions are reversed . . . its pipeline of products is attractive. In particular, the new cholesterol-lowering drug looks as though it may well be a blockbuster. The treatment will also have an important side-benefit for the group; by boosting AstraZeneca's presence in cardio-vascular treatments, it should prevent the share price from being so dependent on a single franchise in future.

Source: Financial Times, Lex Column, 2 August 2000

AstraZeneca is trading at a PE discount based upon 2001 earnings due to the continued patent protection of its best-selling drug, enabling transitorily high current earnings and, thereby, a relatively low present value of future earnings. The PE ratio 'recovers' when the patent protection is lost. The growth in the PE is due not only to the expected loss of Losec earnings, but also to the increase in the present value of future earnings attributable to the drugs pipeline. Moreover, the move from dependence on a single franchise probably lowers the risks perceived by investors, thereby reducing the cost of capital and boosting the PE ratio further.

4.6 Growth in the PE ratio

One useful approach to reconciling the simple PE ratio with its underlying complexity is to focus on the determinants of changes in the PE ratio from one year to the next.[11] A useful framework for this analysis is a formal model that takes the perspective of the rate of return that shareholders expect to achieve over a one-year period. The model is as follows, where the shareholders' expected return (the cost of capital) is defined in terms of income (the dividend yield) and growth (in both earnings and in the PE ratio itself).

$$\text{Shareholders' expected one-year return} = k = \frac{D_1}{P_0} + g_E + g_{PE} + (g_E \times g_{PE})$$

where

$$g_E = \text{growth in earnings} = (E_2/E_1) - 1$$

$$g_{PE} = \text{growth in the PE ratio} = (PE_2/PE_1) - 1$$

The intuition behind this expression is straightforward. The return that shareholders expect is comprised of income and growth. Income is given simply by the dividend yield, which is a cash return from the company as a percentage of the shareholders' investment. Growth is determined jointly by the growth in the company's earnings and by the growth in the multiple at which these earnings are converted into the share price. If the PE ratio is constant, then earnings growth will be equal to share price growth and, therefore, equal also to the shareholder's rate of capital gain. Likewise, earnings might be at a constant level but the PE ratio itself might increase, perhaps because of an increased expectation of future return on equity. In this case, the capital gain will equal the percentage change in the PE ratio. If both earnings and the PE ratio change, however, then the effect on the capital gain will additionally include the effect of one variable on the other (the final term in the equation). So, for example, suppose that the performance as shown in Table 4.5 is expected for a given company.

Table 4.5 PE growth and investment returns

	Year 1	Year 2
Share price at start of year (P_t)	1 100	1 320
Earnings for the year (E_{t+1})	100	110
Dividends paid at year end (D_1)	40	
PE at start of year ($PE_{t+1} = P_t/E_{t+1}$)	11	12
Dividend yield at start of year (D_1/P_0)	4%	
Earnings growth (E_2/E_1) − 1		10%
PE growth (PE_2/PE_1) − 1		9%

Source: Molodovsky (1953)

[11] See Leibowitz (1999) for an expanded discussion of the analysis in this section, including a proof of the derivation of this model. The assumption that earnings are equal to cash flows is not required here.

Using the equation above, the shareholders' expected return over the first year is equal to 24%. This is comprised of income (4%), earnings growth (10%), growth in the rate at which earnings are capitalized (9%) and the combined effect of growth in both earnings and the PE ratio (10% × 9% = 1%). The total return is equal, of course, to the capital gain of 20% plus the dividend yield of 4%.

A more detailed example of this is given in Table 4.6, which displays the underlying data from the declining PE example above.

Table 4.6 Declining PE ratio during temporary period of competitive advantage

	Year											
	1	2	3	4	5	6	7	8	9	10	11	12
Change PE (= g_{PE})		−5.2%	−5.4%	−5.6%	−5.8%	−6.0%	−6.2%	−6.5%	−6.8%	−7.2%	−7.6%	53.3%
Earnings growth (= g_E)		17.5%	17.5%	17.5%	17.5%	17.5%	17.5%	17.5%	17.5%	17.5%	17.5%	−29.5%
$g_E \times g_{PE}$		−0.91%	−0.94%	−0.97%	−1.01%	−1.05%	−1.09%	−1.14%	−1.19%	−1.25%	−1.32%	−15.73%
Dividend yield	3.63%	3.83%	4.04%	4.28%	4.55%	4.84%	5.16%	5.52%	5.92%	6.38%	6.90%	4.50%
Cost of capital	15.0%	15.0%	15.0%	15.0%	15.0%	15.0%	15.0%	15.0%	15.0%	15.0%	15.0%	15.0%

It can be seen that realized earnings growth in excess of the cost of capital is associated with a decline in the PE ratio. For example, in year 6 earnings grow by 17.5% and dividends yield an income of 4.8%. If the PE ratio did not change, then the shareholders would earn a return that is 7.3% in excess of their start of year expectations. The PE ratio therefore declines by 6.2%. Together with a 1.1% joint effect of earnings and PE ratio, this ensures that the share price is, in fact, expected to give shareholders their equilibrium 15% return.

This discussion can be extended still further with a diagram showing that an expected change in the share price reflects an expected change in both earnings growth and in the PE ratio.[12] In contrast to the example above, where a given combination of PE ratio growth and earnings growth is given, Figure 4.4 shows a range of possible combinations of these two variables for a given PE ratio of 6.67.

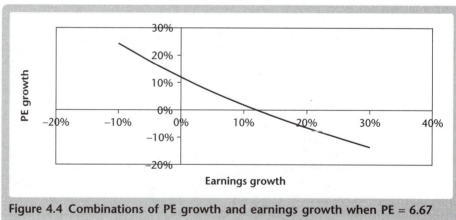

Figure 4.4 Combinations of PE growth and earnings growth when PE = 6.67
Source: Leibowitz and Kogelman (1994)

---

[12] This analysis can be found in Leibowitz and Kogelman (1994) reproduced with permission of the AIMR® (see note 6).

Figure 4.4 demonstrates that any given share price incorporates an implicit assumption about the rate of growth in earnings and in the PE ratio. This assumption gives the shareholders an expectation that they will earn their cost of capital. If either assumption proves to be wrong, then the shareholders' return will prove to be different from their expectation. If, for example, actual performance falls to the right of the line, maybe with an earnings growth of 20% and a PE growth of 20%, then the actual return that shareholders make will exceed their initial expectation.[13] An outcome below the line will have the opposite effect.

This example reinforces the danger in assuming that the PE ratio will remain constant over time. The assumption of a constant PE ratio implies that there is a constant relationship between growth in earnings and growth in share price. In effect, the final two terms on the right-hand side of the expression above are both assumed to be equal to zero. If the rate of earnings growth is expected to be above trend over the coming year, then the assumption of a constant PE ratio will overstate the expected year-end share price and, thereby, overstate the annual return that the shareholders expect to make. Alternatively stated, if the PE ratio and cost of capital are taken as given, then an excess earnings growth rate would imply a negative dividend yield in the expression above. This shows the internal inconsistency of the constant PE ratio assumption. In practice, and as we have seen, the constant PE ratio is applicable only when the expected rate of earnings growth is equal to its sustainable rate.

PE growth

Abby Cohen, the influential Goldman Sachs strategist . . . expects the S&P 500 to rise by 8–10% per year, in line with her estimates of earnings growth. In other words, Ms Cohen no longer thinks the market's price/earnings ratio, currently 27 times prospectively, deserves to expand – even though it has been higher in the recent past.

Source: Financial Times, Lex Column, 29 March 2000

The combination of 8–10% growth in earnings and zero growth in the PE ratio implies that Abby Cohen expects share prices to rise at a rate of 8–10%. Given that the PE ratio has recently been higher, the implication is that earnings had been below their sustainable level, but that growth has now brought them to the trend line. Shareholders' total return is expected to be 8–10% plus the dividend yield.

4.7   Empirical evidence on the PE ratio

In practice, there is considerable variation in the PE ratio across companies. To illustrate this, Table 4.7 (adapted from Penman, 1996) reports average PE ratios for US companies over the period 1968–85.

---

[13] In fact, it will equal 20% + 20% + 4% = 44%, which is a 29% excess return.

Table 4.7 Average PE ratios in the US over the period 1968–85

PE portfolios	Average PE ratio	Implied 'normal' cost of capital
Highest 85–90%	58.82	2%
	25.64	4%
	19.23	5%
	15.87	6%
	13.89	7%
	12.50	8%
	11.49	9%
Medium 50–55%	10.64	9%
	9.80	10%
	9.17	11%
	8.62	12%
	8.06	12%
	7.52	13%
	7.04	14%
	6.49	15%
	5.92	17%
	5.18	19%
Lowest 5%	3.92	26%

Table 4.7 is calculated by ranking PE ratios by size and then grouping companies into portfolios. So, for example, companies whose PE ratios fall between the 50th and 55th percentiles for size of PE ratio have, on average, a PE ratio of 10.64. If this PE ratio is assumed to be normal, then the implied cost of capital for these companies would be 9%, as shown in the final column of the table.

The long-run average rate of return on equities in the US has been in the region of 12%. Given that companies will vary in their specific expected rates of return, this suggests that the average PE ratio of many companies falls within striking distance of a normal level. It is equally clear, however, that many companies in the table have a PE ratio that is inconsistent with a normal return. Indeed, since the data above are averages over a long period, they hide considerable variation between years. Overall, the evidence suggests that PE ratios often deviate from their 'normal' path.

There is considerable evidence that PE ratios do, in fact, behave in the transitory manner that was analysed earlier in the chapter. Consider the evidence from Beaver and Morse (1978), which uses PE portfolios (as above) and compares the PE ratio with earnings growth in the current and the following year (see Table 4.8).[14]

In portfolio 1, with the highest PE ratio, the earnings growth in the current year is negative, whereas that in the following year is highly positive. This is

---

[14] Reproduced with permission from the AIMR® (see note 6). See also Beaver (1998).

Table 4.8 Evidence of temporary fluctuation in PE ratios

PE portfolio	Median PE ratio	Median earnings growth	
		Current year	Following year
1	50.0	−4.1%	95.3%
2	20.8	10.7%	14.9%
3	14.3	9.6%	12.9%
4	11.1	10.0%	8.8%
5	8.9	10.8%	5.2%
6	5.8	26.4%	−3.3%

Source: Beaver and Morse (1978)

consistent with transitory earnings, whereby a fall in current earnings relative to the sustainable level of earnings leads to a transitorily high PE ratio. For portfolio 6, the exact opposite takes place, reinforcing the evidence. For the intermediate portfolios, the effect is less pronounced, indicating that extreme values of the PE ratio are most likely to be associated with transitory current year earnings.

Penman (1996) shows that the effect of transience in current year earnings can be significant. If any given company has a high PE ratio, then this is due either to the company's ability to generate abnormally high earnings in future years, or else it is due to the earnings in the current year being abnormally low. These two explanations are almost exact opposites: either the company is expected to do well, or else it is currently doing badly. The data in Table 4.9 are taken from Penman's study. The terms 'high' and 'low' refer simply to above or below average (i.e. the rows and the columns all add to 50%). Table 4.9 shows that the PE ratio gives the 'correct' signal about two-thirds of the time.[15] A high PE ratio is usually associated with high future earnings growth (and vice versa), but one-third of the time it is associated with low current earnings.

Table 4.9 Does the PE ratio measure earnings growth?

		Value of earnings growth	
		High	Low
PE ratio	High	32.8%	16.7%
	Low	17.1%	33.4%

---

[15] The 'correct' signal is where a high PE ratio is consistent with a value-creating company, and vice versa. The term 'value of earnings growth' in Table 4.9 is used to differentiate higher value-creating companies ('high') from lower ones ('low'). The differentiation is actually based upon the price–book value ratio, which will be reviewed in Chapter 6. The relationships between the PE ratio and the price–book value ratio (which is the basis of Table 4.9) will be explored in Chapter 9.

A further empirical finding is that differences across companies in PE ratios tend to persist over time, suggesting that companies differ consistently in their ability to generate abnormal earnings (Beaver and Morse, 1978). In a follow-up study, Zarowin (1990) found that these differences are due, as would be expected, to differences in the expected rate of earnings growth. Differences in risk are less important, perhaps because the cost of capital varies less than earnings performance across companies.

Summary

The main points from this chapter may be summarized as follows:

- The PE ratio relates the share price to the expected level of earnings in the current year. There are two key determinants of the PE ratio, the cost of capital and the rate of return spread. The cost of capital 'converts' future earnings into a present value. A high cost of capital implies a low PE ratio. In turn, the rate of return spread determines, at any given level of the cost of capital, whether or not the company is creating value. A positive rate of return spread increases the PE ratio above the normal level that is given by the cost of capital.

- A simple PE model can be derived from the DGM, on the assumptions that earnings equal cash flows and that all model parameters are constant.

- The simple PE model can be used to demonstrate that the PE ratio has a 'normal' value of one over the cost of capital, which arises when the rate of return spread is constant and equal to zero, implying value-neutral growth. The conditions for a normal PE ratio imply that: the PE ratio remains constant over time; changes in the rate of future investment do not affect current shareholder value; and there is a one-to-one relationship between retained earnings and changes in shareholder value.

- The normal PE ratio also arises in the no-growth model when there is no new capital investment. In this case, the earnings yield equals the dividend yield.

- In a constant growth model, the PE ratio exceeds its normal value when the return on equity exceeds the cost of capital. In such a case, a given increase in invested capital will lead to a greater increase in shareholder value.

- The PE ratio is constant over time if both the return on equity and the cost of capital remain constant (and also, whenever the two are not equal to one another, the rate of new investment is constant also). In all other situations, the PE ratio will not be constant. Simple PE and dividend yield valuation models are therefore inconsistent with a PE ratio that is expected to change.

- The share price incorporates an assumption about changes in earnings growth *and* changes in the PE ratio. If investors assume a constant PE ratio, then the expected returns are likely to be miscalculated. In general, if earnings rise above their sustainable level, than the PE will fall below its normal level, because a fall in earnings growth must follow, and vice versa.

References

Beaver, W.H. (1998). *Financial Reporting: An Accounting Revolution*. Hemel Hempstead: Prentice Hall.

Beaver, W.H. and D. Morse (1978). 'What Determines Price–Earnings Ratios?', *Financial Analysts Journal*, July–Aug., 65–76.

Danielson, M. (1998). 'A Simple Valuation Model and Growth Expectations', *Financial Analysts Journal*, May–June, 50–7.

Durand, D. (1992). 'What Price Growth?', *Journal of Portfolio Management*, 12(1), 84–91.

Gordon, J.R. and Gordon, M.J. (1997). 'The Finite Horizon Expected Return Model', *Financial Analysts Journal*, May-June, 52–61.

Leibowitz, M. (1999). 'PE Forwards and their Orbits', *Financial Analysts Journal*, May–June, 33–47.

Leibowitz, M. and S. Kogelman (1994). 'The Growth Illusion: The PE Cost of Earnings Growth', *Financial Analysts Journal*, March–April, 36–48.

Molodovsky, N. (1953). 'A Theory of Price-Earnings Ratios', *The Analysts Journal*, 65–80. (Reprinted in the *Financial Analysts Journal*, 51(1) 1995.)

Penman, S.H. (1996). 'The Articulation of Price-Earnings Ratios and Market-to-Book Ratios and the Evaluation of Growth', *Journal of Accounting Research*, 34(2), 235–59.

Zarowin, P. (1990). 'What Determines Earnings-Price: Revisited', *Journal of Accounting, Auditing and Finance*, Summer, 439–54.

5 Financial accounting

Overview
- Fundamental principles of accounting: cash flows vs. accruals
- Accounting information and valuation
- Creative accounting
- A review of financial statements, including NOPAT, EBITDA, free cash flow, etc.

Chapters 2–4 have shown that the value of a company is a combination of, first, the amount of capital invested in the company and, second, the size (and timing) of the rate of return spread that the company is expected to achieve on this capital. These factors were shown to be captured by simple valuation models such as the dividend growth model and the PE ratio.

Very importantly, however, Chapters 2–4 have not addressed the measurement issues that are, in practice, fundamental to the use of any given valuation model. For example, Chapter 4 made the convenient, simplifying assumption that a company is comprised of a single financial asset, and that earnings from this asset are equal to cash flows. This treatment was helpful in reconciling the PE ratio to the underlying valuation framework of the dividend discount model. It was also, however, an unrealistically limited description of a company. In practice, shareholders' capital is invested not in a single financial asset but in a collection of different types of asset, each of which is employed by the company in generating an annual profit stream. In this realistic setting, the measurement of invested capital and return on equity is not straightforward, as has been assumed in earlier chapters. In fact, moving into this 'real world' creates very significant measurement problems, which cause complications in the interpretation and use of valuation models. It is in addressing these problems that the demand for financial statements arises. In effect, the financial statements are a practical attempt to measure invested capital, earnings and return on equity. It will be seen, however, that the accounts are only partially successful in this attempt, making it important to understand the limits of their usefulness.

The essence of the measurement problem is the valuation of assets. In the earlier case of a financial asset, the asset's value was unambiguous because it could be realized readily, and the value of shareholder's invested capital was therefore clear. Suppose, however, that shareholders' cash investment in a company is not used to buy a financial asset but is instead invested by the company in two different ways – in physical plant and in advertising for the company's products.

What now is the value of shareholders' invested capital? The only tangible evidence of value is the physical plant, yet presumably the company has invested in advertising because it expects this to generate an income stream. The value of shareholders' capital depends, in turn, upon the expected size and timing of this income stream. It seems sensible, therefore, to attempt to measure separately the investment made by a company and the return that the investment achieves. This requires the valuation of all assets, whether they be in the form of financial assets, physical plant or advertising expenditure. In turn, it allows the measurement of return, since this is the increase in the value of assets over time.

The aim of accounting, therefore, is to address the need for measures of asset values and income streams. Accounting can be defined as a method for reporting economic transactions and events in the form of statements of financial performance. The most important of these statements are the income statement (otherwise known as the profit and loss account) and the balance sheet. Both of these financial statements are based upon principles and methods that are universally accepted and applied.

Economic transactions and events are recorded using the system of 'double-entry', so-called because (as will be seen) all economic activity is recorded twice in the accounts. The most common application of double-entry is accruals accounting, which has been an unchallenged method of financial reporting since it was first used in fifteenth-century Venice. It was codified by Luca Pacioli, in 1494. The following extract from Pacioli's work indicates how little the fundamental principles of accounting have changed over the course of five centuries:

> Each of the entries made in the journal must be posted twice in the ledger, one to the debit and the other to the credit . . . (and) you shall also have an account for profit and loss . . . (which is) necessary to every business so that the businessman will always know what his capital is, and at the end of the period, how it is progressing.

We need not be concerned with the book-keeping details of journals, ledgers and the like. Such detail need only be of interest to accountants themselves and not to *users* of accounts. Of central interest, however, are the principles of double-entry and accruals, which Pacioli discusses in this extract. It is these principles that give rise to Pacioli's account for profit and loss and his measure of capital (meaning, in effect, his balance sheet). Profit (or income, or earnings) and capital are the cornerstones of the accounting system, since they measure return and investment, respectively.

As a subject of study, accounting is often found to be confusing. This is probably because it has a high 'entry' cost, meaning that it usually takes some time to grasp the underlying principles. In turn, this is because the methodology of accounting is unique, and it requires a specific way of thinking. It is also insufficient to understand any one aspect of the accounting framework, because all parts are related. Once the essentials of the accounting framework are understood, however, than it becomes apparent that a key strength is its underlying simplicity. There are only a limited number of ways in which financial transactions and events can be classified: in fact, all possible economic events or transactions must be recorded as either capital, liability, asset, income or expense.

The initial difficulty in understanding accounting is in understanding how the use of different classifications gives rise to different measures of capital and profit. But the accounting model itself remains an unchanging framework into which every financial transaction and event fits.

This chapter will review accounting on the assumption that the reader has no prior knowledge of the subject. This approach has been chosen because of the nature of the relationships between shareholder value and accounting information. In order to understand these relationships, it is essential to explore the fundamental, underlying principles behind the accruals accounting framework – in particular, to explain why earnings differ from cash flows, and why balance sheet values differ from market values. This can only be done properly by starting from first principles. As explained above, the accruals accounting framework is simple yet complex, and the simple needs to be mastered first. *The experienced accountant will be able to skip through these pages quickly.* As accountants are generally trained to prepare accounts rather than to use them, however, the valuation-oriented discussion of financial accounting presented here should nevertheless be a useful thought-provoker.

The chapter will use a single numerical example throughout. Simple cash-flow-based accounts are presented first, and the limitations of these accounts are then shown to generate a need for accruals accounting, in the form of the income statement and the balance sheet. The strengths and weaknesses of accruals accounting are then explored, with an emphasis on the usefulness of accounting information to the investor.

5.1 Fundamental principles of accounting: cash flows vs. accruals

All forms of accounting are concerned with keeping records of financial transactions and events. In the simplest case, this means recording inflows and outflows of cash, just like a bank statement. As an example of this form of accounting, consider a simple five-year business venture. On day one of the business £10 000 is invested in purchasing a soft drinks vending machine. An agreement is made with a supplier to stock the machine with drinks at 30 pence each, for which an annual service contract fee of £1 500 is payable. Drinks are sold for 80 pence each. The machine has a life of five years, and it is worth nothing when the business venture comes to an end. Over the five years, the business achieves the volume and value of sales shown in the table below. Table 5.1 also shows the costs, net cash flows and cash balance.

This is a simple set of accounts: it is a financial record of the life of the business, and it summarizes all of the financial transactions entered into as well as the financial position at the end of each year. In this example, the accounts appear to report everything needed to understand the financial position of the business. It can be seen that the business has made a profit, since the £10 000 invested in the business has increased to £16 000 by the time the venture is complete. It is also clear how much cash comes in and goes out during each year, and also how much money is in the bank at each point in time. And this is all known

Table 5.1 Vending machine: sales, costs and net cash flow							
Year	Number of cans sold	Sales (£)	Cost of cans (£)	Service contract (£)	Cost of machine (£)	Net cash flow (£)	Cash balance (£)
							1 Jan. 31 Dec.
1	3 000	2 400	−900	−1 500	−10 000	−10 000	10 000 0
2	6 000	4 800	−1 800	−1 500		1 500	0 1 500
3	9 000	7 200	−2 700	−1 500		3 000	1 500 4 500
4	11 000	8 800	−3 300	−1 500		4 000	4 500 8 500
5	18 000	14 400	−5 400	−1 500		7 500	8 500 16 000
Total	47 000	37 600	14 100	7 500		6 000	

in spite of there being no income statement or balance sheet. It is not immediately obvious, therefore, why such financial statements are needed, and what they might add to a simple record of cash flows.

There is, however, an important sense in which the example is unrealistic, which is that it covers the financial record over the whole life of the business, effectively ignoring the practical problem of the uncertainty of investment performance. This overlooks two very important questions that would, in reality, always be asked of any investment. The first question concerns how well the investment has performed so far, and the second concerns how well it is likely to perform in the future. These questions concern the 'stewardship' and the 'investment' roles of the accounts, respectively. They provide a setting where the income statement and the balance sheet provide useful information over and above that available from the simple cash accounts.

To illustrate this, suppose that an investor wishes to buy the vending business at the end of year 3. He or she will want to know whether the business is profitable and, if so, how profitable; and the answer to this question will determine how much the business is worth. This follows, of course, from the discussion in earlier chapters, where it was shown that the rate of return on investment is the critical determinant of value.

At the end of year 3, the cash accounts report that the business started with £10 000 but now only has £4 500. This does not look good, but it is also not a fair picture. It is true the future cash balance of £16 000 cannot be foreseen. It is also, true, however, that at the end of year 3 the business has a machine, which has two years of life remaining and therefore has some sort of value. What is known for sure, therefore, is that the business is worth its cash (£4 500) plus the value of its machine. Cash flows alone do not give the full story about business value, and there is more information contained in the historic financial records than cash flows alone. But how much is the machine worth? And what value can therefore be placed on the business?

Accruals accounting can help to answer these questions, albeit to a limited extent. It is therefore important to digress somewhat to review the methodology of accruals accounting. It will then be possible to return to the question of the value of the business, this time with the additional information given by a balance sheet and income statement.

The first stage is to analyse the balance sheet, which is at the very core of accruals accounting. A balance sheet for the first day of the business venture shows an investment of £10 000 cash as shown in Table 5.2.[1]

Table 5.2 Opening balance sheet

	£		£
Capital	10 000	Cash	10 000
	10 000		10 000

A balance sheet describes the financial position of a business at a given point in time, summarizing everything that the business owns ('assets') and everything that the business owes ('financial obligations'). Importantly, it describes the financial position of the business itself and not that of the owners of the business. The amount on the left-hand side of the balance sheet is 'capital', which is the amount that the owners have put into the business. On the right-hand side of the balance sheet are the assets of the business, which in this case comprise only cash in the bank. The sub-total on the left-hand side of the balance sheet equals that on the right. This will *always* be the case, because a business will always owe precisely as much as it owns. Alternatively stated, when money is invested in a business an obligation to repay the money is recorded and, at the same time, the use to which the money is put is recorded as an asset. This is the underlying logic of double-entry. A business cannot in itself be wealthy, because wealth must belong ultimately to individual people. Double-entry therefore records, first, the effect of an economic transaction or event on the assets of the company and, second, the equal and opposite effect on the company's obligations to its owners. Of course, a company may have obligations to parties other than its shareholders. It may, for example, have liabilities to repay debt, or to settle accounts with suppliers. In this case, shareholders' capital is equal to the net of total assets less total liabilities. The shareholders therefore have a residual claim, meaning that they own all the assets to which no other party has a claim. The shareholders' funds can be regarded as the 'balancing item' that maintains equality between the two sides of the balance sheet.

Returning to the example, the first event in the life of the business was the purchase of a machine. In making this purchase, the business gave up one type of asset (cash) and replaced it with another (a machine). There was no change in the amount that the business owed to its owners or in the recorded total value of that which it owned. The revised balance sheet therefore looks as shown in Table 5.3.

---

[1] Balance sheets can be presented in different formats. In every case, the underlying information is the same, but the presentation of the information differs. The format used here is a horizontal, UK format. An alternative, vertical format will be presented later in the chapter.

Table 5.3 Balance sheet on day 1 of year 1

	£		£
Capital	10 000	Machine	10 000
		Cash	0
	10 000		10 000

This is the balance sheet for the first day that the business is in operation. Note that the balance sheet shows the amounts that are owed and owned at *a specific point in time*. As soon as something happens to the business – such as a can being sold or the machine wearing out – then the amounts owed and owned change, and a new balance sheet is needed. In practice, a new balance sheet is prepared at the end of each financial reporting period, such that a comparison of the balance sheet at (say) the beginning of the year with that at the end will show how the net financial position of the business has changed during the year.

Two things actually happen during the first year of the example – there is a loss in the value of the machine (caused by one year of use) and there is trading activity (sales are made and expenses are incurred). Consider the machine first. If it is *assumed* that the machine wears out at a steady rate over its five-year life, then its value in the accounts declines by £2 000 each year. This annual loss in value of the asset is known as *depreciation*.[2] At the end of year 1 a value of £8 000 is therefore recorded in the balance sheet for the machine, which is the original cost less the amount that has been 'used up'.

What about trading activities? During the first year, the business sold cans worth £2 400 and incurred expenses of £900 for the cans and £1 500 for the service contract. This gives a net cash flow of zero. This does not, however, give a fair picture of the profit for the year, because one-fifth of the machine has been 'used up' in order that the business could carry out its trading activities. It seems reasonable, therefore, to deduct depreciation from the net cash flow in order to calculate profit or loss.

These trading activities may be summarized in an income statement, which is simply a record of all income and all expenses that relate to a given financial period. The income statement for the period of the first year of the business is as shown Table 5.4.

The relationship between capital and profit can now be demonstrated. The balance sheet reports that shareholders' capital at the beginning of year 1 is £10 000. Meanwhile, the income statement reports that £2 000 of this money has now been lost, and so the business must now owe only £8 000 back to its owners.[3] The revised total on the left-hand side of the balance sheet should therefore be £8 000. This may seem like strange logic, but remember that the

---

[2] The term 'depreciation' is applied to tangible fixed assets, such as plant and machinery, while the term 'amortization' is used analogously for intangible fixed assets, such as R&D or goodwill.

[3] Notice that the balance sheet reports the net change in shareholders' financial position, while the income statement reports the gross income and expenditure that underpins the net change.

Table 5.4 Income statement for year 1

		£	£
Sales income			2 400
less costs:	cost of cans	−900	
	service contract	−1 500	
	depreciation	−2 000	−4 400
Profit (loss)			−2 000

assets of the business are only worth £8 000 at the end of the year (£10 000 machine less £2 000 depreciation). The business is therefore only able to refund £8 000 to its owners, and it is the owners who must bear the financial loss. The balance sheet at the end of year 1 is as shown in Table 5.5.

Table 5.5 Balance sheet at end of year 1

	£		£
Capital	10 000	Machine	8 000
Profit	−2 000	Cash	0
	8 000		8 000

Notice two things regarding this balance sheet. First, the profit figure derived from the income statement feeds directly into the balance sheet. It measures the change during the year in the value of the owners' investment in the company. Shareholders' funds equal the sum of capital and profit. Second, the net cash flow was zero, even though profit was not. The difference is the £2 000 loss in the value of the asset, which affects both sides of the balance sheet. It is a reduction in the value of the asset (which is called the *provision for depreciation*) and it is a reduction in the amount that the business owes to its owners (which appears in the income statement and is called the *depreciation charge*). Changes in non-cash balance sheet values are accruals, and they are a mechanism for allowing the measure of profit to differ from that of cash flow.

This difference between profit and cash flow can be considered further by examining the data for year 2. The net cash flow in year 2 is £1 500 and depreciation is £2 000, which gives the income statement shown in Table 5.6.

Notice that there are two different types of cost in this income statement. First, there are costs that are paid for in cash – these are the costs of the cans and the service contract. Second, there is depreciation. This is considered to be a cost in that it reflects the using up of an asset, but it is not a cost in a 'conventional' sense because it does not involve paying out any cash during the year. In fact, the cash for the asset was paid out at the beginning of year 1, although the expense is only *recognized* now.[4] This difference between when cash is paid out and when

---

[4] The term 'recognition' means inclusion in the financial statements.

Table 5.6 Income statement for year 2

		£	£
Sales income			4 800
less costs:	cost of cans	−1 800	
	service contract	−1 500	
	depreciation	−2 000	−5 300
Profit (loss)			−500

an expense is recognized in the income statement is the distinguishing feature of accruals accounting. It is known as a *matching* process, because the idea is to match the cost of an asset to the period in time when the asset is actually used up. In this example, the machine was bought at the beginning of year 1, but the cost of the machine is spread (i.e. matched against revenue) across each year of the asset's life. As has already been seen, this matching process gives a better measure of profit for the year than a simple measure of cash flow.

This can be seen in more detail by examining the accounting treatment of the machine throughout its life, as shown in Table 5.7. When the asset was bought at the beginning of year 1, its value was recorded in the balance sheet. This process of treating a purchase as an asset and recording it in the balance sheet is called *capitalization*. Thereafter, at the end of each year, the value of the asset in the balance sheet was reduced by £2 000. This is depreciation (or *writing-off*). The mechanism of capitalizing and then depreciating an asset allows the cost of the asset to be spread over its economic life.

Table 5.7 Value of the machine in the balance sheet (£s)

	Start year 1	End year 1	End year 2	End year 3	End year 4	End year 5
Balance sheet value	10 000	8 000	6 000	4 000	2 000	0
Depreciation charge	–	2 000	2 000	2 000	2 000	2 000
Cash outflow	10 000	0	0	0	0	0

Notice that the total amount of cash spent on the machine is equal to the sum of the depreciation charges over all five years, but while there is a one-off change in the bank balance, there is an annual effect on profits. In other words, profit and cash flow are different in each year, even though they sum to the same amount when taking all years together. This suggests that any depreciating asset is effectively a *deferred expense*. At some stage or another, the cost of a depreciable asset will be reflected in the income statement. But by the mechanism of capitalizing and depreciating, the *timing* of this recognition can be affected. Looked at another way, whenever a business spends money, it has to decide whether to take this expenditure directly to the income statement for the year or to capitalize it and take it to the balance sheet.[5] If it does the latter, then the expenditure is deferred in the accounts and will be recognized in the income statement in later years. In principle, any business therefore has the choice between recognizing a cash outflow as either an expense or an asset; and the balance sheet is the mechanism by which a cost can be kept out of the income statement for the current year, and then transferred into the income statement in future years.[6]

Asset or expense?

America Online, the world's leading provider of online services, yesterday agreed to pay regulators $3.5m to settle charges it improperly accounted for marketing costs in 1995 and 1996 ... According to the SEC (Securities and Exchange Commission), AOL wrongly capitalised the costs of acquiring new customers – including sending out thousands of free computer discs – reporting them as an asset rather than an expense ... The SEC said the company posted profits for six of eight quarters, instead of the losses it would have reported had the costs been shown correctly ... it discontinued the controversial accounting practice on October 1996 and took a $385m charge to write off the expenses. In settling the charge, AOL did not admit any wrongdoing and stressed the agreement would have no impact on its results since 1997.

Source: Financial Times, Thomas Catán and agencies, 16 May 2000

Capitalizing the costs of new customers allowed AOL to build up an asset of $385m over two years. These costs therefore avoided the income statement, allowing profits to be higher than if expensing had taken place. Since, however, an asset is simply a deferred expense, the income statement was eventually charged with the full $385m when the asset was written off. AOL did not admit wrongdoing, presumably because it regarded the costs as an investment incurred to generate *future* revenue. The mechanism of capitalizing and writing-off would thereby have allowed the matching of revenues and costs in the income statement. There was no impact post-1997 since no asset remained on the balance sheet and all costs had been expensed.

Returning to the data for year 2, the loss of £500, the depreciation of £2 000 and the net cash inflow of £1 500 gives the closing balance sheet shown in Table 5.8.[7]

---

[5] The converse of this is also true. Cash inflows can be recorded on the balance sheet as deferred income (a liability) rather than taken directly to the income statement. Also, expenses (income) can be charged (credited) to the income statement in the current period, with the cash outflow (inflow) taking place in a later period. For example, a provision for future costs gives rise to a current expense and a current liability, without any current cash flow. Similarly, credit sales give rise to income in the income statement and to an accounts receivable asset on the balance sheet. Overall, accruals adjustments can be used to record either income or expenditure in time periods either before or after their associated actual cash flows.

[6] Inventory is an obvious example of this, since it is transferred as an expense to the income statement at the point at which is it sold, allowing profit to be calculated at the date of sale. The same would be true for land, which remains on the balance sheet until it is sold, at which point its cost is netted off in the income statement against its sales price. Even accounts receivable can be viewed as deferred expenses. They are valued in the accounts at their expected recoverable amount which, when received, generates neither a profit nor a loss. If, however, some debts were not collected, then the accounts receivable asset would have to be written-off as an expense.

[7] To keep the example simple, it is assumed that the company's cash balance does not earn interest, and also that no dividends are paid.

Table 5.8 Balance sheet at end of year 2

	£		£
Capital	10 000	Machine	6 000
Profit	−2 500	Cash	1 500
	7 500		7 500

Notice that the profit figure is now the sum of the loss in year 1 (of £2 000) and the loss in year 2 (of £500). This reflects that, over the life of the business (since the original £10 000 was invested) losses are a total of £2 500. This is not a healthy picture, although there is some comfort in that the loss in year 2 is a significant improvement on that in year 1.

Looking ahead to year 3, it is now possible to address the question raised above of how much the business is worth at the end of its third year. There is a net cash inflow of £3 000 and a depreciation charge of £2 000, which gives the business its first year of profit. The associated income statement and balance sheet are as shown in Table 5.9 and Table 5.10 respectively.

Table 5.9 Income statement for year 3

		£	£
Sales income			7 200
less costs:	cost of cans	−2 700	
	service contract	−1 500	
	depreciation	−2 000	−6 200
Profit (loss)			1 000

Table 5.10 Balance sheet at end of year 3

	£		£
Capital	10 000	Machine	4 000
Profit	−1 500	Cash	4 500
	8 500		8 500

At first sight, the business appears to be worth £8 500. This is the value of the owners' stake in the business that is recorded in the balance sheet, and it is the *book value* of the net assets. The fundamental problem with this valuation, however, is that the balance sheet reflects the past (it is said to be based upon 'historic cost').[8] The actual value of the business depends, of course, upon how much

---

[8] Historic costs are commonplace and are used in this example, although in most jurisdictions revaluation to market values is allowable for certain types of asset. See Chapter 6 for further discussion.

net cash flow the business will generate in the *future*. An investor with perfect foresight would know that the business is worth a total of £16 000 at the end of year 5. Yet at the end of year 3, the accounts report an historic book value of only £8 500. The market value of assets can therefore differ from the book value. While it is obvious that the £4 500 cash is actually worth £4 500, the market value of the machine cannot be inferred from the accounts. Remember that the book value of the machine is made up of two things – how much was paid for it, and how much of its value has been depreciated. The effect of depreciation is to spread the *cost* of the machine over its life. This process is independent of the actual market value of the machine, should it be sold. It might have been the case, for example, that the market value of vending machines increased during year 3 of the business, allowing disposal for (say) £9 000. But the accounts do not reflect this. They do not report how much the machine is actually worth, but only how much of the original cost is estimated to have not been 'used up'.

A key reason why the accounts do not reflect market values is the generally accepted need for objectivity and conservatism (or 'prudence'). Nobody can be absolutely sure that the machine could be sold at its estimated market value, and a market value is therefore somewhat subjective.[9] In contrast, there is no question about the price that was originally paid for it. Historic cost is objective, and it can therefore be verified by an auditor of the accounts. In practice, this is important because the accounts would presumably be less reliable if managers were given discretion over assets values. The downside of this, however, is that the book value of assets is unlikely to reflect their true worth, meaning that the accounts generally do not provide the most relevant information for decision making. For example, the estimated market value of £9 000 is of greater relevance to the decision to sell the machine in year 3 than the book value of £4 500. This conflict between *relevance* and *reliability* is a central and critically important theme in accounting. Typically, the value of the business will be greater than the book value of the assets. The difference between market value and book value is called *goodwill*. It is the amount of business value that the accounts do not tell us about.[10]

Fortunately, this does not mean that accounting information cannot be used in valuing companies. While they do not give the 'correct answer', they can nevertheless be useful in either of two ways. First, book value is itself a starting point. The accounts report a cash balance of £4 500 and a machine that is prudently valued at £4 000. Although it is not certain that £4 000 could be realized by selling the machine, a conservative estimate of the value of the business would be £8 500 (£4 500 + £4 000). Second, the income statement provides a basis for forecasting future cash flows. While a cumulative net loss of £1 500 has been made by the end of year 3, the income statements report that the profit trend is sharply upwards. It might therefore be expected that profits will rise into the future. If,

---

[9] This is especially true of intangible assets. See Chapter 6.

[10] Goodwill can arise either because assets are incorrectly valued in the accounts or, alternatively, because the company as a whole is more valuable than the sum of its parts. The second of these possibilities is termed 'pure' goodwill. See Chapters 6 and 7 for an extended discussion.

for example, it is assumed that sales increase by 50% in year 4 (to £10 800) and also in year 5 (to £16 200), then the cash balance would rise to £21 375 by the end of year 5. Overall, then, the accounts might lead us to estimate that the business is worth somewhere between £8 500 and £21 375.[11] This is a wide range, but a more precise figure would have to rely upon an estimation of business prospects. Such an estimation cannot come from the accounts, but only from other sources such as market research.

Returning to the example, the business actually receives a net cash inflow of £4 000 in year 4 and makes a profit of £2 000 after charging depreciation. This is all reflected in the balance sheet at the end of year 4 as shown in Table 5.11.

Table 5.11 Balance sheet at end of year 4

	£		£
Capital	10 000	Machine	2 000
Profit	500	Cash	8 500
	10 500		10 500

Notice that the book value of the investment is now higher than the original investment, since there is a positive value of £500 for cumulative profits. What is more, investors can be confident that the risks of the business have fallen considerably from its early days. Of the total book value of £10 500, £8 500 is in cash and only £2 000 in an asset of uncertain market value. Moreover, the profit continues to increase, which suggests that an even bigger profit will be made in year 5.

Before considering year 5, it will be useful to take one final look at asset values. In particular, notice that throughout the example it has been *assumed* that £2 000 of the value of the machine has been lost in each year. This assumption is subjective. It is an accrual, an accounting adjustment taking place without any corresponding change in the cash position. A different assumption could easily have been made, for example to depreciate the machine by either £1 000 or £3 000 in year 4. This would have increased the book value of the asset to £3 000 or reduced it to £1 000, respectively. In turn, the profit for year 4 would have been increased to £3 000 or reduced to £1 000, respectively. So, a single business can have more than one possible measure of book value and of profit. This is because there is a degree of subjectivity in the assessment of asset values, which also affects the level of the reported profits. The subjectivity is made possible because accruals accounting allows the recording of more than just cash flows.

---

[11] Notice two things about this valuation. First, and simply for convenience, the time value of money is ignored. Strictly, the value at the end of year 5 should be discounted in order for it to be comparable with the current value of the asset. Second, there are actually two distinct types of valuation here. The value of the machine represents an 'exit' option. It is the sales value of the company's asset. The future cash flows, on the other hand, represent the 'staying in business' option. It is the value that the company generates from using the machine. In effect, the sales value is simply an open market estimate of how much a different company believes it can generate by using the asset. In this way, the two valuations are related. This will be discussed further in Chapter 6.

While the cash flows are objective, and must be reported as and when they occur, the valuation of assets and the associated effect on profits is based upon subjective judgement. This difference between profit and cash is not important over the whole life of a business because, as has been seen, everything becomes cash sooner or later. But in individual years during the life of an ongoing business, subjective accounting choices can have a significant effect on reported book values and profitability. Indeed, the very reason why the balance sheet and the income statement convey more useful information than the cash flow statement is that judgement is exercised over the values of assets and liabilities. But this scope to exercise judgement is itself the cause of subjective variation in estimates of profit and capital.

Change in accounting policy

In the year to March 2001, Sony expects net profits to tumble 92 per cent to Y10bn . . . Sony blamed the losses for the three months to June 30 on the strong yen and a one-time accounting charge worth Y101.65bn . . . The charge resulted from a change in US accounting rules that require motion picture groups to record marketing expenses within three months of a film's release, instead of amortising these costs over the life of the movie as before.

Source: Financial Times, Alexandra Harney and Rebecca Bream, 27 July 2000

The change in US accounting rules forced Sony to recognize marketing expenses sooner rather than later, lowering asset values and profits for the current year but relieving future profits by an equal and opposite amount. Importantly, while a change of this type in accruals method affects the way in which economic performance is measured and reported, it is independent of the company's actual cash flows and therefore independent of shareholder value itself.

This problem of subjective valuation only arises, in fact, because the life of the company has been arbitrarily divided into five individual years. The requirement for a company to report its financial performance every year is unrelated to the underlying economics of the company. It is simply a time period deemed to be convenient by investors, tax authorities and regulators of financial reporting. In the example given, the machine was reckoned to have a life of five years. The need to report book value annually therefore required putting a valuation on a part-used asset. In turn, this generated a need for an accruals adjustment to cash flows, in the form of asset capitalization and subsequent depreciation. If the company had reported its financial performance every five years, then no such accrual would have been required, because the value of the asset would have been 0 in the opening and the closing balance sheets. Hence, subjectivity in measuring profit and capital arises because of the need for a periodic measure of financial performance, and the shorter the period, the greater the subjectivity. Alternatively stated, subjectivity varies across industries according to the length of the operating cycle.

The equivalence of profits and cash flows over the whole lifetime of a business becomes apparent at the end of year 5, as shown in Table 5.12. During the year, the business receives a net cash flow of £7 500, and makes a profit of £6 500. The value of the asset reduces to 0. Notice, therefore, that the lifetime

Table 5.12 Profit vs. cash flow over the whole life of the business

	Year 1	Year 2	Year 3	Year 4	Year 5	Total
Net cash flow	−10 000	1 500	3 000	4 000	7 500	6 000
Profit	−2 000	−500	1 000	2 000	5 500	6 000

net operating cash flow equals the lifetime profit. By using accrual accounting techniques, however, profit has been recognized at a different time from when the cash flows took place. This was done to give a better picture of whether or not the business was making money and of how much, therefore, the owners' original investment had changed in value.[12]

The final balance sheet for the end of year 5 is as shown in Table 5.13.

Table 5.13 Balance sheet at end of year 5

	£		£
Capital	10 000	Machine	0
Profit	6 000	Cash	16 000
	16 000		16 000

The £16 000 cash can now be paid back to the owners of the business in full settlement of the business' obligations, and the life of the business ends here.

5.2 Accounting information and valuation

Having reviewed the fundamental principles of accruals accounting, it is now possible to illustrate the relationship between the book value of assets and their market value. Figure 5.1 plots the cash balance, book value of shareholders' funds and market value for the example used above. The market value is simply the value of future cash flows, discounted at a cost of capital of 9%.[13]

This graph demonstrates a number of points. First, market value always exceeds book value which, in turn, always exceeds the cash balance. Typically (though not always), these relationships would be expected to hold. The book value exceeds the cash balance because the company holds non-cash assets. These assets exist because of accruals accounting, which has been used to capitalize a

---

[12] A cash flow statement records the net cash flows over the course of a year, while the income statement records the net of income over expenditure. The two statements can be reconciled via the balance sheet, since the accruals that cause net cash flow and profit to differ are reflected in changing values of shareholders' funds, assets and liabilities.

[13] Note that there is, in fact, only one relevant cash flow, which is the return to shareholders of £16 000 at the end of year 5. Until this point all earnings have been retained. In the absence of dividends, the market value increases by the cost of capital each year, giving a 9% annual return on an initial market value of £10 399.

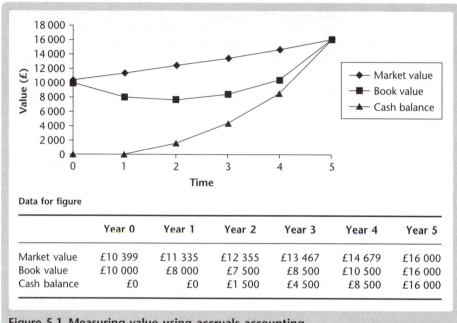

Data for figure

	Year 0	Year 1	Year 2	Year 3	Year 4	Year 5
Market value	£10 399	£11 335	£12 355	£13 467	£14 679	£16 000
Book value	£10 000	£8 000	£7 500	£8 500	£10 500	£16 000
Cash balance	£0	£0	£1 500	£4 500	£8 500	£16 000

Figure 5.1 Measuring value using accruals accounting

cash outflow in the form of an asset with a multi-period life. Second, the book value of the asset is itself somewhat subjective, and it depends over time upon the rate of depreciation applied. If the depreciation rate changes, then the slope of the book value curve will change also. It will still start at £10 000 and it will still finish at £16 000, but its path between these points can vary. The periodic measures of capital and profit are therefore also somewhat variable. Third, at the end of the five-year period, all measures are in agreement, because all assets are in the form of cash. In all other years, there is positive goodwill, because the market value exceeds the book value. At the start of the venture the discounted value of future cash flows exceeds only marginally the book value of the asset. By the end of the first year, however, the present value of cash flows has increased while accounting profit, based only upon transactions up to the end of the year, is actually negative, causing a fall in the book value of capital. The second year sees a further fall, but thereafter historic performance 'catches up' with the future performance that has already been 'anticipated' by the market value.

This example is, of course, limited in some important ways. In particular, it calculates market value on the assumption that future cash flows are known, it includes only one accruals adjustment (depreciation), and it relates to a company with a finite (and short) life. The example nevertheless illustrates the main themes of this chapter. Financial accounting is able to improve upon cash flows as a means of providing information about the value of a company: the book value curve is closer to market value than the cash balance, and the rate at which profits are made can be extrapolated more meaningfully than net cash flows. Financial accounting can only achieve this, however, at the expense of subjectivity in the determination of the value of assets and liabilities, and this subjectivity can be misleading as well as helpful.

5.3   Creative accounting

A good understanding of financial accounting is equivalent to a good understanding of creative accounting, since using accruals to inform users of accounts is the converse of using them to mislead. Table 5.14, which is taken from Schilit (1993), characterizes creative accounting schemes as 'shenanigans' and categorizes them according to their impact upon the financial statements. The use of accruals to either defer or bring forward either income or expenditure is the subject of four of Schilit's shenanigans (numbered in Table 5.14 as 6, 1, 4 and 7, respectively). For example, the deferral of depreciation expenses falls into category 4. The remaining three shenanigans are different in nature. The accounts can be incomplete or incorrect, for example when liabilities known to the company are not accounted for or disclosed (shenanigan number 5) or when income is falsely recorded (shenanigan number 2). The accounts can also be consistent with financial reporting standards, but still misleading. For example, leased assets need not always be capitalized, leading to an effective understatement of both assets employed in the business and debt (shenanigan number 5.4). Finally, financial performance can be disguised by careful and selective use of line items in the financial statements (shenanigan numbers 3.3 and 3.4, see below and also Chapter 7 for further discussion).

Table 5.14 Sources of creative accounting – 'the seven shenanigans'

1. Recording revenue too soon	1. Shipping goods before a sale is finalized 2. Recording revenue when important uncertainties exist 3. Recording revenue when future services are still due
2. Recording bogus revenues	1. Recording income on the exchange of similar assets 2. Recording refunds from suppliers as revenue 3. Using bogus estimates on interim financial reports
3. Boosting income with one-time gains	1. Boosting profits by selling undervalued assets 2. Boosting profits by retiring debt 3. Failing to segregate unusual and non-recurring gains or losses from recurring income 4. Burying losses under non-continuing operations
4. Shifting current expenses to a later period	1. Improperly capitalizing costs 2. Depreciating or amortizing costs too slowly 3. Failing to write off worthless assets
5. Failing to record or disclose all liabilities	1. Recording revenue rather than a liability when cash is received 2. Failing to accrue expected or contingent liabilities 3. Failing to disclose commitments and contingencies 4. Engaging in transactions to keep debt off the books
6. Shifting current income to a later period	1. Creating reserves to shift sales revenue to a later period
7. Shifting future expenses to a current period	1. Accelerating discretionary expenses into the current period 2. Writing off future years' depreciation or amortization

Source: Schilit (1993).

Further interesting discussions of creative accounting schemes can be found in Griffiths (1995) and Smith (1996). Examples range from adjustments to inventory valuations and bad debt provisions to holding assets and liabilities 'off-balance sheet' to the exploitation of favourable methods of accounting for mergers and acquisitions.

While not the focus of this book, the scope for creative accounting is an important reminder that accruals accounting is inherently subjective, and that it can be used to mislead investors as well as to inform them.

How much sales revenue?

US regulators are about to lift a cloud from Priceline.com's share price by effectively endorsing the controversial accounting statements of the internet company . . . Priceline records all the revenue from ticket sales. So if it sells an airline ticket for $500, it books $500 on its top line and deducts the cost of the ticket in its cost of goods sold. This has caused controversy because normal travel agents record only the commission they receive . . . although it does not affect a company's net earnings, the practice is seen by some as giving turnover an artificial lift in an attempt to attract investors seeking strong revenue growth.

Source: Financial Times, Adrian Michaels, 28 July 2000

In this example, as with most cases of creative accounting, Priceline.com has a legitimate choice between two different accounting methods. Its preference for one method of revenue recognition over another does not affect reported profit or underlying value, but it may influence investors' perceptions of value. Specifically, stock market value would benefit if investors focus uncritically on valuation using a sales revenue multiple (a common valuation model for internet stocks).

5.4 A review of financial statements[14]

In concluding this chapter, the simple financial statements presented above can now be extended into a more complete review of financial reporting practice. The following financial statements are published by the accounting firm KPMG in a report that illustrates how international accounting standards are used (KPMG, 2000). They will be used here to highlight a few important characteristics of the primary financial statements.

---

[14] The presentation of the financial statements differs somewhat (though not greatly) between countries. There can also be significant differences between countries in the required methods of recognition, measurement and disclosure of financial statement data. International standards for financial statements are governed by the International Accounting Standards Committee (IASC), while national standard-setting bodies include the Financial Accounting Standards Board (FASB) in the USA, and the Accounting Standards Board (ASB) in the UK. Regarding the presentation of financial performance in the income statement, the relevant financial reporting standards are IAS 1, SFAS 130 and FRS 3, respectively. For further information, the respective web sites for these organizations are iasc.org.uk, fasb.org, asb.org.uk.

Table 5.15 Consolidated income statement (for the year ended 31 December 2000, €'000s)

	Continuing operations		Discontinuing operations		Total consolidated	
	2000	1999	2000	1999	2000	1999
Revenue	99 360	95 186	8 043	24 693	107 403	119 879
Cost of sales	(52 694)	(55 171)	(7 351)	(22 675)	(60 045)	(77 846)
Gross profit	46 666	40 015	692	2 018	47 358	42 033
Gain on sale of discontinuing operation	–	–	736	–	736	–
Other operating income	1 020	265	–	–	1 020	265
Distribution expenses	(17 784)	(18 012)	(106)	(295)	(17 890)	(18 307)
Administrative expenses	(15 458)	(15 066)	(177)	(492)	(15 635)	(15 558)
Other operating expenses	(3 893)	(1 800)	(71)	(197)	(3 964)	(1 997)
Profit from operations	10 551	5 402	1 074	1 034	11 625	6 436
Net financing costs	(849)	(1 196)	–	–	(849)	(1 196)
Income from associates	467	587	–	–	467	587
Profit before tax	10 169	4 793	1 074	1 034	11 243	5 827
Income tax expense	(2 979)	(1 404)	(365)	(352)	(3 344)	(1 756)
Profit after tax	7 190	3 389	709	682	7 899	4 071
Minority interest	(376)	(219)	–	–	(376)	(219)
Net profit from ordinary activities	6 814	3 170	709	682	7 523	3 852
Extraordinary item	(679)	–	–	–	(679)	–
Net profit for the year	6 135	3 170	709	682	6 844	3 852
Basic earnings per share (euro)	1.85	0.90			2.08	1.13
Diluted earnings per share (euro)	1.77	0.89			1.98	1.11

Source: KPMG (2000) www.KPMG.co.uk

The income statement shown in Table 5.15 can be seen as an expansion of those given earlier. The top half of the statement reports performance from the operating activities of the company, with the operations that are ongoing being identified separately. Operating costs are split between those that are relatively direct (i.e. the cost of sales that varies in proportion to output) and those that are relatively indirect (i.e. the other costs that are mostly fixed over the reporting period). The *gross profit* percentage captures the per unit gain on the sale of products and services, while the *profit from operations* is the 'bottom line' of the company's operating (or 'trading') activities. The company's financing costs, taxation charges and interests of minority shareholders are then deducted from operating profit, giving net profit from ordinary activities. Finally, if a company has gains or losses during the year that are of an unusual, one-off nature, then these are reported separately as extraordinary items. This is because inclusion of these in operating profit would distort the underlying trend in the company's performance.[15] The net profit attributable to shareholders is the bottom line of the income statement, and it is divided by the number of shares in issue to give earnings per share (or eps).[16]

Which profit measure?

Both Smithkline Beecham and Glaxo Wellcome have managed to produce strong interim results ahead of Monday's shareholder meetings to approve their merger . . . [but] while Glaxo's figures seemed to show a good recovery, with pre-tax profits and earnings up 20 per cent, they needed an accounting pick-me-up to give them a rosier complexion. Sales of investments raised £199m, of which £55m was tucked into operating income, and without that gain the advance was more pedestrian. Still, that cash appears to have been well spent in boosting marketing efforts. These have translated into higher sales, notably in the US.

Source: Financial Times, Lex Column, 28 July 2000

Where to 'draw the line' in calculating profit is rarely straightforward. Glaxo Wellcome's 20% increase in pre-tax profits include an investment gain that is unrelated to the core business and to trend profitability. At the same time, it has expensed marketing costs that are an investment in enhancing revenues both now and in the future. The separate disclosure of these items allows investors to form their own judgements about the current and future profitability of the company. (Earnings measurement is discussed at length in Chapter 7.)

The income statement can be viewed from either of two perspectives. First, the shareholders' perspective requires a focus on *profit after tax*, since this represents the net income available for distribution to shareholders. Second, there is the combined perspective of shareholders and debtholders, whereby the appropriate income measure is the amount available for either interest or dividend payments. This measure is often termed NOPAT, which stands for net operating profit after tax. It is the remainder after deducting tax at the corporate rate from operating profit.[17] It equals the sum of profit after tax and net interest payments after tax, and it is independent of the capital structure of the company.[18]

A final, commonly used income statement measure is EBITDA, which stands for earnings before interest, tax, depreciation and amortization. In other words, it

---

[15] These are known as exceptional items in the UK. See Chapter 7 for further analysis.

[16] The method of calculating eps is laid out in IAS 33. Diluted eps is calculated on the basis that all contingently issuable shares (e.g. share options, convertibles) are in fact issued.

[17] Ideally, this measure should be operating profit *plus* other income such as income from associates, but *excluding* interest paid. In this way it represents the total income from the company's net assets, and thereby the return to equity and debt. An alternative way to measure NOPAT, therefore, is to add back to profit after tax the interest expense multiplied by one minus the tax rate. This equals profit after tax plus interest after tax.

[18] Consider, for example, a company with operating profit of £100 and a tax rate of 40%. NOPAT is £60. If the company is all equity financed, then profit after tax is £60 also. If there is also debt finance, then the interest on the debt is allowable against tax. An annual interest payment of £25 gives profit before tax of £75, and profit after tax of £45. The net interest payment is £15 (60% of £25) which, added to the profit after tax of £45, gives the NOPAT of £60. This can illustrate the independence of NOPAT from capital structure.

is operating profit with the non-cash flow expenses of depreciation and amortization added back. The rationale for EBITDA is three-fold. First, there is unavoidable subjectivity (and therefore potential distortion) in the calculation of depreciation and amortization. A more reliable earnings measure, it can be argued, is one that is closer to cash flow, and that therefore excludes depreciation and amortization. The problem with this line of reasoning, however, is that *all* accruals can be viewed as subjective, non-cash-flow items, intended to enhance the usefulness of the earnings measure. If the benefits of accruals are accepted, then it is not clear why some accruals should be reversed whilst others are left unchanged. This is particularly so because EBITDA favours companies with high capital expenditure. If companies are, in effect, not charged for capital expenditure in the income statement, then their purported income stream is unrealistically high. A second (and more convincing) justification for EBITDA is that depreciation and amortization expenses are not cash flows, and they represent allocations of historic costs rather than expectations of future capital expenditure. They might therefore be an inappropriate basis from which to assess the ongoing profitability of a company's operation. Of greater relevance to this assessment is the current cost of acquiring fixed assets (i.e. capital expenditure rather than depreciation). This suggests, again, that a company's EBITDA should not be viewed in isolation from its capital expenditure requirements. Finally, a third justification for EBITDA is that it measures a company's flexibility to respond to changing market conditions. Again, since depreciation and amortization are not cash flows, EBITDA is a better measure than operating profit of the cash flow that a company is making available for new investment. This said, an alternative measure to EBITDA in this context is operating cash flow, which is discussed below. In summary, EBITDA has some merits as a measure of financial performance, but there are qualifications associated with all three of the justifications for its usage.[19]

The income statement does not, however, capture all of the changes in shareholders' funds during any given year. In fact, it is possible for economic gains and losses to be taken direct to balance sheet reserves without first passing through the income statement. The rationale for this is to distinguish operating performance from gains and losses unrelated to operations. The latter are captured in the statement of recognized gains and losses, and they include items such as revaluation gains on properties, or exchange differences arising on the translation of the net assets of foreign subsidiaries into the reporting currency.[20] It is the total recognized gains and losses, together with changes caused by the injection or withdrawal of equity capital (including dividends), that equate the opening and closing values of shareholders' funds in the balance sheet. In Table 5.16, the €7 627 change in shareholders' funds from 1999 to 2000 equals net profit (€6 844) plus other recognized losses (€29) less dividends (€1 243) plus new capital and other charges (€2 055).[21]

---

[19] There is also a further justification in the specific context of the amortization of goodwill, that will be explored further in Chapter 7.

[20] If all gains and losses do not pass through the income statement, then the financial statements are said to be not 'fully articulated' (or not 'clean surplus'). This is discussed further in Chapter 9.

[21] The detail of the change in capital and reserves is provided in a footnote to the accounts, which is not reproduced here.

Table 5.16 Consolidated balance sheet (as at 31 December 2000, €'000s)

	2000	1999
Assets		
Property, plant equipment	31 350	31 049
Intangible assets	2 745	1 661
Investment property	5 570	1 050
Investments in associates	2 025	1 558
Other investments	3 637	3 379
Deferred tax assets	143	432
Total non-current assets	45 470	39 129
Investments	1 243	1 568
Inventories	18 965	15 399
Income tax receivable	–	294
Other receivables	18 400	20 532
Cash and cash equivalents	2 415	1 850
Total current assets	41 023	39 643
Total assets	86 493	78 772
Equity and liabilities		
Issued capital	15 045	14 550
Share premium	4 613	3 500
Reserves	1 044	706
Retained earnings	19 383	13 702
Total capital and reserves	40 085	32 458
Minority interest	1 196	820
Liabilities		
Interest-bearing loans and borrowings	20 942	17 116
Employee benefits	1 907	1 730
Deferred government grants	1 000	1 500
Provisions	660	550
Deferred tax liabilities	2 717	521
Total non-current liabilities	27 226	21 417
Bank overdraft	334	282
Interest-bearing loans and borrowings	4 390	6 476
Income tax payable	71	–
Other payables	12 181	16 119
Provisions	1 010	1 200
Total current liabilities	17 986	24 077
Total equity and liabilities	86 493	78 772

Source: KPMG (2000) www.KPMG.co.uk

Table 5.16 presents assets and liabilities in increasing order of liquidity (i.e. in order of convertibility into cash). For example, assets are listed in a progression from property to cash. The total value of assets is €86 493, with shareholders' funds of €40 085 representing 46% of the business, and the remaining 54% being funded by minority shareholders, debtholders and other creditors.[22] Not all of these sources of funding should be viewed as financing the business, however, because some (such as trade creditors, tax liabilities, etc.) do not demand a return on capital. It is not always straightforward to identify the providers of 'true' finance, although a common definition is shareholders' funds, plus minority interests, plus interest-bearing debt (both non-current and current). This total can be termed *capital employed*, and the equal amount of total assets less non-finance liabilities can be termed *net assets*. The balance sheet can be used to estimate the total capital invested in the business. The ratio of debt to capital employed is called leverage (or gearing), and it measures the extent to which a given amount of shareholders' investment is matched by finance from other (usually fixed-interest) sources.

Finally, the cash flow statement (Table 5.17) is a summary of the cash inflows and outflows during the course of a reporting period.[23] There are three distinct categories in the cash flow statement, which are operations, investing and financing. The first two categories are closely related, with the former focused on ongoing operating activity and the latter on associated investing activities. Taken together these categories are concerned with net assets, while the third category, financing, is concerned with the opposite side of the balance sheet, capital employed.

An important valuation metric derived from the cash flow statement is 'free cash flow'. This is a measure of the net cash flow between a company and its providers of finance. It is defined as operating cash flow after tax less investing cash flow (where the latter can include increases in the company's cash balances). From the cash flow statement above, the first step in deriving free cash flow is to add net interest back to operating cash flow (since interest is a financing flow). If the tax rate is estimated at 30% (from the income statement), then net interest is €879 and operating cash flow after tax is €4 889. If the investing cash outflow (€6 845) and the increase in cash (€435) are subtracted from this, then free cash flow is calculated to be (€2 391) – or, alternatively, (€1 956) if the change in cash is treated as a financing flow. This net operating cash outflow from the company is necessarily equal and opposite to the company's net financing cash inflow. Specifically, €2 391 equals the financing cash inflow of €3 270 from the cash flow statement less the net interest cash outflow of €879. Free cash flow is the basis of the discounted cash flow valuation model, as will be discussed in Chapter 10.

---

[22] If a company does not wholly own one of its subsidiaries, then the shares not owned are said to belong to 'minority shareholders'. When the consolidated accounts for the group of companies are prepared, the whole of the net assets of the subsidiaries are added together, and the minority shareholders are reported as a separate class of equity claimants on these assets.

[23] This is true of the 'direct' format for the cash flow statement, which is presented above. In contrast, the 'indirect' format reports operating profit with adjustments for 'non-cash' items, such as depreciation.

Table 5.17 Consolidated statement of cash flows (for the year ended 31 December 2000, €'000s)

	2000	1999
Operating activities		
Cash receipts from customers	109 538	93 295
Cash paid to suppliers and employees	(102 853)	(85 238)
Cash generated from operations	6 685	8 057
Interest paid	(1 255)	(1 734)
Income taxes paid	(741)	(1 048)
Cash flow before extraordinary item	4 689	5 275
Payments for extraordinary expenses (net of tax)	(679)	–
Cash flow from operating activities	4 010	5 275
Investing activities		
Proceeds from sale of plant and equipment	1 025	381
Proceeds from sale of investments	2 723	565
Interest received	145	238
Dividends received	200	291
Disposal of subsidiary, net of cash disposed of	10 890	–
Acquisition of subsidiary, net of cash acquired	(2 125)	(808)
Acquisition of property, plant and equipment	(15 031)	(1 938)
Acquisition of investment property	(1 000)	–
Acquisition of other investments	(2 150)	–
Development expenditure	(1 522)	(515)
Cash flow from investing activities	(6 845)	(1 786)
Financing activities		
Proceeds from the issue of shares	1 630	–
Proceeds from the issue of convertible notes	5 000	–
Proceeds from the issue of redeemable preference shares	2 000	–
Proceeds from other non-current borrowings	1 724	–
Repurchase of own shares	–	(280)
Repayment of borrowings	(5 000)	(1 500)
Payment of finance lease liabilities	(531)	(562)
Payment of transaction costs	(310)	–
Dividends paid	(1 243)	(520)
Cash flow from financing activities	(3 270)	(2 862)
Net increase in cash and cash equivalents	435	627
Cash and cash equivalents at 1 January	1 568	966
Effect of exchange rate fluctuations on cash held	78	(25)
Cash and cash equivalents at 31 December	2 081	1 568

Source: KPMG (2000) www.KPMG.co.uk

Summary

The main points from this chapter may be summarized as follows:

- Accruals accounting converts economic transactions and events into financial statements by using the universally accepted methodology of double-entry. The process of accruals (matching) allows revenues and costs to be assigned to the time period in which they are most relevant in calculating capital and profit. Accruals are, in effect, adjustments made to underlying cash flows in order to reflect better the historic financial performance of the business.

- The main products of accruals accounting are the balance sheet and the income statement. A simple record of cash flows, without accruals, is the cash flow statement.

- The accounts provide information for both stewardship (how well has an investment performed?) and for investment (what does historic performance say about future performance?).

- A balance sheet always balances. This is because the amount of money that a business owes to its providers of finance, at any given point in time, must always be equal to the book value of the assets in which the finance has been invested. This is the underlying logic of double-entry accounting.

- The balance sheet is a simple record of historic transactions and it does not anticipate the future creation of value. There is therefore a difference (called goodwill) between the book value of assets and the market value of the company. Assets are generally valued conservatively at the lower of historic cost or net realizable value. Conservative, reliable valuation is preferred in practice to more subjective, yet more economically relevant valuation.

- Within the financial accounting model, any operating cash outflow may be treated as an expense (i.e. written-off) or as an asset (i.e. capitalized). These are the only two options. If expensed, the cash outflow immediately becomes part of the calculation of profit or loss for the year. If capitalized, then the expense is effectively deferred, and will become part of the calculation of profit or loss in future years when it is depreciated, amortized, sold or written-off. Similarly, any cash inflow must be either a liability (for example a bank loan or deferred income) or it must be income in the current period. The balance sheet can therefore be interpreted as a means of recording deferred expenses and deferred liabilities.

- Profit in any period of time differs from cash flow, due to both accruals and finance payments. Accumulated profit over the whole life of a company will, however, equal net cash flow over the same period.

- The financial accounting system gives us a balance sheet and an income statement. Between them, these two statements provide a better basis than cash flow alone for the estimation of value.

- Key outputs from the financial statements include the following measures of economic performance: gross profit, EBITDA, NOPAT, profit after tax, capital employed and free cash flow.

References

Griffiths, I. (1995). *New Creative Accounting: How to Make Your Profits What You Want Them To Be*. London: Macmillan.

KPMG (1999). *International Accounting Standards: Illustrative Financial Statements*. London: KPMG.

Schilit, H.M. (1993). *Financial Shenanigans: How to Detect Accounting Gimmicks and Fraud in Financial Reports*. New York: McGraw-Hill.

Smith, Terry (1996). *Accounting for Growth: Stripping the Camouflage from Company Accounts* (2nd edn). London: Century Business.

6 Interpreting the balance sheet

Overview
- Interpreting the price-book value ratio
- An economist's measure: Tobin's q
- Theoretical foundations of asset values and goodwill
- Asset valuation in practice: an analysis of balance sheet components
- Factors affecting the usefulness of the balance sheet
- Empirical evidence on the usefulness of book values

This chapter will explore the use of the balance sheet in equity valuation. The chapter starts with an evaluation of the price–book value ratio, outlining its usefulness and limitations. This leads into an analysis of the reasons why, in theory, balance sheet value differs from shareholder value. It is shown that the difference arises for two reasons. The first of these concerns the market values of individual assets, and the second concerns goodwill for the company as a whole.

If the balance sheet does not report shareholder value, then the question arises what it does actually report, and how it can therefore be interpreted. The chapter proceeds by analyzing each component of the balance sheet, identifying associated valuation problems and drawing implications for the use of the balance sheet by analysts. Two possible uses for balance sheet data are explored. The first concerns aggregate book value, with respect to which a series of adjustments is recommended. The second focuses on the separate components of the balance sheet, identifying their respective uses in valuation models.

6.1 Interpreting the price–book value ratio

It was shown in Chapter 3 that shareholder value differs from book value whenever the rate of return spread is expected to differ from zero. This is because the return that the assets are expected to generate differs from that which shareholders are able to achieve in alternative investments. Put differently, the value of the company will differ from the cost of its assets whenever the company invests in projects that do not have zero net present value. The drinks vendor example from Chapter 5 is reproduced in Figure 6.1 as an illustration of this.

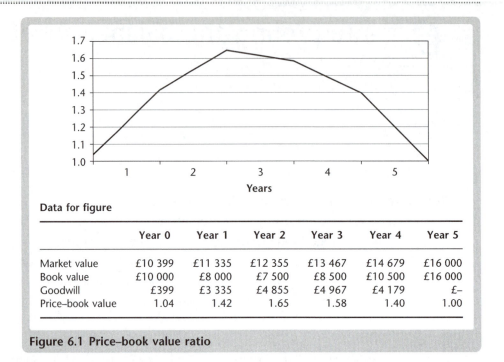

Data for figure

	Year 0	Year 1	Year 2	Year 3	Year 4	Year 5
Market value	£10 399	£11 335	£12 355	£13 467	£14 679	£16 000
Book value	£10 000	£8 000	£7 500	£8 500	£10 500	£16 000
Goodwill	£399	£3 335	£4 855	£4 967	£4 179	£–
Price–book value	1.04	1.42	1.65	1.58	1.40	1.00

Figure 6.1 Price–book value ratio

The price–book value ratio at the outset of the investment is 1.04, which arises because the net present value of the investment is equal to 4% of the invested capital. In other words, while the book value is simply equal to the amount of the invested capital, the market value reflects the expected economic gain, and the price–book value ratio therefore shows the extent to which expected future gains are not reflected currently in the accounts. In subsequent years, however, the price–book value ratio becomes less straightforward to interpret. In year 2, it increases. The market value is now 13.3% higher than its starting level, due to the 4% initial gain and the subsequent 9% return during the year.[1] The book value has fallen, however, because the machine has depreciated and net cash flows are zero. The net cash inflow that was the basis of the positive net present value remains in the future, and it is not yet reflected in book value. In year 3, a similar situation to year 2 causes a further increase in the price–book value ratio, but thereafter the growth in book value exceeds that in market value and the price–book value ratio declines. Ultimately, book value captures all of the value of the company, and the price–book value ratio equals one, making it once again straightforward to interpret.

In this example, the company has a finite life and is comprised of a single asset. Nevertheless, the implications of the example are equally valid for a company with an indefinite life that is constantly renewing its asset base. At any point in time, the price–book value ratio is simply the ratio between the present value of the company's assets and the book value of those assets.

---

[1] This 9% gain is simply the 'unwinding' of the discount rate, since expected returns equal actual returns.

From the perspective of an investor, this description of the price–book value ratio has an important limitation. If the aim of the investor is to determine the share price, then what is needed is a method for getting from book value to share price, rather than a statement of what the price–book value ratio represents once it has been calculated. This raises a problem, however. Consider the dividend yield and the PE ratio. In each case, it was shown in earlier chapters that shareholder value depends upon the level of dividends or earnings that a company is able to generate. The same is not true of book value. The assets that a company acquires are *inputs* to its operations, while the earnings that the company generates with the assets are the outputs, with which dividends are paid and from which value is derived. The price–book value ratio therefore has a different interpretation to the dividend yield or the PE ratio. Instead of expressing the value of the company in terms of the determinants of that value, it expresses the value of the company relative to the cost of the inputs. Shareholder value is not a function of book value in the way that it is a function of dividends or earnings.

There is, however, a relationship between shareholder value and book value in terms of the return that a company is able to generate from the assets that it has in place. This relationship is not simple, though, because the return itself depends upon the method of valuation used for a company's assets. To illustrate this, Table 6.1 shows the effect of a change in accounting policy on the data from the example above. The change is simply in the rate at which the company's machine is depreciated. It can be seen that the revised accounting policy involves the asset being written off more heavily in its later years, with the effect that profits are higher in early years and lower in later years. In turn, this causes the book value to be higher throughout. It does not, however, affect the market value of the company at all. Recorded goodwill is therefore higher and the price–book value ratio is lower at all stages of the company's life (except at the beginning and the end, when both policies give the same book value).

Table 6.1 Price–book value ratio with change in accounting policy

	0	1	2	3	4	5
Previous depreciation charge	–	£2 000	£2 000	£2 000	£2 000	£2 000
Revised depreciation charge	–	£1 000	£1 500	£2 000	£2 500	£3 000
Market value	£10 399	£11 335	£12 355	£13 467	£14 679	£16 000
Book value	£10 000	£9 000	£9 000	£10 000	£11 500	£16 000
Goodwill	£399	£2 335	£3 355	£3 467	£3 179	£0
Price–book value ratio	1.04	1.26	1.37	1.35	1.28	1.00

The effect of this change in accounting policy on the return on equity is illustrated in Table 6.2, using data from the final year of the company's life. Consider first the data for the original accounting policy. This shows that, if the book value of assets is £10 500 at the start of year 5, then a 52.4% return on equity is required if book value at the end of year 5 is to equal the market value of £16 000. In turn, and with a cost of capital of 9%, this implies a price–book

Table 6.2 The effect of a change in accounting policy on the return on equity

	Original policy	Revised policy
Book value at start of year 5	£10 500	£11 500
Book value at end of year 5	£16 000	£16 000
ROE year 5	52.4%	39.1%
Market value at start of year 5	£14 679	£14 679
Market value at end of year 5	£16 000	£16 000
Economic return year 5	9.0%	9.0%

value ratio of 1.40 at the start of the year, and 1.0 at the end of the year. This is because a gain of 52.4%, when discounted at 9%, is equal to a present value gain of 40%.[2] Contrast this with the revised policy, where the required ROE is only 39.1%, which is associated with a lower price–book value ratio of 1.28.

There is no economic difference between the two cases, and the market value of the company is the same. The difference in the accounting policy causes the difference in the price–book value ratio and in the required ROE.

As in previous chapters, the importance of being able to measure the ROE is central. The difficulty of this measurement task is only now becoming apparent, however, since the example illustrates that historic and forecast ROEs can vary independently of market value, simply by changing accounting policy. Indeed, the dependence of book value and ROE on one another seems to threaten the usefulness of both measures. Investors cannot infer shareholder value from book value without knowledge of expected ROEs, but the measurement of ROE is itself dependent not just upon economic fundamentals but also upon the measurement of book value.

The answer to this conundrum lies in the possibility of selecting a method of valuation in the accounts that gives rise to an ROE measure with a straightforward economic interpretation. This was the case for the opening book value in the example above, where the price–book value ratio of 1.04 captured the economic return of 4%.

One possible method of asset valuation is 'replacement cost'. This gives a price–book value ratio commonly referred to as 'Tobin's q', as will now be explored.[3]

6.2   An economist's measure: Tobin's q

The term 'replacement cost' refers, quite simply, to the amount that a company would have to pay, at the present time, to replace any one of its assets.

---

[2] This relationship between the price–book value ratio and the return on equity is simplified by the fact that market value equals book value at the end of the year. In general, the relationship is more complicated. This subject will be returned to in Chapter 8.

[3] James Tobin is a Nobel Prize winning economist. Tobin's q is discussed in a series of papers, for example Tobin (1969). A recent, extensive analysis of stock market valuation that is based upon Tobin's q is Smithers and Wright (2000).

Replacement cost is relevant to economic decisions because it concerns the costs currently attributable to a company's output. For example, if inventory could be replaced at a cost of $100 and sold for an income of $120, then replacement would be a rational economic decision.

In the special case where assets are valued at their replacement costs, the price–book value ratio is known as Tobin's *q*, as follows

$$Tobin's\ q = \frac{shareholder\ value}{replacement\ cost\ of\ assets}$$

Alternatively stated, Tobin's *q* is a measure of the rate of return spread, in the form of a ratio. In the simplest case where the cost of capital (k) and the rate of return on the replacement cost of assets (R_{RC}) are both constant, then shareholder value is a capitalized constant profit stream, as follows

$$shareholder\ value = \frac{R_{RC} \times replacement\ cost\ of\ assets}{k}$$

$$Tobin's\ q = \frac{R_{RC}}{k}$$

Tobin's *q* can be used to add some economic insight into the meaning of the price–book value ratio. Suppose, by way of illustration, that a company decides to enter a market. It can do this in one of two ways. It can either acquire an existing company in the market, or else it can acquire assets and build a new company from a zero base. The choice between these two alternatives depends upon the costs attached to each. In principle, an acquisition can be achieved by purchasing the target company at its shareholder value, whereas creating a new, equivalent company can be achieved at the replacement cost of the company's assets. The choice is summarized, therefore, by the value of *q*. If *q* is equal to 1, then the two costs are equal and both options are equally attractive. Or, viewed another way, if *q* is equal to 1 for an existing company, then its expected return on capital equals its cost of capital. The replacement cost of its assets is such that the company would be expected to earn a zero rate of return spread, and the acquisition of further assets would not create value.

For any given company, a value of *q* in excess of 1 suggests that the industry in which the company competes is abnormally profitable.[4] There would appear to be an incentive for another company to enter the industry by replicating the assets of the incumbent company or, alternatively, there is an incentive for the incumbent company itself to expand. This increase in industry supply might be expected to lead to a decline in market prices, thereby reducing both companies' shareholder value and the value of *q*, perhaps to the extent that further entry of new companies becomes unattractive. In other words, one possible interpretation of *q* greater than 1 is that a company has an unsustainable

---

[4] Strictly, *q* is relevant to marginal investment decisions, whereby the incremental investment cost of a new asset is compared with its incremental economic return. It is quite possible (for example) for the marginal *q* to equal 1 while the average *q* exceeds 1, since the marginal *q* might decline with increasing investment.

competitive advantage. This is, of course, the same situation that was described in Chapter 4 under the heading 'declining PE ratio during temporary period of competitive advantage'. It simply reinforces that the source of the temporarily high PE ratio is the abnormal returns expected over a short time period.

An alternative interpretation of a value of q in excess of 1 is that a given company has a sustainable competitive advantage within its industry. This advantage might reside in the company's brand name and reputation for quality, or in the ability of its employees to work together to extract excess value from the company's assets, or perhaps from a monopolistic or technological advantage that enables it to exclude other new entrants into the industry (a 'barrier to entry'). In such a situation, the company is likely to trade on an abnormally high PE ratio, reflecting its ability to earn in excess of its cost of capital. Again, the relationship of this situation to the PE ratio was described in Chapter 4.

It is also possible, of course, for the value of q to fall below 1. This would suggest that either the company or the industry is inherently unprofitable. If the former, the other companies in the industry might have q values in excess of 1. The difference in the q values reflects the difference in the companies in their ability to create value with a given asset base. If the latter, then all companies would be expected to have low q values, indicating industry decline and the likely exit of the least profitable companies.

These economic insights provided by Tobin's q are helpful, especially in relating book value to the PE ratio and the share price, and in understanding the economic dynamics of value creation. The benefit of valuation at replacement cost is that book value represents the current cost of investing in the business, such that the expected ROE has a straightforward economic meaning. What holds for Tobin's q does not, however, necessarily hold for the price–book value ratio in general. The two are by no means equivalent, because valuation in the accounts is generally not at replacement cost. Indeed, it may not even approximate replacement cost. Moreover, the notion of a replacement cost is rather abstract, because it is not always clear what is being replaced. It is also hypothetical, because it is based upon what could happen, rather than on what has happened.

An obvious question, therefore, is whether *actual* asset values and price–book value ratios can be given an economic interpretation similar to that of Tobin's q. In the numerical example used earlier, the rate of return spread was modest, leading to a price–book value ratio of 1.04 in the first instance. The considerable subsequent increase in the ratio arose because of the method of accounting, which caused a decline in book value and a subsequent delay in the book value catching up with market value. This delay was due to the conservatism of the asset valuation, and the (related) duration of the asset. In turn, this conservatism led to the required rate of return spread being very high towards the end of the asset's life.

In order to examine the methods of asset valuation used in practice, it will first be helpful to explore further the underlying conceptual difficulties posed by asset valuation. This will provide some intuition into why the aggregate book value of assets might not have a simple economic interpretation, and why it might therefore give rise to an ambiguous measure of the return on capital.

6.3 Theoretical foundations of asset values and goodwill

In general, an asset is something that has economic value, which can take the form of claims on goods, services or money. Goods are tangible and include land, buildings, materials and so on. Services are intangible and include items as diverse as human labour, electricity supply and insurance policies. Finally, money is itself a claim on goods and services, and it can be defined broadly to include items such as traded securities and accounts receivable.

Whenever a company acquires goods or services, it has two options for recording the transaction in the accounts. The first is to expense the goods and services, and the second is to capitalize them. In principle, the distinction between these two cases is very clear. A cash outflow is expensed when the economic benefit of the good or service is consumed within the current financial reporting period. Alternatively, it is capitalized if, at the balance sheet date, there are economic benefits yet to be consumed. In this case, an asset is recorded in the accounts. The need to value assets arises, therefore, whenever the economic benefits of a good or service are split across more than one financial reporting period. Alternatively stated, the value of assets (net of liabilities) is a measure of shareholders' existing investment in the company, after all the prior gains and losses on their capital have been accounted for. It is therefore a measure of the amount against which shareholders expect to earn a return.

Following this line of reasoning, the International Accounting Standards Committee defines an asset as follows (IASC, 1989):

> A resource controlled by the enterprise as a result of past events and from which future economic benefits are expected to flow to the enterprise.

The concept of an asset is therefore clear in principle. So, too is that of a liability, which is defined as the exact opposite of an asset. In practice, though, the shareholder value of a company is likely to differ from its book value. This is because the implementation of the above definition requires the resolution of two practical measurement issues. The first is whether or not the asset does actually have any value, and the second is how much this value is. If there is any uncertainty about the existence and amount of future economic benefits, then the valuation of the asset becomes subjective, and conservative accounting practice dictates that the book value should be at the lower end of estimates, or maybe even at 0.[5] For example, if the value of claims to intangible benefits such as research and development (R&D) cannot be measured with reasonable certainty, then cash

---

[5] There are good reasons for this conservatism, notably that company managers are constrained from presenting over-optimistic performance, based on their own hopes of the future rather than on their verifiable historic performance. Beaver (1991) notes, however, that 'the past and the present is the only basis we have for estimating the future. Hence, the term, *based on past transactions and events*, is not necessarily constraining'. Beaver points out that while all accruals contain some implicit assumption about future events, 'there is not a well-articulated statement of what types of information (i.e. past transactions and events) are acceptable upon which to condition the estimated effect of future events on existing assets and liabilities'. In practice, the recognition of future events in the financial statements is rather *ad hoc*.

outflows will in practice be expensed rather than capitalized, giving a book value of 0. Since reliable measurement can be problematic, the accounts are biased towards conservative valuation, with future liabilities more likely to be included in the financial statements than future assets. On balance, book value is therefore likely to be an under-estimate of shareholder value.

This issue of whether or not asset values can be measured reliably can be analysed insightfully at a conceptual level. There are, in fact, three fundamental reasons why asset valuation is inherently problematic. The first two concern the difficulty of valuing individual assets, while the third concerns the relationship between the separate values of individual assets and the total value of the company as a whole (i.e. goodwill). Each of these will be reviewed in turn.

The first valuation problem is that markets exist only for a limited number of assets. For example, while it is straightforward to buy and sell finished goods, it is less easy to trade part-finished goods (or, indeed, part-used fixed assets). A fully manufactured product has a market, and therefore a price, while a set of dedicated components of the product does not have a market until manufacture is finished. In such a case, inventory does not have a market price, and its value has to be estimated by some other means. Similarly, there is no established market for unfinished research and development work, or for unique brand names, or for any other asset that is not traded frequently. This is the problem of incomplete markets. In essence, the problem is that if markets do not exist, then prices do not exist. There is therefore no external, objective basis for asset valuation, and some alternative, subjective basis has to be adopted. In some cases, the difficulty posed by the absence of prices is such that assets are not valued at all. This is in spite of the many examples where expenditure in the current period is undertaken with a view to benefits in future periods, for example with R&D, advertising, training and the like. Such expenditure is written-off through the income statement rather than capitalized on the balance sheet, in spite of its obvious asset-like nature. Attempting to value intangible assets such as these is deemed to be simply too subjective and prone to error.

The second fundamental valuation problem is that different prices can exist for the same asset. For example, a retailer can expect to buy goods from wholesalers for less than they can be sold to consumers. What, then, is the correct price for valuing the retailer's inventory: purchase cost or sales price? The problem worsens when an asset is used to generate an income stream. Suppose that a taxi driver buys a car. The purchase cost will exceed the re-sale value. But the car was purchased as a means of generating income. Arguably, therefore, it has a value equal to the discounted future stream of the income less expenses that it generates.

There are, then, at least three possible current values for any single asset. These are the cost of replacing the asset (which is entry price or *replacement cost*), the value of the asset to the business in its current use (this is *present value*) and, finally, the sales value (this is the exit value, or *net realizable value*).[6] The reason

---

[6] [The *net realizable value* is the sales value net of any selling costs.] It is natural to think in terms of the minimum replacement cost, the maximum present value and the maximum net realizable value. In practice, of course, a company may pay higher than minimum cost and achieve lower than maximum value. A range of values is therefore possible.

why these different valuation options arise is that markets are not perfect. There are transactions costs, such as sales taxes and distribution costs, causing entry and exit prices to differ. There are also companies with varying degrees of monopolistic control, causing sales prices to exceed costs. And, finally, there are differences in the extent to which customers and suppliers are properly informed, for example when someone without specialist knowledge sells an antique to a dealer. For all these reasons of market imperfection, asset valuation can be based upon one of three options. If we add to this the complication arising when markets are incomplete and prices unavailable, then the practical difficulties of valuing individual assets become considerable. In effect, the basis of asset valuation becomes *ad hoc*, depending upon the generally accepted suitability of any given basis of valuation, and also upon the availability of data for the basis that is preferred.

When, moreover, the company as a whole is considered, rather than the individual assets that comprise the company, a further difficulty arises. This is the problem of goodwill that, in essence, is due to the whole being greater than the sum of the parts. If all of a company's assets are valued independently of one another (on whatever basis), then the sum of their valuations is likely to fall short of the total shareholder value of the company.

Goodwill is defined as simply the difference between shareholder value and book value. In principle, therefore, goodwill can arise for one of two reasons. Either it is 'pure' goodwill, or else it arises because of 'measurement error' in the assets. Suppose, for example, that a company has two assets. Each has a market value of $100, while the company as a whole has a market value of $250. If the assets are valued at their market value, then 'pure' goodwill is $50. If, however, the assets are valued conservatively at, say, $80 each, then goodwill is $90. The difference of $40 is included in goodwill, but is more properly regarded as measurement error in the individual asset values.

There is a fundamental issue here. The company's share price reflects the combined value of all of its assets. An intractable valuation problem is that this total value cannot be disaggregated across each of the assets individually. This is due to synergy between assets. A company does not create value simply by holding assets. It creates value by means of a judicious *combination* of expenditure decisions, in areas as diverse as recruitment, product development, plant construction, advertising, service delivery and operations management. It is the combined effect of each of these resource allocations that gives rise to an income stream, and thereby to a value for the company as a whole. Viewed in this way, it is unclear what the term 'value' means when applied to individual assets in the balance sheet. An individual asset may have a market price, as discussed above, but its value to the company will depend inextricably upon its relationship with all other resources deployed by the company. This difficulty is summarized by Thomas (1975) as follows:

> Inputs to a process interact whenever they generate an output different from the total of what they would yield separately. For instance, labor and equipment interact whenever people and machines working together produce more goods than the total of what people could make with their bare hands and machines could make unattended. As this example suggests, interaction is extremely common. Almost all of a firm's inputs interact with each other – their failure to do so would ordinarily signal their uselessness.

Surprising as it may seem, it can be proved that whenever inputs interact, calculations of how much revenue or cash flow has been contributed by any individual input are as meaningless as, say, calculation of the proportions of a worker's services due to any one internal organ: heart, liver or lungs.

Whatever the method of valuation chosen for individual assets, goodwill is likely to exist. If markets are imperfect, such that a company can earn a positive abnormal return, then the value of the company will exceed the sum of the entry prices of its assets. The opposite will also be true, of course, but in such a case the conservative basis for preparing accounts should cause assets to be written-down to their recoverable value. For this reason, goodwill is much more likely to be positive than negative.

As was seen in Chapter 5, the goodwill existing at any particular point in time is sooner or later converted into book value. As this conversion takes place, so new goodwill is likely to be created. At any point in time, the book value of a company is therefore a lagged measure of the shareholder value.[7] Or, viewed another way, the balance sheet values separable assets that have current market prices. Goodwill, on the other hand, is the non-separable component of value that is based upon expected future events, and that cannot be expressed in terms of current market prices.

Adding goodwill to existing assets

Last week, a group of the largest US mall operators, all of them Real Estate Investment Trusts, announced the formation of MerchantWired, a venture intended to provide a technology infrastructure for retail centres. The move suggests that some property investors have understood that the sector is among the best placed to benefit from the so-called new economy . . . MerchantWired says it plans to provide retailers with a so-called virtual private network allowing high-speed connectivity between different stores. This will allow a retailer with sites not only at, say, the 45 Macerich shopping centres nationwide, but also at those of the other mall company partners, to communicate quickly between stores. MerchantWired also promises to deliver high-speed data connectivity, secure access to the internet, and video/internet broadcasting capabilities, the last of which offers great potential for brand-led promotions at many sites simultaneously.

Source: Financial Times, Norma Cohen, 26 May 2000

The creation of MerchantWired recognizes the opportunity to use information technology to enhance the *collective* value of retail centres. It is the connections between the centres that allows each of them to benefit from one another, and for the whole to be greater than the sum of the parts – for example, by enhancing the economic viability of brand promotions, or by pooling and sharing data on consumer demand. MerchantWired therefore offers growth in goodwill, but not in the separable value of individual assets.

---

[7] See Edwards and Bell (1961) for an expanded analysis of this point, and see Beaver and Ryan (1993) for related empirical evidence.

Are people assets?

The immediate explanation for the failure (of the merger between Germany's Deutsche Bank and Dresdner Bank) lies in Dresdner's assessment of what Deutsche really planned to do with DrKB (Dresdner Kleinwort Benson) . . . Bernhard Walter, Dresdner chairman, and his colleagues concluded that Deutsche's intention was not to integrate DrKB into its investment banking operations – as Dresdner believed had been promised – but to dispose of most of it. This was too much for Dresdner. DrKB was Dresdner's most valuable asset, having contributed more than half the group's 1999 pre-tax profits . . . Employees at DrKB in London and Frankfurt were under few illusions about their possible fate. Seven members of the investment bank's equity division, specialising in utilities, defected to Salomon Smith Barney. Then T.J. Lim, co-head of global markets and one of DrKB's few globally respected investment bankers, left to rejoin his old employer, Merrill Lynch. In total, about 100 investment bankers handed in their notice at DrKB between January and early April, according to Horst Muller, a Dresdner board member.

Source: Financial Times, Tony Barber, Tony Major and William Lewis, 12 April 2000

Since a company can have little in the way of legally enforceable 'ownership' of its employees, it cannot consider them to be assets in the financial statements sense. Yet DrKB, which is described above as 'Dresdner's most valuable asset', is very much a people business. Its separable net assets, such as computer hardware and office leases, are limited in number and in value, and profits are generated only through the skills of its employees. People are therefore the key source of goodwill. They form part of the value of the business as a whole and they interact with the company's assets to generate a profit stream, but they are not themselves assets of the company and, as the example illustrates, they are always free to walk out of the door.

6.4 Valuation in practice – an analysis of balance sheet components

In practice, and consistent with the discussion above, there is not a 'general theory' of valuation that is applied universally across each category of asset and liability in the accounts. Most valuations represent the joint product of the application of the fundamental principles of conservatism and accruals. In cases where these two principles are not in conflict with one another, then valuation is straightforward: assets are created by accruals and they are not modified by conservatism. Examples of this are rare, although one such would be the market valuation of financial assets. In other cases, conservatism prevails, such that (for example) R&D is expensed rather than capitalized, and gains caused by increases in the market values of assets are not recognized until the asset is sold and the gains are realized. Most assets are 'valued' as deferred costs, rather than market values. Indeed, market valuation is often used only when required by conservatism, because the net realizable value falls short of book value (i.e. not all costs are 'recoverable').

In order to illustrate this discussion, the main balance sheet components will now be reviewed in some detail. The review will cover each of the main components of the balance sheet, including property, plant and equipment, intangible assets, inventory, accounts receivable and debt and financial assets. Conclusions will be reached for, first, the valuation usefulness of each of the balance sheet components, second, the meaning and interpretation of aggregate book value.

An obvious starting point for this analysis is land, since the valuation of land in the accounts is typically straightforward, yet it also illustrates two universal difficulties with balance sheet values. These difficulties concern, first, the use of historic cost and, second, the distinction between cost and value.

Land is often valued in the accounts at its historic cost, such that its book value neither increases nor decreases over time. This treatment is conservative to the extent that land values rise rather than fall, and it is objective, because the amount paid for the land is known and verifiable.[8] From the perspective of the analyst, however, historic cost is not a very useful valuation base. More specifically, it is not relevant to the economic choices that the company faces, and it is therefore also not relevant to valuation. The company can choose to either retain the land or dispose of it. If it retains it, then the value of the land is embodied in the cash flow stream that the company can generate from the use of the land. If the company disposes of the land, then the relevant value is the current market price, and not the historic market price. Indeed, the historic cost can only be relevant if the market price has remained unchanged over time. This problem of historic cost is not specific to land, of course, but is general to all of a company's assets. Moreover, it gives rise to a secondary problem. At any point in time, the balance sheet value of any asset category is an aggregation of a whole range of assets falling into that category. A company might have bought land in London in 1940, New York in 1970 and San Francisco in 2000. The accounts in the year 2000 will therefore aggregate one current market value with two historic costs, one more distorted than the other. This aggregation compounds the difficulty of extracting economically relevant data from the accounts. The book value is the aggregation of different pieces of land bought at different times and at different values. Unlike current market prices, such values cannot be added together in any meaningful way.[9]

Even market prices are of limited use, however, since the economic choice typically made by companies is not to dispose of land but to use it. Land is something that the company needs to have in order to conduct business, but not something that the company is in the business of trading.[10] The current market price of land is therefore unlikely to be directly relevant to the analyst in most cases, since land is just one of a number of interacting *inputs* in the generation of future profits. It is a cost, and thereby only a *part* of the present value equation. While it is true that the ultimate disposal of the land will lead

---

[8] Under international and UK accounting standards, property can be revalued to its market value. This is not permissible in the US, where historic cost is mandatory.

[9] It should be noted that specific assets will experience significant variation in market prices, and that a general price index is able to capture only an average price change across a sample of goods and services. See Whittington (1983) for further discussion.

[10] An exception to this is investment properties, which are held with a view to re-sale. This is recognized in both UK and international accounting standards, where such properties can be carried at market value in the balance sheet. Under US accounting standards, however, investment properties must be treated in the same way as any other property and carried at historic cost.

to a cash inflow, and that valuation at market prices tracks economic gains or losses on the land itself, the relevance of land to corporate valuation is therefore limited. It tends to be come indirectly to the extent that current values are used in measuring return on capital (see the discussion above of Tobin's q). Indeed, if the company did find itself needing to dispose of land holdings, then the market price at the most recent balance sheet date might prove to be unhelpful anyway. The very reasons why the company is in trouble might also be good reasons to expect the value of the land to have fallen.[11]

The same problems of valuation occur for plant and equipment as for land. In addition, however, there is the problem that plant and equipment can be expected to lose value over several accounting periods, causing the accruals-based accountant to attempt to match the cost of an asset over each period of its life. The choice of a specific method of depreciation raises two valuation problems. The first is subjectivity, and the second is arbitrary valuation. Both of these will be considered in turn.

It is often argued that historic cost is highly objective. In practice, however, the amounts originally recorded at historic cost are subsequently amended by the subjective judgement of management and auditor. Paton (1922) highlights the problem:

> Most writers outside the field of accounting consider that the word 'cost' closes the discussion of objectivity. Nothing could be further from the truth.

Sterling (1970) reinforces this view as follows.

> The distinction between objectivity and subjectivity is highly confused . . . the fact that two different accountants could arrive at two different costs with a variation of several hundred percent should raise some general questions about the objectivity of cost valuation.

Depreciation is an example of this subjectivity. The amount of depreciation in any one year depends upon the accountant's *assumptions* about the useful economic life of the asset, the residual value of the asset at the end of its life, and the rate of usage of the asset during its life. Each of these assumptions is subjective, and any variation will give rise to an alternative book value for a fixed asset.

It might be thought that there must be some 'correct' method of depreciation, such that the issue of subjectivity is simply one of measurement error. In fact, the problem is rather more fundamental than this, as has been demonstrated by Thomas (1969). If the aim of depreciation is to match the cost of an asset against the benefits derived from the use of the asset, then the correct method of depreciation requires knowledge of two things. The first is the amount of the benefit, including the time periods during which it occurs. In other words, when will the company receive its cash inflows derived from the ownership and use of the asset? This requires a prediction of the future which cannot, of course, be known. The second piece of required knowledge is the relationship between asset usage and cash flow generation. In other words, to what extent can the output of the company be attributed to the use of the asset? This, again, is unanswerable.

---

[11] For example, depressed retail conditions would affect both the likelihood that a retail company will dispose of its stores and also the likely realizable value of those stores.

It is the same allocation problem that has already been outlined in the context of goodwill. Any asset contributes to value creation in conjunction with other assets. It does not have a separable, individual contribution. It follows from this that there is no method of depreciation that is 'correct'.[12] Any number of different depreciation methods may be argued to be equally acceptable. The effect, however, is to make the book value of a depreciating asset something of questionable economic relevance. Not only is the method of depreciation subjective, but no single method can be argued to be correct. Under these circumstances, book value is nothing other than an unexpired cost. It is an historic cost (or a current cost for revalued assets) that has not been expensed in prior years, but that will be expensed in future years. In itself it has very little meaning. Arguably, its purpose from a valuation perspective is indirect, and comes via the income statement. As was seen in Chapter 5, the depreciation expense is intended to adjust operating cash flows in order to provide an economically meaningful measure of accounting earnings. This indirect role for the book value of depreciable assets will be reviewed in Chapter 7.[13] For the time being, it can simply be noted that the book value of depreciable assets is unlikely to be a reasonable measure of either the current market price of the assets or of the value of their contribution to the ongoing business.

These issues are of greatest relevance to intangible assets, which have the same types of valuation problem as tangible assets, but to an even greater degree. It will be recalled that asset valuation is subject to incomplete and imperfect markets. Market incompleteness is common for intangible assets because they tend to be either unique in nature (such as R&D or brand names), or else inseparable from the company (such as advertising, training or the corporate brand name). Intangible assets are therefore rarely traded and typically without market prices. Moreover, the markets for intangible assets are often highly imperfect, meaning that the relationship between value and cost can vary dramatically. Alternatively stated, expenditure on intangible assets is often a key source of value creation (or, indeed, value destruction). This is evidenced by the growing recognition that a company's greatest 'assets' include its people, its brand and its information systems and knowledge base. For example, pharmaceutical companies are able to earn abnormally high profits if, and only if, they generate successful, patent-protected drugs; and technology stocks are abnormally profitable if, and only if, their spending on new product development is successful.

Underlying the problems of incomplete and imperfect markets for intangible assets is the uncertainty of expected future returns. In practice, since few intangible assets can be valued with any degree of certainty, the principle of conservatism requires them to be given a value of 0 in the accounts. Even if expenditure on intangible assets is value creating, it is likely to be expensed rather

---

[12] Although see the discussion of economic depreciation in Chapter 8.

[13] It is possible, for example, that the allocation of historic cost is not the most appropriate measure of depreciation in the income statement. An alternative would be to charge a notional cost equal to the current annual market rate for hiring the asset in question. This might give a better measure of whether or not the company is generating an economic return at current market prices, rather than on the basis of allocated historic cost.

than capitalized, leading to a simultaneous increase in shareholder value and decrease in book value, with both effects increasing the price–book value ratio.

Some exceptions to expensing can arise in practice. For example, some jurisdictions will allow R&D expenditure to be capitalized, thereby allowing cost (though not value) to enter the balance sheet.[14] Also, in some cases an intangible asset has a clearly defined cost and life, such as an operating licence purchased in a government auction. More generally, the acquisition of intangible assets from other companies provides evidence of an objective market price, thereby allowing capitalization. An important example of this is purchased goodwill, which arises simply as the difference between the acquisition cost of a company and the book value of that company's net assets.[15] Strictly, however, the objectivity of the valuation of goodwill depends, in fact, upon the objectivity in valuing the acquired company's net assets, since the value of goodwill is calculated as a residual. Indeed, whenever an acquisition is made, there is no simple way in which the value of intangible assets such as brand names can be measured independently of goodwill. In general, any intangible asset that does not have a separable market value is, in effect, a sub-set of goodwill and (following the logic of the earlier discussion of goodwill) it cannot be given a meaningfully 'correct' value in the balance sheet. In practice, therefore, the balance sheet values of intangible assets should be interpreted with care, especially when they lack a verifiable market value.

Billion dollar brands   **FT**

Rank	Company	Country	Brand value 2 000 ($bn)
1	Coca-Cola	US	72.5
2	Microsoft	US	70.2
3	IBM	US	53.2
4	P&G	US	48.4
5	Nestle	Switzerland	40.3
6	Intel	US	39.0
7	Nokia	Finland	38.5
8	General Electric	US	38.1
9	Unilever	UK	37.1
10	Ford	US	36.4

Source: Interbrand/Citibank

---

[14] International and UK accounting standards both allow the capitalization of development costs, while US accounting standards require that both costs are written off as incurred (with some exceptions for software development).

[15] In general, goodwill is capitalized and amortized. In the US, the maximum amortization period is normally 20 years, while international accounting standards allow up to 40 years, and UK standards *can* allow an indefinite life (a practice likely to be adopted in the US also under current proposals). This gives rise, of course, to an inconsistency between the book value of purchased goodwill compared with internally generated goodwill, with the latter always given a book value of zero. It also leads to subsequent difficulties in interpreting the balance sheet. This is because goodwill is typically treated as a depreciating asset, which allows subjectivity in the rate at which it is charged to the income statement, and a disconnection between its book value and its 'true' economic value. This problem will be reviewed further in Chapter 7.

The Coca-Cola brand is still reckoned to be worth a phenomenal $72.5bn (£48.3bn) in terms of its earnings potential. But its value has tumbled 13 per cent in the last year, while the value of Microsoft's brand is estimated to have increased 24 per cent to $70.2bn . . . The evidence of Microsoft's looming supremacy comes from Interbrand, the branding consultancy, which is in its second year of analysing earnings forecasts for the world's best-known consumer brands and translating those forecasts into brand valuations . . . Until now, companies such as Coca-Cola, H.J. Heinz and Kellogg had been around so long that their brands looked indestructible, and seemed destined to command the top slots in the global league table for as long as anyone could foresee. It is still hard to imagine a day when these famous names will cease to dominate the supermarket shelves. But when a brand as powerful as Coca-Cola can lose 13 per cent of its value in just a year, it is possibly time to ask whether the lifespan of these brands is infinite, or something less.

Source: Financial Times, Richard Tomkins, 18 July 2000

There is an understandable interest in attempting to value brands. In effect, this requires identifying and valuing a sub-set of a company's goodwill, which is ambitious given that goodwill arises from a complex interaction between assets, people, reputation, technology, competition and so on. The reported volatility in Coca-Cola's brand value can be attributed both to the inherent and unavoidable difficulty in valuation, as well as to genuine changes in value. The size of the estimated change does, however, highlight that brand values can, in principle, change very quickly and by very large amounts.

Moving now to a discussion of current assets, it appears that, in principle, the problems posed by matching are more tractable for inventory than for fixed assets (especially intangibles). After all, if the purpose of matching is to assign expenses into the time periods in which revenues are recognized, then it seems obvious enough that inventory should remain on the balance sheet for as long as it remains within the company, and then be transferred to the income statement at the point when it is sold. In practice, however, subjectivity in the valuation of inventory generates ambiguity in the interpretation of book value.

Inventory is valued at either its cost or its net realizable value, whichever is the lower. In other words, an entry cost is used whenever a profit is expected, and an exit price is used only when a loss is recognized. The method of valuation is therefore conservative, because losses are recognized but profits are not. The book value (when at historic cost) is therefore likely to fall short of the market value. This conservative treatment arises in spite of the relative ease with which market prices can be estimated for inventory. It also arises despite the obvious economic relevance of market prices for inventories which, in contrast to fixed assets, are the traded output of the company's operations.

The cost of inventory is defined to include all expenses incurred in bringing the inventory into any given location and condition, and it can therefore offer scope for subjective interpretation whenever these costs are significant. In addition to materials, the book value of inventory includes (for example) transportation costs, direct labour costs, and allocations of overheads, such as depreciation, insurance, electricity and the like. This is simply an application of matching, whereby all of these costs should 'attach' themselves to the inventory in the balance sheet, until the time period when revenue is recognized and all costs are expensed. The subjectivity in deciding the amount and timing of capitalization and expensing is compounded by the effect of changes in the prices of inputs over time. For example, a company can transfer cost to the income statement on the basis of the most recent prices paid for raw materials, and the most recent amounts for all inclusive cost items. This would be a last-in-first-out (LIFO) basis of inventory valuation, and (if prices are rising) it would normally leave a relatively low balance sheet value. Alternatively, a first-in-first-out (FIFO) basis would leave relatively expensive inventory on the balance sheet, with a correspondingly low inventory expense in the income statement. Other methods could also be used, and the choice of method contributes further to the subjectivity of book values.[16]

In summary, the book value of inventory will generally be significantly lower than its market value, and it may differ also from its replacement cost, depending upon factors such as changes in raw material prices and the length of operating cycle. Inventories can nevertheless provide useful information to analysts in one of two ways. First, they represent an investment of shareholders' funds, and are therefore a basis from which a return has to be made, although the extent to which their book value represents the actual cost of the investment will vary. For example, FIFO would be a better measure than LIFO in the balance sheet, because the book value is based upon the most recent inventory costs. An efficiency measure that captures this relationship is inventory turnover, as follows[17]

$$days\ of\ inventory = \frac{inventory}{cost\ of\ goods\ sold} \times 365\ days$$

This relationship states simply how many days of inventory a company is holding. Other things being equal, the greater the number of days, the less efficient the company's operation, because the greater is the amount of capital employed for a given return.[18]

The second use for inventory values is in providing information concerning future cash flows and earnings. Used carefully, changes in inventory levels can be a lead indicator of financial performance. For example, an increase in raw material days might suggest that the company is expecting higher sales, whereas an increase in finished goods might indicate that demand had been over-estimated, suggesting that forecasts should be revised downwards. Large inventory levels may also suggest the possibility of future stock write-offs, especially in industries that are subject to rapid changes in fashion or technology. The amount and timing of write-offs are subjective and to some extent discretionary. A company is more likely to postpone write-offs when profit performance is poor, and

---

[16] International accounting standards allow LIFO, FIFO or a weighted average method of costing. LIFO is common in the US, though not permitted in the UK.

[17] It is not necessary to multiply by 365 days. Inventory turnover can be expressed as 'number of times that inventory turns over during the year' or, as above, in terms of days of inventory.

[18] It should be noted that this ratio compares current inventory levels with the cost of sales over the past twelve months. This represents a mis-match to the extent that expected activity levels differ from those just achieved. If, for example, a company is growing, then inventory management will appear more inefficient than it really is, because inventory levels have increased in anticipation of growing sales.

to write-off enthusiastically when times are good. This is classic profit 'smoothing' behaviour. The coincidence of increasing inventory levels and poor profit performance should therefore give investors an additional reason for concern.

Inventory growth

Stockpiles of unsold goods among factories, wholesalers and retailers in the US surged in June, matching May's gain, the fastest rise since November. It was unclear whether the jump reflected the reaction of producers and distributors to a sudden slowdown in consumer spending, or their preparations for stronger sales ahead. But economists warned that the June rise – the 18th consecutive monthly increase in inventories – could translate into a fall in growth in the third quarter.

Source: Financial Times, Peronet Despeignes, 15 August 2000

In itself, an increase in inventory levels sends the ambiguous signal that either demand has unexpectedly slowed or that it has been expected to rise. The resolution of this ambiguity requires the use of additional evidence, such as survey data on consumer confidence or on producer's output plans.

The final category of operating asset in the balance sheet is accounts receivable, which can be regarded as one step away from cash. The question for valuation is relatively simple. It is whether (and when) the money due will be received. The book value of accounts receivable is comprised of the amount of the unsettled credit sales, less a provision for amounts that are expected never to be collected. The provision is therefore a subjective 'prediction' of future events.

In a similar fashion to inventories, a standardized measure of the amount of accounts receivable on the balance sheet is calculated in days, as follows:[19]

$$debtor\ days = \frac{accounts\ receivable}{sales} \times 365\ days$$

Similarly to inventory, an increase in debtor days can be worrying for two reasons. First, accounts receivable are unproductive assets, and the greater the amount of accounts receivable on the balance sheet, the higher the return on investment required from all other assets. In short, inefficient credit control adversely affects value creation. Second, an increase in debtor days can be a signal of a difficult economic environment. It might, for example, arise because the company is offering more generous credit terms to customers, which suggests that demand is weak and competition tough. Alternatively, it might signal that customers are either having difficulty paying, or else they are lengthening their payment periods on the basis of greater relative bargaining power. In contrast, there could be other, more benign interpretations, such as a change in product mix.

---

[19] Since accounts receivable arise only on credit sales, any sales made in cash should ideally be excluded from the denominator. In practice, this is rarely done, partly because the relevant data are typically not available in published accounts, but partly also because the amount of cash sales is usually small (an exception being retail sales), and it will only distort the ratio if it changes year on year.

Are asset values recoverable?

Last week the retailer Sogo filed for protection from its creditors with almost Y1 900bn (£11.8bn) of debts. This week, Seiyo, a property group, filed for liquidation with Y517bn debts. The size of these failures has startled investors. 'The question people are asking is whether Japanese banks have an adequate arsenal against these bad loans,' says James Fiorillo, an analyst at ING Barings. The banks insist they do. They have already written off more than Y50 000bn of bad loans in recent years, out of the estimated Y70 000bn of problem loans inherited after the bursting of the 1980s bubble. In Seiyo's case, its woes were well known and its main creditors – including Dai-Ichi Kangyo, Industrial Bank of Japan, Sumitomo Trust and Mitsui Chuo Trust – insist that this year's results will not be affected because they had written off its loans . . . But what has fuelled investor concern is that Japanese banks have been over-optimistic about their bad loans before . . . Among the factors making Japanese banks less willing to forgive debt are a new law making it easier for a company to file for bankruptcy, and tighter accounting standards. Meanwhile, the government is also less willing to use public funds to keep companies alive, even in politically sensitive sectors such as construction or retailing. 'The long-held perception . . . that major Japanese companies are too big to fail is no longer valid,' argues Standard and Poor's, the US credit rating agency.

Source: *Financial Times*, Gillian Tett, 20 July 2000

While the value of loans recorded in banks' balance sheets is an objective statement of how much has been lent, the provision that is netted against these loans is a highly subjective forecast of recoverability. The view of the banks is that impending bad loans have been anticipated and written-off through the income statement, resulting in conservative financial statements. The alternative view, however, is that the value of accounts receivable in the balance sheet is overstated, and that losses can be expected. The example highlights the reliance of the balance sheet on the prediction of uncertain future returns, with respect to which the company management has 'inside' information on its own customer base, whereas external investors have to rely on information such as experience from previous economic cycles.

There is a fundamentally important difference between valuing financial and non-financial net assets, which is simply that the former are already denominated in terms of money. It remains the case, however, that debt is valued at its historic cost rather than its market value, with the latter fluctuating according to changes in the market rate of interest. This is arguably unimportant if the debt is to be held until maturity (or if it is short term). Nevertheless, the company does have the opportunity to redeem its debt, and then to re-finance itself at different rates (or, indeed, to switch debt for equity). The balance sheet provides incomplete information relevant to this opportunity.

An additional incompleteness concerning net debt is the extent to which a company is engaged in off-balance sheet finance. This could arise, for example, if leased assets are not capitalized, or if debt-laden subsidiaries are not consolidated. A similar issue, though not concerned directly with debt, is whether or not a company has made adequate provision for expected cash outflows. For example, potential liabilities for oil or chemical companies may be understated if inadequate provision has been made for environmental clean-up costs, and the balance sheets of tobacco companies would be similarly distorted if provisions for litigation costs were excluded.

Financing growth

Six months on from Vodafone's epic bid for Mannesmann, cracks are starting to appear in the new group's ability to meet mounting spending commitments. Despite paying for the £113bn acquisition with shares rather than cash, Vodafone inherited debts that have swollen group borrowings to an estimated £20bn. These would be difficult enough to service at the best of times. Full-year results due on Tuesday are expected to reveal operating profits last year of just £2.64bn – less than twice the likely annual interest bill . . . The auction of third generation mobile phone licences in the UK forced the company to pay £6bn just to stay ahead in its domestic market. Another £2bn is probably needed to build the network, and all this money will be required long before the anticipated increases in profitability per customer promised by the next generation of services. The success of the UK auction in raising money for the Treasury has also encouraged other governments to consider the true value of their own licences. Multiplied across Vodafone's vast portfolio of international assets, the cost of bidding for all the necessary licences and meeting the infrastructure costs could reach a total of £58bn, according to some analysts . . . To set against that, Vodafone also has plenty of valuable assets. It has just sold Mannesmann's engineering interests for €9.4bn . . . and is thought to have raised about €7.5bn by selling its stake in France's Cegetel.

Source: Financial Times, Dan Roberts, 26 May 2000

The assessment of debt takes on a special importance in this example, not least because of the sudden and dramatic increase in borrowing. The ratio of operating profit to interest payments (the 'interest cover') is less than two, suggesting a small comfort margin should profits fall or interest rates rise. The growth in debt might also lead to an increase in either or both the cost of equity or debt, commensurate with the increased risks to both suppliers of finance, and possibly leading to a decline in enterprise value. To off-set these concerns about debt, Vodafone is disposing of assets. In contrast to the company's debts, the balance sheet is unlikely to reveal to investors any significant information on the market values of these assets.

6.5 Factors affecting the usefulness of the balance sheet

This discussion suggests a number of reasons why book value might be misleadingly different from shareholder value. In particular, a company's balance sheet is of diminished economic relevance to the extent that any of the factors in Table 6.3 prevail.

To the extent that any given company has limited exposure to any of these factors, then its balance sheet is likely to be of greater economic relevance. Even if the factors are significant, however, appropriate adjustments can sometimes be made to balance sheet data in order that its valuation usefulness is enhanced. For example, it may be appropriate to capitalize and amortize 'revenue investments' such as advertising, R&D and training, thereby treating them consistently

Table 6.3 Causes of distortion in book values

Cause	Explanation
Existing assets were not acquired recently	Greater divergence between historic cost and current value
Asset base is mostly fixed rather than current	Greater impact of subjective depreciation and amortization
'Assets' are mostly intangible	Less likely that assets are recognized
Significant value of off-balance sheet assets	Balance sheet understates net assets and capital employed
Operating cycles are long	Increases scope for subjectivity of accruals accounting to affect measurement of annual economic performance, in particular through impact on asset values and provisions.

with tangible fixed assets. This is not as problematic as it may seem. Analysts are not constrained in their use of accounts in the same way that companies and auditors are, notably in that conservatism need not interfere with the attempt to measure economic performance. Revenue investments represent cash outflows made in the expectation of future returns. If these outflows are capitalized then management is, in effect, held to account for investments made. For the purposes of recognition in the analyst's financial statements it does not matter, in fact, whether the investment will be recovered or not. The aim is to show economic performance, whether good or bad, in the period in which it occurs. There is, of course, subjectivity on the part of the analyst in separating revenue expenditure from investment. There is also the potential for mis-representing performance to the extent that poor investments are capitalized, thereby deferring losses into future periods. Nevertheless, the aim of deriving a clear distinction between revenue and capital is clear and worthwhile.

Further adjustments can also be made by analysts to 'correct' for the other difficulties with book value outlined in this chapter. Where possible, the analyst can adjust book values of assets and liabilities to their market prices, to the extent that this better represents shareholders' invested capital. Likewise, written-off goodwill can be re-capitalized (see the analysis in Chapter 7) and off-balance sheet assets (if known) can be recognized.

As a final comment, it is important that these adjustments should not bring 'pure' goodwill on to the balance sheet. The value of goodwill is the value of future economic performance, as will be discussed in more detail in Chapters 7 and 9. It represents the *return* on shareholders' investment in net assets, and it should not be confused with the balance sheet, which measures the investment itself. This point returns to the argument at the beginning of this chapter that assets are inputs only to a company's operations, and not the value of returns. An implication is that brand values, R&D and the like should be valued at cost, and not at market value, since this maintains the conceptual distinction between investment and return. Some intangible assets do, however, have an open market value. If this is the case, then valuation in the accounts at market value is appropriate, because a company can dispose of the assets, and this disposal value represents an opportunity cost for investors. The invested capital of shareholders should incorporate this opportunity to 'cash-in' the asset. In principle, therefore, only 'pure' (non-separable, non-tradable) goodwill should be excluded from the balance sheet.

6.6   Empirical evidence on the usefulness of book values

In practice, there is considerable variation in the price–book value ratio across different companies. To illustrate this, Table 6.4 (adapted from Penman, 1996) reports average price–book value ratios for US companies over the period 1968–85.

Table 6.4 is calculated by ranking price–book value ratios by size and then grouping companies into portfolios. So, for example, companies whose price–book value ratios fall between the 50th and 55th percentiles for size of price–book value ratio have, on average, a ratio of 1.22.[20]

There is plenty of evidence concerning this observed variation in the price–book value ratio. In trying to explain the ratio, a number of studies have examined the extent to which the value of assets is not captured on the balance sheet. For example, Aboody, Barth and Kasznik (1999) find that the upward revaluation of assets in the UK is positively associated with future operating performance, which suggests that managers' decisions to increase book value is a signal to investors that the company is under-valued. Amir, Hamis and Venuti (1993), using

Table 6.4 Price–book value ratios for US companies over the period 1968–85

Price–book value portfolios	Average price–book value ratio	Price–book value portfolios	Average price–book value ratio
Highest 5%	6.20	45–50%	1.13
	3.66		1.05
	2.82		0.98
	2.33		0.92
	2.00		0.85
	1.76		0.79
	1.58		0.72
	1.43		0.64
	1.31		0.54
50–5%	1.22	Lowest 5%	0.39

Source: Adapted from Penman (1996)

---

[20] Price–book value ratios below 1 are not unusual. For example, negative goodwill is common in industries in decline, where the break-up value of a company can exceed the present value of its expected earnings.

revaluations reported by overseas companies in reconciling their performance to US GAAP, find that US price–book value ratios are partly explained by the under-valuation of assets. Further evidence in Barth and Clinch (1998) suggests that revaluations should be interpreted differently according to the type of asset that is being valued. In particular, they find that the revaluation of operating assets (plant and equipment) is more closely associated with price–book value ratio than the revaluation of land and other property, suggesting that assets more closely related to the output of a company are also more closely related to the company's value.

Other studies have examined the value of intangible assets that are not recognized on the balance sheet. Sougiannis (1994) estimates that, on average, a 1 dollar increase in R&D expenditure is associated with a 5 dollar increase in shareholder value, implying that value is created in spite of R&D expenditure not being capitalized. Lev and Sougiannis (1996) estimate the value of the R&D 'asset' and show it to be a reconciling difference between shareholder value and book value. Similarly, Aboody and Lev (1998) and Barth *et al.* (1998) show that software capitalization and estimates of brand values, respectively, also help to explain price–book value ratios.

There is some evidence concerning the usefulness of working capital information in predicting financial performance. Bernard and Noel (1991) test whether the book value of inventory is useful in forecasting financial performance. They find that, for the typical manufacturing company, an unusual increase in raw materials and work-in-progress is generally associated with an increase in future sales. This increase is incremental to that which could be predicted on the basis of current sales alone. It suggests that changes in raw materials and work-in-progress are lead indicators of demand, because they reflect the company's expectation of a change in sales beyond current levels. In contrast, however, Bernard and Noel also find, for both manufacturing and retail companies, that an unusual increase in finished goods inventories is predictive of unusually low future earnings, and vice versa. This suggests that an unexpected increase in finished goods implies that demand actually turned out to be lower than expected, but that an unexpected decrease in finished goods implies higher demand, and maybe additionally unmet demand due to unavailable inventory. Lev and Thiagarajan (1993) reach a similar conclusion, and they also show that the importance of the change in finished goods depends upon the growth rate of the company. In particular, if the company is growing slowly, then the negative effect on the share price of an unexpected increase in finished goods inventory is greater, because investors are more likely to attribute the increase to worsening economic fundamentals, than simply to a one-off error in estimating current demand.

In a similar analysis to Bernard and Noel, Stober (1993) examines whether the book value of accounts receivable can also be used to enhance forecasts of financial performance. Stober finds that, in the very short term, an unexpected increase in receivables is predictive of an increase in sales, but that the longer-term effect is negative for earnings. This is most likely because an increase in accounts receivable signals a decline in earnings quality, for the reasons discussed above.

Summary

The main points from this chapter may be summarized as follows:

- The price–book value ratio is simply the difference between the present value of the company's assets and the book value of those assets.

- A company's share price is not determined by the book value of its assets. It is determined by the amount and timing of the expected returns that the assets generate. This differentiates the price–book value ratio from either the PE ratio or the dividend yield. Assets are inputs to a company's operations, whereas earnings and dividends are the resultant outputs. In the PE ratio and the dividend yield, the share price depends upon the present value of expected future earnings and dividends, respectively. In the price–book value ratio, the share price depends upon the rate of return that relates the book value of assets to the present value of the cash flows that they generate.

- The rate of return that relates shareholder value to book value depends upon two factors: the underlying economic return of the company; and the method of accounting used by the company. In general, subjectivity in accounting implies that the price–book value ratio does not have a straightforward economic interpretation.

- The valuation of assets in the accounts is complicated by a number of factors. Market prices for a company's assets often do not exist, or else they are different according to whether the company is buying or selling. Net assets are valued conservatively and assets that cannot be valued reliably are expensed. Moreover, shareholder value generally exists in a form that cannot be attributed to individual assets, because of the interaction between assets in the generation of cash flows. Overall, accounting policies tend to reduce the book value of assets relative to their market value, with the resultant difference being unattributable to any underlying economic cause.

- In principle, the book value of assets can be useful to investors in one of two ways. First, aggregate book value is a measure of the shareholders' investment in the company, and it forms a basis for the analysis of return on equity and, thereby, shareholder value. Second, the individual components of the balance sheet can each be used to assist in the forecasting of future earnings and, thereby, in the determination of the current share price. In practice, the difficulties of asset valuation make an unadjusted aggregate measure of limited use, forcing the investor to analyze balance sheet components individually.

- Recommended adjustments to book values include the following, whenever significant and consistent with the economic fundamentals of the company: capitalization and subsequent amortization of 'revenue investments' such as advertising, R&D and training; market valuation of assets and liabilities, to the extent that shareholders' invested capital is better represented; write-back of goodwill amortization; and capitalization of off-balance sheet assets. The aim of these adjustments is to move the balance sheet value of net assets closer to an economically meaningful measure of invested capital (and thereby to achieve a better measure of 'pure' goodwill).

References

Aboody, D., M.E. Barth and R. Kasznik (1999). 'Revaluation of Fixed Assets and Future Firm Performance: Evidence from the UK', *Journal of Accounting and Economics*, 26, 149–78.

Aboody, D., and B. Lev (1998). 'The Value Relevance of Intangibles: the Case of Software Capitalization', *Journal of Accounting Research*, 36(supplement), 161–91.

Amir, E., T.S. Harris and E.K. Venuti (1993). 'A Comparison of the Value-Relevance of US versus Non-US GAAP Accounting Measures Using Form 20-F Reconciliations', *Journal of Accounting Research*, 31, 230–64.

Barth, M., M.B. Clement, G. Foster and R. Kasznik (1998). 'Brand Values and Capital Market Valuation', *Review of Accounting Studies*, 3, 41–68.

Barth, M. and G. Clinch (1998). 'Revalued Financial, Tangible and Intangible Assets: Associations with Share Prices and Non Market-Based Value Estimates', *Journal of Accounting Research*, 36, 199–233.

Beaver, W. (1991). 'Problems and Paradoxes in the Financial Reporting of Future Events', *Accounting Horizons*, 5(4), 122–34.

Beaver, W. and S. Ryan (1993). 'Accounting Fundamentals of the Book-to-Market Ratio', *Financial Analysts' Journal*, Nov.–Dec., 50–6.

Bernard, V. and J. Noel (1991). 'Do Inventory Disclosures Predict Sales and Earnings?' *Journal of Accounting, Auditing and Finance*, Spring, 145–81.

Edwards, E.O. and P.W. Bell (1961). *The Theory and Measurement of Business Income*. Berkeley: California University Press.

IASC (1989). *Framework for the Preparation and Presentation of Financial Statements*.

Lev, B. and T. Sougiannis (1996). 'The Capitalization, Amortization and Value-relevance of R&D', *Journal of Accounting and Economics*, 21, 107–38.

Lev, B. and S.R. Thiagarajan (1993). 'Fundamental Information Analysis', *Journal of Accounting Research*, 31(2), 190–215.

Paton, W.A. (1922). *Accounting Theory*. New York: Ronald Press.

Smithers, A. and S. Wright (2000). *Valuing Wall Street*. New York: McGraw-Hill.

Solomons, D. (1995). 'Criteria for Choosing an Accounting Model', *Accounting Horizons*, 9(1), 42–51.

Sougiannis, T. (1994). 'The Accounting Based Valuation of Corporate R&D', *Accounting Review*, 69(1), 44–68.

Sterling, R.R. (1970). *Theory of the Measurement of Enterprise Income*. Lawrence, Kansas: University Press of Kansas.

Stober, T.L. (1993). 'The Incremental Information Content of Receivable in Predicting Sales, Earnings, and Profit Margins', *Journal of Accounting, Auditing and Finance*, Fall, 447–73.

Thomas, A.L. (1969). *The Allocation Problem in Financial Accounting Theory*. Sarasota, Florida: American Accounting Association.

Thomas, A.L. (1975). 'The FASB and the Allocation Fallacy', *The Journal of Accountancy*, Nov., 65–8.

Tobin, J. (1969). 'A General Equilibrium Approach to Monetary Theory', *Journal of Money, Credit and Banking*, 1, 15–29.

Whittington, G. (1983). *Inflation Accounting: An Introduction to the Debate*. Cambridge: Cambridge University Press.

7 Measuring earnings

Overview ● Economic measures of shareholder return
● Stewardship and investment: the need for accounting earnings
● Reconciling economic earnings with accounting earnings
● The need for three types of earnings measure
● From comprehensive income to normalized earnings
● Goodwill
● Empirical evidence on earnings measurement

This chapter will address the theory and practice of earnings measurement. The approach taken will be to first define 'economic earnings' and 'permanent earnings', which will be shown to be theoretical benchmark earnings measures, against which the strengths and weaknesses of actual earnings data can be assessed. The chapter will review theoretical and practical issues in earnings measurement, including the assessment of one-off economic gains, the effect of changes in asset valuation and the treatment of goodwill. The chapter concludes with recommendations on how accounting earnings should be measured and understood for valuation purposes, including recommendations on a method for extracting and understanding a measure of 'normalized' earnings.

7.1 Economic measures of shareholder return

Economic earnings are a total measure of how much shareholders' economic position changes over a given period of time. The classic definition of economic earnings is that of Sir John Hicks, a Nobel Prize winning economist. Hicks defines the purpose of earnings (or income) measurement as follows (Hicks, 1946):

> The purpose of income calculations in practical affairs is to give people an indication of the amount they can consume without impoverishing themselves. Following out this idea, it would seem that we ought to define a man's income as the maximum value which he can consume during a week, and still expect to be as well off at the end of the week as he was at the beginning. Thus, when a person saves, he plans to be better off in the future; when he lives beyond his income, he plans to be worse off. Remembering that the practical purpose of income is to serve as a guide to prudent conduct, I think it is fairly clear that this is what the central meaning must be.

Although Hicks defines income with respect to an individual, it is straightforward to translate the definition for a company. Earnings are the maximum amount that can be distributed to shareholders during a period while maintaining the capital value of expected future cash flows. If the capital value of the company is neither higher nor lower at the end of the year than it was at the beginning, then shareholders can consume any surplus without making themselves any worse off.[1] In effect, therefore, economic earnings are a measure of the investment performance of the company. Economic earnings can be consumed while maintaining the value of shareholders' claims to future consumption, or else they can be re-invested in the company, thereby increasing shareholders' future claims.

If the stock market sets the price of a share equal to its intrinsic value, then economic earnings are equal to the dividend that a company would pay during a year if the year-end share price were to equal the beginning-of-year share price. Or, equivalently, they are the actual dividend paid plus the actual change in the share price. Economic earnings can therefore be thought of in terms of 'total shareholder return' (or TSR) and, as has been seen already in Chapter 2 they are the basis from which the dividend discount model (DDM) is derived.

Total shareholder return

The FT's European Company Performance survey . . . ranks Europe's top companies according to their total returns to shareholders over the past year and the past five years. Total return is defined as the percentage capital gain (or loss) received by a shareholder over the period, assuming all dividends distributed by the company are immediately reinvested in the company's shares . . . The companies presented with awards by FTSE last night were: Gruppo Editoriale L'Espresso, the Italian media business, which was ranked first over one year, with a total return of 600 per cent, and also over five years, with a total return of 6,000 per cent; Nokia, the Finnish mobile phone manufacturer, ranked second over five years, with a total return of 3,400 per cent; Skandia, the Swedish life assurance company, ranked third over five years, with a return of 2,200 per cent . . . This survey is based on total return because it is straightforward, encompasses a huge amount of valuable information about a company, and answers the question which, for better or worse, is upmost in the mind of most shareholders: what has this company done for me?

Source: *Financial Times*, Martin Dickson, 23 June 2000

A straightforward application of economic earnings is in the measurement of investment performance. In this FT survey, stock market performance is ranked according to a simple combined measure of capital gain and dividend payout. Shareholders in Gruppo Editoriale L'Espresso, for example, could liquidate and consume 600 per cent of their investment made one year ago and still be as well off as they had been at that time.

(Note that the method of adjusting for dividends makes the [contentious] assumption that the company could have re-invested dividends at the same rate of return as on existing capital, as opposed to shareholders investing at a return equal to the cost of capital. See the discussion in Chapter 3.)

---

[1] Strictly, this requires that interest rates are constant.

While economic earnings are the appropriate measure of the change in share-holders' wealth, they are not directly relevant to the main purpose of investment analysis, which is the determination of share prices. This can be understood by contrasting the market's expectation of economic earnings at the start of a year with the actual performance achieved during the year. At the start of the year, the market's expectation of economic earnings will simply be equal to the share price multiplied by the cost of capital, since economic earnings are the normal return that shareholders expect.[2] If, as events turn out, the company has an unusually good year, then realized economic earnings will include what might be termed a 'windfall' – an unexpected, one-off gain. Economic earnings for the current year will therefore be unusually high relative to future years.[3] In terms of Hicks' statement of the purpose of earnings measurement, the measure for the current year is therefore not a good 'guide to prudent conduct', since it is not a good indicator of the earnings that we can expect in future years. This problem gives rise to a second definition of economic earnings, which is given by Hicks as 'the maximum amount the individual can spend this week, and still expect to be able to spend the same amount in each ensuing week'.[4] This is *permanent earnings*. It represents a constant annual return. It equals the cost of capital multiplied by the share price, and is therefore the level of earnings consistent with a normal PE ratio. The definition of permanent earnings gives the same value as economic earnings when expressed in terms of expectations but it differs when, in a practical sense, realized performance is used as a guide to future performance. This practical difference is described by Hicks as follows:

> The income *ex post* of any particular week cannot be calculated until the end of the week, and then it involves a comparison between present values and values which belong wholly to the past. On the general principle of 'bygones are bygones', it can have no relevance to present decisions. The income which is relevant to conduct must always exclude windfall gains; if they occur, they have to be thought of as raising income for future weeks (by the interest on them) rather than as entering into any sort of effective income for the present week.

To illustrate, suppose that a company has a cost of capital equal to a return on capital of 12.5%, and a retention ratio of 60%. This is shown in the first column of Table 7.1, where the share price of $1 200 at time 0 represents a first year dividend of $60, growing at a constant rate of 7.5%, as follows:

$$\textit{Total expected return (cost of capital of 12.5\%)}$$
$$= \textit{dividend yield (5\% = \$60/\$1 200)}$$
$$+ \textit{growth rate (7.5\% = 12.5\% return on capital} \times \textit{60\% retention ratio)}$$

---

[2] This must be the case, unless the share is mis-priced. As was discussed in Chapter 2, the share price adjusts, in the light of expected dividends, to reflect an expected gain equal to the cost of capital.

[3] In turn, this leads to an abnormally low PE ratio, as was discussed in Chapter 4.

[4] Hicks also defines a third, and final, measure which is permanent earnings adjusted for inflation: 'the maximum amount the individual can spend this week, and still expect to be able to spend the same amount *in real terms* each ensuing week'. See Whittington (1983) for a comprehensive analysis of the implications of inflation for the measurement of earnings.

Table 7.1 Economic earnings vs. permanent earnings with one-off unexpected gain

(Cost of capital = 12.5%; retention ratio = 60%)	Expectation at time 0	Actual data at time 1	Windfall
Share price (time 0)	1 200		
Dividends (time 1)	60	72	12
Share price (time 1)	1 290	1 308	
Change in share price	90	108	
Economic earnings	150	180	30
Permanent earnings (time 0)	150		
Permanent earnings (time 1)	161.25	163.5	2.25

Expected economic earnings are equal to 12.5% of the share price. They are $150, which is the sum of the expected change in the share price ($90, given by the growth rate of 7.5%) plus the dividend payment ($60, given by the dividend yield of 5%). Permanent earnings are also equal to the cost of capital multiplied by the share price, because the value of the company is equal to that of an annual dividend payment of $150 in perpetuity.[5]

The final two columns of Table 7.1 illustrate a windfall gain in the first year. The company actually achieves a return on capital of 15%, although for the first year only, and 12.5% is again expected thereafter. With a constant retention ratio, the actual share price therefore increases by 9%, rather than the 7.5% that had been expected originally.[6] In turn, this re-investment leads to an increase in permanent earnings, which are now $163.5 at the beginning of year 1, as opposed to an expectation at time 0 that they would be $161.25. The difference between this actual level of permanent earnings and the expected level is $2.25, which equals the retained windfall multiplied by the cost of capital. This is consistent with Hicks' statement above. Windfalls affect future cash flows indirectly, because they increase invested capital and, thereby, the absolute level of future returns. The actual amount of the windfall is included in economic earnings, because it represents a gain over the period, but it is excluded from permanent earnings, because the gain is not sustainable and therefore not indicative of future earnings capacity.

It is therefore *sustainability* that differentiates economic earnings from permanent earnings. In this example, the company cannot earn $180 per annum indefinitely. Permanent earnings, not economic earnings, are therefore the

---

[5] Additionally, and if earnings are assumed to be equal to cash flows, then expected economic earnings are equal in this example to the expected accounting earnings of the period. This is simply because the return on investment has been assumed to be equal to the cost of capital, implying a zero rate of return spread and therefore a book value equal to shareholder value. The discussion of economic earnings would be equally valid if the rate of return spread was (for example) positive, implying shareholder value in excess of book value. Equally, accounting earnings might differ from net cash flows. The concept of economic earnings is independent of any method of accounting.

[6] The share price exceeds expectations by $18, which is the amount of re-invested windfall earnings.

natural focus for analysts in forecasting economic performance and determining the share price. This is consistent with the discussion in Chapter 4. If the PE ratio is not at its normal level, then the level of current earnings cannot be sustainable. This does not mean that current earnings are not a good measure of economic performance during the current year, but only that they are not a good predictor of future earnings. The term 'earnings quality' is frequently used to capture this issue of sustainability. For example, if investors have a high degree of confidence that an earnings stream is likely to be sustained or to grow, then these earnings are of high quality.

There is also an additional issue concerning sustainability. The example above assumed that all of the unexpected gains during the year were entirely one-off. The expectation of the company's return on capital from year 1 onwards did not change as a result of the realized performance during the first year. This is surprising in so far as unexpectedly good performance would generally lead to an upward revision in the expectation of future performance. In other words, it might be expected that some of the unexpected gains would be sustainable, at least for a few years.[7] This would imply that permanent earnings are higher than estimated above, although still lower than economic earnings. It would also make economic earnings an even less effective indicator of sustainable economic performance than it has already been shown to be. This can be demonstrated by assuming that the unexpected gain is entirely sustainable, rather than entirely one-off. In other words, the revised expectation is that the company will achieve a 15% return in perpetuity. This causes the share price at the end of the year to rise dramatically to $2 242, as shown in Table 7.2.[8]

Table 7.2 Economic earnings vs. permanent earnings with sustainable unexpected gain

(Cost of capital = 12.5%; retention ratio = 60%)	Expectation at time 0	Actual data at time 1	Windfall
Share price (time 0)	1 200		
Dividends (time 1)	60	72	12
Share price (time 1)	1 290	2 242	
Change in share price	90	1 042	
Economic earnings	150	1 114	964
Permanent earnings (time 0)	150		
Permanent earnings (time 1)	161.25	280.29	119.04

Economic earnings of $1 114 now greatly exceed permanent earnings of $280, and they are very clearly not a good indicator of sustainable performance. While

---

[7] This is consistent with the analysis in Chapter 4 of the PE ratio during a period of temporary competitive advantage.

[8] With a 60% retention rate, the constant growth rate for the company is 9%. Year 2 dividends are therefore expected to be $78.5, and the spread between dividend growth and the cost of capital is 3.5%, giving a valuation of $2 242. The assumptions of the DGM are maintained.

it was shown above that economic earnings include the unexpected gain of the current period, it is now shown that they also include the (formerly) unexpected gains of all *future* periods. The change in the share price, which feeds directly into economic earnings, reflects both the *actual* achievements of the current year and the *expected* achievements of future years.

In summary, economic earnings are an inappropriate base from which to forecast future performance, because they are unlikely to be sustainable and are therefore ill-suited to valuation models that focus on the forecasting of annual income streams.

Windfall gains

Bids in the German (telecom licence) auction have already reached almost DM80bn (£24.6bn), exceeding the British total. The German government is facing domestic political pressures to spend the unexpected windfall, just as the UK government did earlier this summer. In both countries, governments are determined to use the proceeds to repay debt. This is the correct approach. A one-off windfall should not be used to fund a recurring spending item. That would force governments either to reverse policy, or watch the public finances deteriorate, when the money ran out. One-off spending on infrastructure, or to fund the transition costs of a policy change, might be justified in some circumstances. But the best use of the money is to pay off national debt. This reduces interest payments in future years, freeing up money for spending on other priorities. In the German case, annual interest payments would fall by around DM5bn if the auction were to raise DM100bn . . . In considering the impact of these huge gains on public finances, it is important to remember that governments are only selling the lease of an asset. Accounting for this in the first year – as Eurostat wants governments to do – would result in a large budget surplus, which would be misleading. Accruing the sum over the 20-year term of the lease would be better.

Source: Financial Times, Leader, 15 August 2000

In this example, the economic earnings for the German government exceed significantly permanent earnings, due to a large windfall gain from the mobile licence auction. The author's argument that the gain should not be used to fund recurring expenditure is consistent with the view of Hicks, as is the suggestion that the gain should be used to offset a recurring interest burden on the national debt. The author argues further that the accounts should not show a one-off gain, but that instead the gain should feed through over the 20-year life of the licences. In effect, this treats the gain as the opposite of a depreciating asset, and it uses accruals accounting to show a smoothed, sustainable income stream, as opposed to a potentially misleading one-off gain.

7.2 Stewardship and investment: the need for accounting earnings

Economic and permanent earnings are both derived from the share price. For example, permanent earnings are given simply by multiplying the share price by the (constant) cost of capital. Both measures are therefore best regarded as the *output* of the analyst's valuation task, rather than the *input*. In contrast, accounting earnings are the measure of change in shareholders' wealth given by the accounts. They are the earnings measure that is available in practice, and that precedes the determination of the share price, and thereby precedes also the derivation of economic and permanent earnings.

Accounting is sometimes described as performing two roles, relating to stewardship and investment. These roles are relevant to economic and permanent earnings, respectively, and they can be used to introduce the relationships between these earnings measures and accounting.

Stewardship concerns how well a company's economic resources have been managed. Economic earnings may therefore be regarded as having a stewardship role because they measure the overall change in shareholders' economic position, regardless of whether or not the rate of change is sustainable. In contrast, permanent earnings have an investment role. They are a measure of the expected future return on a new or existing investment in the company, and they are therefore concerned directly with the sustainability of performance. In contrast with the stewardship measure, which focuses on changes in wealth, the investment measure focuses on the ongoing level of wealth creation, and it can (in theory) be multiplied by a constant (the PE ratio) in order to determine the share price.[9]

At first sight, accounting earnings perform a stewardship role. They are calculated in much the same way as economic earnings, by taking the difference between the value of net assets at the beginning and end of a period of time.[10] They differ, of course, in using book values rather than shareholder values, but they are similar in attempting to record the change in shareholders' wealth, and in not purporting to represent sustainable performance. They are also similar in that any measure of periodic performance for an ongoing business must, to some extent, anticipate the future. This is because assets are only valuable because of the future economic benefits they are expected to bring. For example, the value of accounts receivable relies upon the assumption that the amounts due will actually be collected. More generally, the valuation of land, buildings, inventories and other assets implies future realization. Yet, as was explored in Chapter 6, the accounts do not capture shareholder value fully. They are incomplete in their valuation of future events, and therefore incomplete as a statement of the shareholders' economic investment at any given point in time. In turn, therefore, the change in book values that is measured by accounting earnings does not actually capture the change in shareholders' wealth. The method of asset valuation is therefore the fundamental difference between economic earnings and accounting earnings. For example, a company can write-off against earnings cash outflows such as research and development, advertising and employee training, thereby reducing accounting earnings even though shareholder value is likely to rise. An alternative would be to capitalize these expenses at their estimated

---

[9] See Black (1980 and 1993) for an elaboration of this point. The appropriate PE ratio can vary, of course, to incorporate expectations of growth in the current level of sustainable earnings.

[10] The calculation of accounting earnings is typically visualized in terms of income and expenditure, although this is equivalent (allowing for dividends) to thinking in terms of changes in shareholders' capital/net assets.

value to the company, which is more likely to reflect economic earnings. A company might also maintain in the accounts the historic cost of assets, rather than reflecting ongoing changes in their actual market values. Again, this would fail to record changes in economic value. The accountant's approach to measuring earnings is summarized neatly by Treynor (1972), as follows:

> The accountant defines it (earnings) as what he gets when he matches costs against revenues, making any necessary allocations of cost to time periods; or as the change in the equity account over the period, before capital transactions. These are not economic definitions of earnings, but merely descriptions of the motions the accountant goes through to arrive at the earnings number.

The problem here is that earnings, whether accounting or economic, are derived from asset values. If accounting earnings are to have economic meaning, then presumably book values must bear some relationship to economic values. If the relationship breaks down – for example when R&D is written-off rather than capitalized – then the economic meaning of accounting earnings is unclear. The accounts summarize historic transactions and events, allocating them to the current period in the income statement, or else deferring them to future periods by allocating them to the balance sheet. As was discussed in Chapters 5 and 6, book value in the accounts does not therefore attempt to capture market value. The problem that this creates for the use of accounting earnings in security analysis is again summarized by Treynor (1972):

> If earnings is the difference between the worth of the firm at the beginning and the end of the accounting period, then analysis of a firm's worth logically precedes measurement of earnings, rather than the other way around. The present joint process by which the accountant arrives at earnings by estimating or measuring the change in value over the accounting period, and the analyst in turn uses these earnings to estimate value at the end of each period, is in some danger of being logically circular ... in attempting to estimate the value of the firm, the analyst is using earnings data which in turn depend importantly on accountants' estimates of the value of some of the firm's major assets. If estimation of economic value requires earnings data, and earnings data requires estimates of economic value, how do we get the joint process off the ground?

There is a clear need to search for economic relevance in the accounting measure of earnings.[11] Given that economic earnings is the 'true' change in the value of an investment, an obvious step is to undertake a formal reconciliation of the definitions of accounting earnings and economic earnings. This will enable both the strengths and the weaknesses of accounting earnings to be made more explicit.

---

[11] Beaver and Demski (1979) analyse this conundrum. They show that, in a world of perfect and complete markets, income is unambiguously measurable from present values. In such a setting, however, there is actually no need for financial statements. If the setting is more realistic, however, then accounting earnings are an ambiguous measure. Beaver and Demski conclude that accounting earnings are at best one of a number of inputs into a valuation model, and that they are useful if they are more informative than cash flow data, but that they should not be viewed as an income measure in a fundamental sense.

7.3 Reconciling economic earnings with accounting earnings

Since book values determine accounting earnings, while economic earnings are derived from shareholder values, the difference between book value and shareholder value must reconcile the two earnings measures. Chapter 6 identified two sources of this difference. The first of these is between the book values of assets and their market values, and the second between the collective market values and shareholder value (i.e. 'pure' goodwill).

Consider first the difference between book values and market values. There are, in fact, two reasons why a *change* in an asset's book value differs from a change in its market value. The first (and most obvious) arises when the market value of the asset changes, but the accounts do not reflect this. Suppose, for example, that a company values land at historic cost. If the land value increases, then there is an economic profit, but not an accounting profit. Gains of this type are referred to as *holding gains*, because they arise simply through the holding of assets. As time passes, of course, the gains will eventually be realized, and thereby recognized in the accounts. If, for example, the land is sold five years after it is purchased, then the whole of the holding gain becomes realized in the year 5 accounts. This, then, is the second type of book value change that is not also an economic profit. Accounting earnings for year 5 include all the holding gains from year 1 onwards, while economic earnings include only the gain that actually occurred in year 5. This gain in year 5 itself is the common ground between the two definitions of earnings. Any asset that is bought and sold in the same accounting period will generate an economic profit equal to accounting profit. It follows that companies with shorter operating cycles and shorter asset lives are likely to show a closer relationship between economic earnings and accounting earnings.

Table 7.3 illustrates this discussion. It is assumed that a company consists only of two parcels of land, both of which are bought in the first year for $10 000 each. The first parcel is sold in year 4, and the second in year 7. Both increase in market value by $2 000 in each year.

Economic profit measures the actual gain in the market value of the company's assets. It is therefore $4 000 in each of the first three years, and then $2 000 after the first parcel of land is sold. It does not matter when the sale takes place,

Table 7.3 A comparison of accounting earnings and economic earnings

	Year							Total
	1	2	3	4	5	6	7	
Book value (end of year)	20 000	20 000	20 000	10 000	10 000	10 000	–	
Market value (end of year)	24 000	28 000	32 000	18 000	20 000	22 000	–	
Accounting profit	–	–	–	8 000	–	–	14 000	22 000
Economic profit	4 000	4 000	4 000	4 000	2 000	2 000	2 000	22 000

in that the profit on the sale has already been recognized before it is actually realized. In contrast, accounting profit recognizes the whole of the economic gain in the year in which it is actually realized. In year 4, the accounting profit of $8 000 includes the unrealized holding gains of the previous three years ($6 000) plus the realized holding gain of the current year ($2 000). In contrast, economic profit is $4 000, and it includes the realized holding gain on the land that is sold ($2 000) plus the unrealized holding gain on the land that remains unsold ($2 000). Over the seven-year life of the company, the total accounting profit equals the total economic profit, but only the latter allocates the economic gains correctly to the years in which they actually took place.

In addition to these issues of tracking the market value of assets, there is a further measurement problem with accounting earnings. This arises because the balance sheet excludes any goodwill that is not attributable to individual assets. Goodwill refers to the capacity of the company to generate abnormal returns *in the future*, because it represents the expected 'earnings power' of a collection of assets, combined with a given set of managerial skills. If the stock market changes its expectations of the company's capacity to generate future returns, then the share price will change, and so too will goodwill and economic earnings. This is independent of the book value of assets and it does not, therefore, affect accounting earnings.

This discussion of the theoretical differences between accounting earnings and economic earnings is summarized by Solomons (1961) as follows:

> Accounting income
> + Unrealized changes in the value of tangible assets which took place during the period, over and above value changes recognized as depreciation of fixed assets and inventory mark-downs[12]
> − Amounts realized this period in respect of value changes in tangible assets which took place in previous periods and were not recognized in those periods
> + Changes in the value of intangible assets during the period, hereafter to be referred to as changes in the value of goodwill
> = Economic income

This reconciliation helps to explain the economic relevance in accounting earnings. Of the three reconciling items above, the first two relate to holding gains. In principle, accounting earnings can be adjusted for both of these items. Holding gains can be excluded if they belong properly to past years. Indeed, the historic record can be adjusted by adding these gains back. It is also possible to estimate holding gains from the current period and add these to accounting earnings. It cannot, however, be expected that accounting earnings should go beyond the market values of assets in order to explain goodwill. The third item above is unrelated to historic performance, and therefore unrelated to the financial statements. While accounting earnings can be helpful in estimating the change in goodwill (and thereby the change in the share price), there is no sensible way

---

[12] Depreciation and other write-offs are changes in book values, and they are included in the calculation of accounting income. It is any *additional* changes in market value that accounting income does not record, arising whenever market value changes do not track book value changes.

of adjusting accounting earnings to include this change. This observation leads Barton (1974) to focus on goodwill, and not holding gains, as the defining theoretical difference between accounting and economic earnings:

> Accounting income is ex post; it measures achievements to date and is based on market transactions and events that have actually occurred in the past. Economic income is *ex ante*; it evaluates expectations of future income and refers to transactions that have not yet occurred . . . This is the essential difference between the two concepts.

To summarize, accounting earnings do not include unrealized holding gains from the current period, but they do include realized holding gains that should properly belong to previous periods. The reason for this is that book values are conservative, and they generally do not recognize gains until they are realized. The effect is that accounting earnings in any one year are actually a composite of some economic gains from the past and a portion of those from the present.[13] In addition, accounting earnings do not incorporate goodwill, which is the stock market's estimate of the 'abnormal earning power' of the collective assets of the company. Goodwill is the fundamental reason why accounting earnings cannot track economic earnings.

Do the accounts record economic gains?

Four years ago Rolls-Royce assured investors it was no longer a standard engineering stock and held out the prospect of double-digit annual earnings growth as it reaped the benefits of its rising share of the growing aero engine market. Yesterday, the company came back down to earth as it was forced to concede that next year's earnings would be flat. In part, it is a victim of its own success . . . Its Trent engines, widely recognised as the most technologically advanced on offer, are selling so well that it is having to invest heavily to ensure it can meet rising production levels in coming years. It now has a 25 per cent share of the future market, measured in terms of engine deliveries, but to get there it has had to give away margin and offer some attractive financing terms. The earnings growth projections are underpinned by the argument that Rolls-Royce can grab most of the spares and maintenance business from those engine sales, which typically does not feed through for six to seven years, but offers juicy operating margins of up to 60 per cent. The problem is that the company had promised the balance in its aero engine business would swing towards the aftersales market for years, and investors have grown tired of waiting . . . Rolls-Royce's other main failing is that it keeps giving investors nasty surprises . . . The problems in its industrial power division, which makes gas turbines, were known, but the £120m provision that was announced at yesterday's interims to fix them was not. 'What relative value can we commit to the earnings when we keep getting all these exceptionals thrown in?' asked Will Mackie at UBS Warburg.

Source: Financial Times, Mark Odell, 25 August 2000

---

[13] There are defensible reasons for the inherent conservatism in financial accounting, along with the emphasis on realization and on consistency of treatment within any one company. In particular, the subjectivity implicit in the estimation of future events can be problematic. It allows managers discretion in the reporting of business performance, which could be used at the expense of investors, and it can also affect the distribution of economic gains between competing parties, such as shareholders, employees, the government and (in regulated industries) customers. See Ijiri (1971) for an expanded discussion of the benefits of historic cost accounting.

The aero engine industry has a long operating cycle, because the manufacturer continues to generate returns over the life of an engine – indeed, engines themselves are often sold inexpensively because the customer then becomes tied in to an expensive service schedule. The sale of an engine therefore generates both an immediate accounting profit and also an additional economic profit (or goodwill), in the form of an expected future profit stream. In the case of Rolls-Royce, there is undoubtedly considerable economic profit arising from the technologically advanced Trent engines. Yet there is also a high degree of uncertainty about the amount of this profit, and neither the management nor the accounts have given investors much of a lead.

7.4 The need for three types of earnings measure

The discussion so far leads to the conclusion that there are three, conceptually distinct, measures of accounting earnings, each of which is relevant to equity valuation.

First is the stewardship measure, which includes all of the changes in shareholders' capital that are measured in the accounts.[14] This is often termed 'comprehensive income' to make it clear that all gains and losses are included. Accruals accounting goes some way towards ensuring that comprehensive income does, in fact, allocate economic performance across periods in a meaningful way, for example through capitalization and depreciation. This allocation is incomplete, however, and comprehensive income can be adjusted to 'correct' for the inherent conservatism of financial statements. In particular, holding gains can be recognized as they occur, rather than when they are realized, and intangible investment expenditure can be capitalized (where justified) and amortized. This adjusted stewardship measure can be used to compare analysts' earnings forecasts against realized performance. It can also be used as a track record of the total gains and losses made by a company.

The second measure is normalized earnings, which has an investment focus. Accounting earnings are only of direct relevance to share prices if they are predictive of future economic performance. For example, if a company has consistently achieved steady earnings growth in the past, then there may be good reason to suppose that it will continue to do so in the future. This is where the concept of permanent earnings is applicable. It is possible to break comprehensive income down into different components of performance, with each component having different implications for future performance. For example, sales achieved in past years are important in so far as they help to predict the growth and sustainability of future sales, whereas a one-off gain in the current year is not directly relevant to future performance. This process of adjusting bottom-line accounting earnings to derive a measure of sustainable performance is termed 'normalization'. In effect,

---

[14] With the exception, of course, of new equity issues or capital repayments, which do not directly concern economic performance.

normalized earnings are the accounting equivalent of permanent earnings, since non-recurring gains and losses are excluded.

Finally, there is the earnings forecast, which is based upon normalized earnings but which necessarily makes additional use of information beyond the financial statements. In effect, the adjustment from normalized earnings to an earnings forecast is an adjustment for goodwill (i.e. for expected changes in the future economic environment), and it reflects the intrinsic limitations of using the financial statements for valuation purposes. The accounts are a record of historic performance, and they cannot be expected to predict the future. If a company is expected to grow its sales, or if it has invested in new technology that will bring down its operating costs, then *future* profits will be enhanced. In due course, the effect will be felt in the historic financial statements, but there is no sensible way in which the current financial statements can be adjusted to incorporate this future performance. The adjustments outlined below therefore deal only with the first and the second of the earnings measures outlined here, even though it is the third (the earnings forecast) that is forward-looking and underpins the share price. In effect, the adjustments are intended to enhance the analyst's ability to forecast accurately, and they therefore emphasize the relationships between the three measures.

Forget the past, it's the forecast that matters

After celebrating earnings that beat Wall Street estimates by 12 cents, Hewlett-Packard executives woke up to a severe hangover yesterday. The morning after the earnings celebrations, they watched their stock sag more than 9 per cent amid downgrades from some analysts and worries over the prospects of the high-end of their Unix server line . . . The issue was not so much the quantity but the quality of the results. The first grumbles came as Mr Wayman (HP chief financial officer), told analysts that 4 cents of the key 97 cents earnings figure was made up of non-operating income, consisting of unspecified 'other income' and interest. The second blow came when HP reported 13 per cent growth in revenues in its Unix server lines, below the expected 15 per cent and well below the growth rates reported by Sun Microsystems and its other competitors in the increasingly competitive market.

Source: Financial Times, Andrew Heavens, 18 August 2000

On the basis of a 'stewardship' measure of performance, it is clear that Hewlett-Packard performed extremely well, exceeding market expectations. On a normalized basis, however, analysts were concerned about the sustainability of non-operating income, which qualified the perception of earnings quality. Most important, however, the reported growth below market rates for Unix servers led to a downgrade in earnings forecasts, and thereby to a fall in the share price.

7.5 From comprehensive income to normalized earnings

The measurement of comprehensive income has been discussed implicitly in Chapter 6. If the adjustments to book value recommended in Chapter 6 can be made, then the problem of holding gains identified in the current chapter are addressed. Adjusted comprehensive income therefore provides an effective stewardship measure from which analysts can derive an investment-focused measure of normalized earnings.[15] To illustrate the derivation of normalized earnings, an extended income statement is presented Table 7.4.[16]

Table 7.4 Statement of financial performance			
	£000	£000	£000
Operating (trading) activities			
Revenues (turnover)			
Continuing operations		550	
Acquisitions		50	
Discontinued operations		175	775
Cost of sales			(620)
Other expenses			(104)
Excess of revenues over expenses:			
Revenues (turnover)			
Continuing operations		50	
Acquisitions		6	
Discontinued operations	(15)		
Less: provision	10	(5)	51
Financing and other treasury operations			
Interest on debt			(18)
Other gains and losses			
Loss on disposal of discontinued operations	(17)		
Less: provision	20	3	
Profit on sale of properties in continuing operations		9	
Revaluation of trade investments		(3)	
Revaluation of fixed assets		4	
Exchange differences on foreign currency net investments		(2)	11
Taxation			(14)
Minority interests			(2)
Total [increase (decrease) in equity other than from investments by or distributions to owners]			28

Source: Based upon Johnson and Lennard (1998)

[15] A well-known set of recommended adjustments to earnings is provided by the Institute of Investment Management and Research (IIMR, 1993). These adjustments aim to provide standarized guidance on deriving an earnings measure that focuses on trading performance, as opposed to capital gains and losses. The IIMR standard defines 'headline' earnings only, meaning that it recommends adjustments that can be made unambiguously and consistently by all analysts, such that there is a common point of reference in interpreting corporate performance. This common reference point is argued to be important for the initial stock market reaction to earnings announcements. The IIMR standard refers also to a second adjusted earnings measure, which it terms 'maintainable earnings'. This is a measure that cannot be unambiguously standardized because it depends upon the subjective judgement of the individual analyst. It is this concept of maintainable earnings that parallels the discussion in this section of the chapter, since the focus here is on a fully adjusted measure, regardless of whether all analysts interpret the recommended adjustments similarly. The IIMR standard and the current chapter can therefore be regarded as different but consistent.

[16] The method of reporting financial performance differs across jurisdictions. It is governed by IAS 1 internationally, FAS 130 in the USA and FRS 3 in the UK. There has, however, been some harmonization in recent years, and the similarities are more marked than the differences. The illustration above is a format suggested by an international working party (Johnson and Lennard, 1998). For present purposes, it is a reasonable consensus representation, and it does not differ materially from most existing practices.

The 'bottom line' of this statement (£28 000) is the measure of comprehensive income. All other line items are components of comprehensive income, and each has been presented separately because it has different implications for normalized earnings.

The major component of financial performance is likely to be the sales, expenses and profits associated with operating activities. There is likely to be a strong relationship between each of these variables in past years with the forecasts for future years. If an operation becomes discontinued, however, then its performance is relevant to the current year only, and separate disclosure therefore allows forecasts to take this into account.[17] Similarly, if a new operation is acquired during the year, then there is a step-change in the scale of the entity, and separate disclosure is again helpful. In particular, it is likely that the accounts record only a part-year of the acquired operation's performance, such that scaling-up is needed for the forecast. It is also likely that an acquired business will undergo significant short-term change. It might, for example, be restructured in order to realize the expected synergy gains from the acquisition. It is also likely that the acquisition will affect the analyst's forecasts for both interest and taxation charges.

In contrast to these operating (or 'core') activities, financial performance can be due to a range of other factors, each of which has different implications for future profitability. In particular, under the heading 'other gains and losses' is a series of disclosures not directly related to operating performance. The first item is a loss on the disposal of an operation, which is likely to be one-off in nature and therefore of limited relevance to ongoing earnings.[18] A disposal gain would be equally one-off, and it would represent the realization of previously unrecorded goodwill. Genuinely one-off gains and losses of this type affect future earning indirectly, in the sense used by Hicks (1946), and it is only this indirect effect that should be included in normalized earnings. This is especially important in view of the possible large size and high volatility of these items, that would otherwise lead to serious distortions in the pattern of earnings performance.

It can be difficult, however, to judge the extent to which a gain or loss is one-off. The separate disclosure of different types of gain makes the task easier, but some degree of subjective judgement is inescapable. The statement of financial performance above includes a profit on the sale of properties in continuing operations. While the continuation of the operation suggests that this source of gain might be ongoing, the amount of future gains cannot actually be determined without knowledge of the company's property portfolio, the outlook for property prices, and the company's intentions with respect to its property. Related to this

---

[17] The example provided in the above statement of financial performance highlights the need to track provisions, such as that for the loss on the discontinued operation. In the previous year's accounts, a provision of £10 000 was made for operating activities, which turned out to be £5 000 too small. In contrast, the £20 000 provision for the loss on disposal turned out to be £3 000 too generous. The net effect of the discontinued operation on the current income statement is only £(2 000).

[18] Though note that the measurement of the loss is somewhat subjective. It would be possible, for example, for some costs that properly belong to the ongoing business to be written-off against the disposal, with the hope that analysts are led to predict higher sustainable earnings.

is the revaluation of trade investments and of fixed assets. Similarly to the gain on the property sale, these are holding gains, not directly related to operating performance.[19] They differ from the property gain in that they have not yet been realized. This makes them less certain, but it does not make them any less relevant to the measurement of economic performance. Again, they are disclosed separately because of their differing implications for future performance. It might be argued, for example, that gains and losses on trade investments (and, indeed, on financial assets generally) are more likely to be volatile and unpredictable than gains on property, suggesting that the former are lower quality earnings. Likewise, holding gains in general may be regarded less favourably than operating gains. A practical example of this is the investment banking industry, where the fee income from asset management operations is more highly valued than capital gains from trading.[20]

A final comment on normalized earnings is that the distinction between operating performance and capital gains and losses can itself be somewhat difficult to interpret. A capital loss on the disposal of an asset might reflect that the asset has been under-depreciated over its life, implying an over-statement of operating performance in prior years. The appropriate treatment would be to restate prior performance and to question the depreciation assumptions built into existing forecasts. A similar exercise of judgement is also required for provisions made for restructuring. In the case of some companies, provisions of this type are very unusual and thereby 'deserving' of exclusion from normalized earnings. This impact on forecast earnings is indirect, and similar in nature to the effect of capital expenditure. In other companies, restructuring provisions are made frequently and should be regarded no differently from other operating expenses.

Earnings quality

Looking at the interim earnings of Cathay Pacific Airways, Hong Kong's de facto flag carrier, it would be easy to conclude that the boom times are back in Hong Kong. The airline reported a record net profit of HK$2.18bn (US$279m) in the six months to the end of June, up sharply from HK$108m a year before. But while its cargo business soared and passenger yields grew significantly, much of the improvement in Cathay's bottom line came from savage cost-cutting . . . It was a theme reflected across other sectors. While there is little doubt that Hong Kong's economy is recovering and bottom lines are expanding, many of the earnings gains are being driven by cost-savings rather than rapid expansion in revenues. Demand in several sectors remains ▶

---

[19] See Edwards and Bell (1961) for an extended, insightful discussion of the importance of separating operating and holding gains. Edwards and Bell advocate the use of replacement cost in the income statement rather than historic cost. For example, suppose that a retail company buys an item of inventory for $50 and then holds it for six months. Over this period the wholesale market price for the inventory (i.e. the replacement cost) increases to $70. If the product is sold after six months for $100, then the company makes a profit of $50. Edwards and Bell would split this profit into a one-off holding gain of $20, and a sustainable economic gain of $30.

[20] Further examples of holding gains and losses that are difficult to predict include exchange differences on foreign currency net investments, pension fund surpluses and deficits, and changes in the value of financial instruments.

weak, preventing companies from increasing prices to lift margins . . . Mr Fu at Merrill Lynch says that, overall, interim earnings were in line with the early stages of an economic recovery. After a recession, companies typically have to work on growing volumes before they can recover pricing power.

Source: Financial Times, Joe Leahy, 25 August 2000

An analysis of the components of Cathay's income statement suggests that its profit growth may not be sustainable, since it arises from cost-cutting rather than revenue growth. On the other hand, if the information in the financial statements is combined with experience from past economic cycles, then it is plausible to expect continued growth, this time from demand strength and renewed control over pricing.

A second example of the analysis of earnings quality comes from the financial statements of Microsoft and Intel:

That Microsoft makes money from selling software and Intel from selling computer chips is irrefutable. But both companies are also creaming off a hefty income from investments – and the scale of the contribution to earnings has begun to make analysts feel uncomfortable. Intel's second-quarter results, announced on Tuesday, included $2.4bn of operating income, up from $2.32bn in the equivalent period of last year, and a massive $2.34bn of interest and investment income, eight times the 1999 figure. Microsoft's earnings, for the fourth quarter of its fiscal year, also benefited from strong investment income: $1.13bn in the quarter, or more than 30 per cent of taxable income for the three months. For those with longer memories, the prominence of investment gains in earnings is a worrying reminder of the Japanese bubble of the late 1980s, when so-called 'financial engineering' by industrial companies was so prevalent that it was given a name, zaiteku. The circumstances in the US are different. Neither company is hiding anything, and neither is dependent on financial investments . . . Both companies argue, however, that investment income will be a recurring item . . . The problem is that investment income is not easy to predict, even for the companies themselves. Intel alerted analysts ahead of its results to expect a much higher investment gain than usual, mainly because of sales of stock in Micron Technology. That led to an unseemly spat with Wall Street . . . Both companies' shares would suffer if analysts began to apply a similar yardstick to their investment earnings as they do to pure high-tech investment companies such as CMGI or Safeguard Scientifics. Those companies were among the hardest hit by the rerating of technology stocks, whereas Intel emerged from the deflating internet bubble almost unscathed, in spite of its exposure to the same sorts of investments. At the very least, that should be a reminder to investors to seek reassurance from the likes of Intel and Microsoft that the quality of their earnings is not strained.

Source: Financial Times, Andrew Hill, 20 July 2000

If a significant percentage of a company's earnings come from non-operating activities, then investors generally have good reason to be concerned. In the first place, operating activities constitute a company's core competence, and therefore typically the source of its value added. In the second place, operating activities are likely to be ongoing, almost by definition, whereas non-operating gains and losses are more likely to be transitory. Investment gains, in particular, are likely to be low-quality earnings, because financial markets can be volatile and unpredictable, and also because prices adjust very quickly in financial markets, making it especially difficult to earn sustainable excess profits. This is reflected in the different ratings applied to high-tech investment companies, as opposed to the high-tech companies themselves (see the discussion in Chapter 3 of the difference between the cost of capital and the return on equity).

> As a final illustration of earnings quality, consider the following, simple example, which shows the benefits of a sustainable 'no surprises' profit stream:
>
> Jack Welch's final year at the helm of General Electric began in trademark style, with the US manufacturing and services conglomerate yesterday reporting record second-quarter earnings per share that beat Wall Street projections by one cent . . . Mr Welch once again demonstrated the predictability that has become the hallmark of GE's earnings, helping it to become the world's most valuable company, at nearly $520bn.
>
> *Source: Financial Times, Richard Waters, 14 July 2000*

7.6 Goodwill

Should the amortization of purchased goodwill be included in normalized earnings? This is a question over which there is considerable disagreement amongst practitioners. In attempting to answer the question, it is first helpful to consider the meaning of purchased goodwill, both on the balance sheet and in the income statement.

Table 7.5, which is based upon Johnson and Petrone (1998), approaches the subject of purchased goodwill by reconciling the book value of the acquiree's net assets with the acquisition cost paid by the acquirer.

Table 7.5 illustrates that purchased goodwill can, in practice, arise for a number of reasons. Assuming for the moment that the fair value of recognized net assets is measured correctly, then purchased goodwill has four components.[21] First, there is the value of unrecognized net assets, such as R&D. Second, there is the 'pure' goodwill of the acquiree, when viewed as a standalone operation. Third, there is the 'combination' goodwill, that arises if the combined organization is able to generate greater value from its assets than had been achievable in the independent companies. The value of this combination goodwill plus the standalone value represents the break-even price for the acquirer in making the acquisition. In practice, more or less than this break-even might be paid, and this over-/under-payment is the fourth and final component of purchased goodwill.

An important difference between purchased goodwill and internally generated goodwill is, simply, that the former is purchased. Internally generated goodwill

Table 7.5 Components of purchased goodwill

Book value of acquiree's net assets . . .	*Plus* fair value adjustments, *equals* . . .
Fair value of acquiree's recognized net assets . . .	*Plus* fair value of unrecognized net assets, *equals* . . .
Fair value of acquiree's total net assets . . .	*Plus* internally generated goodwill, *equals* . . .
Standalone value of acquiree . . .	*Plus* merger/synergy gains, *equals* . . .
Value of acquiree to acquirer . . .	*Plus/minus* over-/under-payment by acquirer, *equals* . . .
Cost of acquisition	

Source: Adapted from Johnson and Petrone (1998)

---

[21] The term 'fair value' refers to the market price of individual assets in arm's length transactions between fully informed buyers and sellers.

represents value creation, because the company is worth more than the cost of its assets. Purchased goodwill does not represent value creation, unless the fourth component above is an under-payment for the acquisition.[22] From the perspective of portraying economic reality in the accounts, the treatment of value-neutral purchased goodwill in the balance sheet and in the income statement should give rise to a zero rate of return spread. In contrast, internally generated goodwill should lead to a positive rate of return spread, as the value of the goodwill is realized over time.

How, then, is purchased goodwill actually treated in the financial statements? Typically, it is amortized by an arbitrary amount over an arbitrary time period.[23] This is due to the impracticality of reliable measurement of the value of goodwill. It is a pragmatic, conservative treatment that writes off the goodwill gradually, just like other purchased fixed assets. In addition to the amortization, there are two other effects of purchased goodwill on the income statement. These are the financing costs of the acquisition (which arise to the extent that debt finance is used) and the cost of expenditure incurred to maintain (or to grow) the value of the goodwill. This latter category includes advertising, training and other costs incurred in order to enhance the future cash flows from the existing asset base. These income statement effects are illustrated in Table 7.6. The data are based on the assumption that neither the original nor the acquired businesses are either creating or destroying value. The original business had a share capital of $1 000 and an ROE of 20%. The acquisition was financed by debt, with an interest cost of 20%. The cost of the acquisition was $100, of which $50 is goodwill to be amortized over ten years. The acquisition generates 20% ROE each year.

Table 7.6 The effect of purchased goodwill on the income statement

Operating profit from original business	$200
Operating profit from acquired business	$20
Amortization of goodwill	$(5)
Interest cost from acquisition	$(20)
Earnings	$195

The acquisition is non-value creating. The income statement should not, therefore, show shareholders to be either better or worse off. In fact, they are shown to be worse off. This is due to the amortization of goodwill. If, in fact, the

---

[22] The break-even sales price for the acquiree is the standalone value. If synergy gains exist, then there is a range of sales prices that represent an economic gain for both the acquiree and the acquirer. The term 'under-payment' used above does not imply that the acquiree has been 'short-changed', but only that there are synergy gains captured by the acquirer.

[23] This is true of international and US accounting standards (IAS 22 and APB 17, respectively). In the UK, purchased goodwill would normally be amortized over a period of up to 20 years, although it is allowed to be capitalized indefinitely on the condition that its value is reviewed annually for impairment (FRS 10). Current proposals suggest a future policy similar to the UK. Universally, the book value of purchased goodwill cannot be revised upwards.

investment is value neutral, then the goodwill will generate a return of 20% in perpetuity. The goodwill is not a depreciating asset, and it is therefore misleading to write it off through the income statement. The amortization of the goodwill should not be regarded as a 'cost' of the investment. The cost of the investment in this example is the interest cost. Alternatively, if equity financing had been used, then profit would have been increased after the acquisition, but only by enough to match the corresponding increase in the shareholders' required return. Again, this would be value neutral. In this example, the amortization of goodwill is misleading, and it should be excluded from the analyst's measure of normalized earnings.

In general, the treatment of goodwill amortization depends upon the view that the analyst takes of the book value of the purchased goodwill. In turn, this depends upon the expected future performance of the acquired company. Consider each of the components of purchased goodwill identified in Table 7.5. It might be the case that the acquired intangible assets, such as R&D, lose their value over time. Equally, the intrinsic goodwill of the acquired company might well erode, perhaps with the loss of customer loyalty or the departure of key employees. Finally, the hoped-for synergies from the acquisition might fail to materialize. In each of these cases, purchased goodwill is properly treated as a depreciating asset, and the income statement should properly include both the financing cost and the amortization. The only issue is how well the amortization expense actually matches the loss in value of the purchased goodwill.

Finally, another issue emerges, which is the extent to which the acquiring company is able to maintain, and even to make grow, the value of the purchased goodwill. It is likely that such maintenance or expansion would require additional, post-acquisition expenditure by the acquirer. Indeed, such expenditure can be viewed as evidence that the value of purchased goodwill is, in fact, being maintained. In order to be consistent with the analysis of book values in Chapter 6, the analyst's adjusted balance sheet should capitalize all investment outlays (whether tangible or intangible) that *increase* goodwill. In contrast, if the value of purchased goodwill is neither increased nor decreased but simply maintained by ongoing expenditure (for example, advertising), then this expenditure should be written-off. Capitalizing it would, in effect, be double counting the company's assets.[24]

This discussion of goodwill highlights the subjective nature of the analyst's adjustments to the balance sheet. No two analysts are likely to agree on the ongoing value of goodwill, and therefore on the appropriate income statement treatment. Nevertheless, the discussion also highlights that the simple amortization of goodwill is arbitrary and most unlikely to yield meaningful results. While the analyst's judgement must be recognized as subjective, it must be considered preferable to a system that requires no judgement at all.

---

[24] In principle, the maintenance of a goodwill asset in the balance sheet in some cases is best represented by the amortization of the purchased goodwill (on the basis that is has a finite life) and the simultaneous capitalization of expenditure that creates new goodwill. If the value of the goodwill is unchanged, then this has the same net effect as writing off the expenditure as incurred but leaving the goodwill asset unamortized.

Purchased goodwill: asset or expense?

BAA is going to concentrate on its core business: operating airports. This is a good idea, given its disastrous acquisition of World Duty Free . . . Profit before tax in the year to March fell by 27 per cent to £377m. The £147m goodwill writedown on the acquisition of World Duty Free is official acknowledgement that BAA seriously overpaid.

Source: Financial Times, Lex Column, 6 June 2000

Purchased goodwill arises simply as the difference between the purchase price of the acquisition and the fair value of the underlying assets. The goodwill asset in the balance sheet might therefore be either a 'genuine' valuation of the excess profit stream that the company has acquired, or alternatively a measure of how much the company has over-paid for the acquisition. If the former, then amortization is likely to be inappropriate and misleading. If the latter (as in this case), then the goodwill is not an asset at all and should be written off. Amortization in this case would be equally misleading, but for different reasons.

7.7 Empirical evidence on earnings measurement

The relationship between share prices and earnings has been the subject of considerable empirical research, some of which has been reviewed already in Chapter 4. The evidence presented here falls under two broad headings. First, it is shown that estimates of permanent earnings have a closer relationship with share prices than unadjusted measures of earnings. Second, evidence is presented concerning the underlying determinants of earnings permanence, which relate both to economic fundamentals and to subjectivity in methods of accounting.

The general relationship between share prices and permanent earnings is consistent with theoretical predictions. By measuring earnings permanence in a variety of ways, studies have confirmed some fundamental relationships. In particular, price–earnings ratios are higher when current earnings are more permanent, the cost of capital is lower and growth in future earnings is higher.[25] A study by Lang (1991) shows further that earnings are valued more highly to the extent that they are more helpful in resolving uncertainty about future earnings. For example, in contrast to a well-established and well-understood company, earnings for a new company are more helpful in revising expectations of future earnings, because they provide relatively more information about the company. The direction of changes in earnings is important also. In general, and because conservatism anticipates losses 'up-front' but does not anticipate profits, Basu (1997) finds that negative earnings changes are less likely to be permanent than positive earnings changes. For example, a loss incurred by a large provision or by an asset write-off is unlikely to persist.

Research has also shed light on the components of earnings, and on their relationship with permanent earnings. At the simplest level of disaggregation,

---

[25] Studies that support these conclusions include Kormendi and Lipe (1987), Easton and Zmijewski (1989) and Collins and Kothari (1989).

Swaminathan and Weintrop (1991) show that if investors have knowledge of revenues and expenses, rather than just of earnings, then they will have a better understanding of share price behaviour. This is because revenues and expenses are likely to behave differently over time, and knowledge of each therefore allows a more accurate forecast of earnings. Likewise, Strong and Walker (1993) show that the disclosure of exceptional and extraordinary items is useful to investors because it improves the estimation of permanent earnings. They show that exceptional and extraordinary items are far more likely to be 'one-off' than other components of earnings, such that they should be excluded from normalized earnings. More generally, Elliott and Hanna (1996) note that write-offs have become increasingly common over the past 20 years, and that while investors tend to focus on earnings before write-offs, their perception of earnings quality is lowered when write-offs persist over time. Fairfield, Sweeney and Yohn (1996) find that the disaggregation of earnings between operating and non-operating is also helpful to investors. Similarly, O'Hanlon and Pope (1999) and Dhaliwal, Subrayanyam and Trezevant (1999) find that net income is more closely related to future cash flows and income than the all-inclusive comprehensive income measure. This supports the conclusion reached above that net income is a closer approximation to permanent earnings than comprehensive income.

Summary

The main points from this chapter may be summarized as follows.

- Earnings are a record of financial performance that can be relevant to the estimation of future performance, and thereby to the determination of share price.
- Economic earnings are equal to the cash flow received during a period plus the change in present value over the period (otherwise known as total shareholder return, TSR). They are a 'true' statement of the economic gain made during a period, although they include 'windfall' gains and losses and are therefore an unreliable guide to future performance.
- Permanent earnings are equal to the sustainable component of economic earnings, and they are adjusted for windfall effects. The share price can be calculated as permanent earnings divided by the cost of capital. Permanent earnings are therefore given by a 'normal' PE ratio. They are the 'ideal' measure for security analysis, against which the practical strengths and weaknesses of accounting earnings can be measured.
- Accounting earnings provide information relevant to the determination of share prices, but their usefulness is subject to a number of important qualifications.
- Accounting earnings are derived from book values. The adjustments to book value recommended in Chapter 6 improve the effectiveness of accounting earnings in recording economic gains and losses.
- It is inescapable, however, that accounting earnings cannot be expected to measure economic earnings, since balance sheet values exclude goodwill. Accounting earnings are best regarded as a measure of a company's progress towards the realization of its goodwill.

- There are three, conceptually distinct, measures of accounting earnings, each of which is relevant to equity valuation. First is comprehensive income, which is a stewardship measure including all of the changes in shareholders' capital that are measured in the accounts. Second is normalized earnings, which is an investment-focused measure of sustainable performance. Normalized earnings make use of the separately reported components of comprehensive income (notably operating gains and holding gains) recognizing that each has different implications for future performance. Finally, there is the earnings forecast, which is based upon normalized earnings, but which necessarily makes additional use of information beyond the financial statements.

- Amortized goodwill should normally be excluded from normalized earnings, unless there is reason to expect the value of purchased goodwill to erode over time.

References

Barton, A.D. (1974). 'Expectations and Achievements in Income Theory', *Accounting Review*, Oct., 664–81.

Basu, S. (1997). 'The Conservatism Principle and the Asymmetric Timeliness of Earnings', *Journal of Accounting and Economics*, 24, 3–37.

Beaver, W.H. (1998). *Financial Reporting: An Accounting Revolution* (3rd edn). Hemel Hempstead: Prentice Hall.

Beaver, W.H. and J.S. Demski (1979). 'The Nature of Income Measurement', *Accounting Review*, Jan., 38–46.

Black, F. (1980). 'The Magic in Earnings: Economic Earnings versus Accounting Earnings', *Financial Analysts Journal*, Nov.–Dec., 19–24.

Black, F. (1993). 'Choosing Accounting Rules', *Accounting Horizons*, 7(4), 1–17.

Collins, D. and S.P. Kothari (1989). 'An Analysis of Intertemporal, and Cross-Sectional Determinants of Earnings Response Coefficients', *Journal of Accounting and Economics*, 11, 143–81.

Dhaliwal, D., K.R. Subrayanyam and R. Trezevant (1999). 'Is Comprehensive Income Superior to Net Income as a Measure of Firm Performance?', *Journal of Accounting and Economics*, 26, 43–67.

Easton, P.D. and M.E. Zmijewski (1989). 'Cross-Sectional Variation in the Stock Market Response to Accounting Earnings Announcements', *Journal of Accounting and Economics*, 11, 117–41.

Edwards, E.O. and P.W. Bell (1961). *The Theory and Measurement of Business Income*. Berkeley: California University Press.

Elliott, J.A. and J.D. Hanna (1996). 'Repeated Accounting Write-Offs and the Information Content of Earnings', *Journal of Accounting Research*, 34(Supplement), 135–55.

Fairfield, P.M., R.J. Sweeney and T.L. Yohn (1996). 'Accounting Classification and the Predictive Content of Earnings', *Accounting Review*, 71(3), 337–55.

Hicks, J.R. (1946). *Value and Capital*. Oxford: Clarendon Press.

IIMR (1993). *The Definition of IIMR Headline Earnings*. London: IIMR.

Ijiri, Y. (1971). 'A Defense for Historical Cost Accounting', in R. Sterling, *Asset Valuation and Income Determination*. Kansas: Scholars Book Co.

Johnson, L.T. and A. Lennard (1998). *Reporting Financial Performance: Current Developments and Future Directions*. New York: FASB.

Johnson, L.T. and K.R. Petrone (1998). 'Is Goodwill an Asset?', *Accounting Horizons*, 12(3), 293–303.

Kormendi, R. and R. Lipe (1987). 'Earnings Innovations, Earnings Persistence, and Stock Returns', *Journal of Business*, 60(3), 323–45.

Lang, M. (1991). 'Time-Varying Stock Price Response to Earnings Induced by Uncertainty About the Time-Series Process of Earnings', *Journal of Accounting Research*, 29(2), 229.

O'Hanlon, J.A. and P.F. Pope (1999). 'The Value-Relevance of UK Dirty Surplus Accounting Flows', *British Accounting Review*, 31(4), 459–82.

Solomons, D. (1961). 'Economic and Accounting Concepts of Income', *Accounting Review*, 36, 374–83.

Solomons, D. (1995). 'Criteria for Choosing an Accounting Model', *Accounting Horizons*, 9(1), 42–51.

Strong, N. and M. Walker (1993). 'The Explanatory Power of Earnings for Stock Returns', *Accounting Review*, April, 385–99.

Swaminathan, S. and J. Weintrop (1991). 'The Information Content of Earnings, Revenues and Expenses', *Journal of Accounting Research*, 29(2), 418–27.

Treynor, J. (1972). 'The Trouble with Earnings', *Financial Analysts Journal*, Sep.–Oct., 41–3.

Whittington, G. (1983). *Inflation Accounting: An Introduction to the Debate*. Cambridge: Cambridge University Press.

8 Measuring the return on capital

Overview
- Return on Equity (ROE) and Return on Capital Employed (ROCE)
- Differences between economic return (IRR) and accounting return (ROE)
- The special case where the IRR equals the ROE
- The general case where the IRR is a weighted average of the ROEs
- How to interpret and use ROE data in practice

Earlier chapters have shown that the value of a company depends upon its return on capital relative to its cost of capital. Understandably, therefore, analysts are highly concerned with the return on capital that companies have achieved historically.

While the return on capital has an unambiguously important role in valuation *theory*, however, it is essential to recognize the difficulty of deriving a good measure of the return on capital in practice. This chapter will explore this measurement problem, focusing on the economic meaning and interpretation of accounting-based measures of the rate of return. In particular, the return on equity (ROE) and the return on capital employed (ROCE) will be contrasted with their economic counterpart, the internal rate of return (IRR). This will highlight the extent to which the ROE and ROCE are useful, in practice, as a basis for measuring the rate of return spread.

8.1 Return on equity (ROE) and return on capital employed (ROCE)

The return on capital measures the efficiency with which assets are employed to generate income. It provides useful information that is unavailable from book values or income measures alone. Consider, for example, the viewpoint of shareholders. The book value of shareholders' funds alone does not measure shareholder value, not least because it records the cost of the resources employed by the company rather than the expected net cash flow stream. Earnings, meanwhile, do attempt to measure the net cash flow stream, but they do not capture the amount of shareholders' capital that is employed. If, for example, one company achieves higher earnings than another, then this may simply be because it has a greater amount of invested capital, and not because it generates higher earnings *per dollar* of invested capital. In principle, therefore, the measurement of shareholder value creation cannot depend solely upon asset values or on earnings, but only on a measure that combines both, and that can be compared with the cost of capital. For shareholders, the return on equity (ROE) therefore appears to be the appropriate measure. It is a rate of return that expresses earnings per dollar of invested equity capital, as follows[1]

$$return\ on\ equity_{t+1} = \frac{profit\ after\ tax_{t+1}}{book\ value\ of\ shareholders'\ funds_t}$$

Alternatively, the return on capital employed (ROCE) is the appropriate measure of the joint return generated by both equity and debt investors.[2] In calculating the ROCE, the appropriate numerator is either operating profit or net profit after corporate tax (NOPAT, see Chapter 5) and the corresponding denominator is the combined book value of equity and debt (which is capital employed, see also Chapter 5)[3]

$$return\ on\ capital\ employed_{t+1} = \frac{NOPAT_{t+1}}{capital\ employed_t}\ or\ \frac{operating\ profit_{t+1}}{capital\ employed_t}$$

The ROE and the ROCE have the convenient property that they can be broken down into two components, the first measuring the profitability of the company, and the second measuring the efficiency of asset usage. Consider the ROCE as an illustration, as follows

$$return\ on\ capital\ employed_{t+1} = profit\ margin_{t+1} \times asset\ turnover_{t+1}$$
$$= \frac{operating\ profit_{t+1}}{sales_{t+1}} \times \frac{sales_{t+1}}{capital\ employed_t}$$

If, for example, a company has capital employed of $50 000 at the beginning of the year, and it generates sales of $100 000 and operating profit of $15 000 then its ROCE is 30%, as follows

$$return\ on\ capital\ employed = 30\% = \frac{15\ 000}{100\ 000} \times \frac{100\ 000}{50\ 000}$$

The profit margin measures the ability of the company to convert sales revenues into bottom-line profits. Asset turnover, meanwhile, measures how efficiently the company is able to use its asset base in order to generate the sales in the first place. The effect of multiplying the profit margin by the asset turnover is to cancel the sales term, and to express directly the efficiency with which assets are employed to generate profit. The above formula allows, for example, a high-margin,

---

[1] Strictly, the denominator should be *average* capital employed, since earnings are a compound return during the year. A simple means of estimating the average capital employed is to take the average of the opening and closing balance sheet values.

[2] A further variant is the return on operating assets, where the return from cash and other financial assets are excluded. In this case, the appropriate income measure is NOPAT, though measured using operating profit before income from financial assets. The corresponding capital measure is equity plus net debt, where the latter equals debt minus financial assets.

[3] The use of operating profit has the benefit that it is not influenced by the rate of taxation, which can be regarded as (mostly) unrelated to operating activity and beyond corporate control. It can also be used internally as a way of assessing divisional performance. In contrast to NOPAT, however, operating profit overstates the actual return to providers of capital.

low-turnover business (such as luxury cars) to be compared with a low-margin, high-turnover business (such as food retail).

This break-down of the ROCE is known as the DuPont formula, because it was used in the early twentieth century by senior managers of the DuPont Corporation, who wanted a measure of the relative performance of their operating companies. In effect, they were acting as portfolio managers, and were measuring the return generated by each of their investments. Surplus cash flows would be re-invested in the operating companies that were generating the highest ROCEs, and taken away from those that were less efficient. The ROCE therefore served as a guide in allocating new capital. Additionally, it was a management control measure, enabling the managers to understand where corrective action needed to be taken in order to enhance performance.[4]

The interpretation of the ROCE in this way relies heavily, of course, upon the method of measuring sales, profit and asset values. Suppose that the method of accounting had been different in the example above. Operating profit might then have been $20 000 (perhaps because of using a slower rate of depreciation) which would have led to an ROCE of 40%. Alternatively, a higher initial valuation of the assets, say $75 000 would have reduced the ROCE to 20%. In practice, the scope for variation in the ROCE is unlikely to be this large. The fact remains, however, that the economic relevance of the ROCE depends upon the values of profit and assets, which is in turn dependent upon subjective methods of accounting. In the same way, therefore, that the measurement of profit depends upon asset values, so too does the ROCE.

This subjectivity in measuring and interpreting the return on capital is problematic. Chapters 3 and 4 demonstrated that the return on capital plays a central role in valuation models. In particular, it was shown to be the main driver of value in the dividend yield and PE ratio valuation models. In order to reconcile these simple models to the underlying dividend discount model (DDM), however, it was essential to effectively ignore measurement issues and to define the return on capital as the cash flow of a period divided by an economic value of invested capital at the beginning of the period. Chapters 5, 6 and 7 have demonstrated, however, that there are no easy solutions to the practical problem of measuring economic performance, implying that there are no simple ways to operationalize valuation models. In particular, the method of accruals accounting was shown to generate useful but subjective and conservative measures of book value and earnings. An implication is that while the accounting return on capital is an attempt to measure 'true' return on capital, it is necessarily an imperfect measure. Book values are not economic values, and accounting and economic earnings do not coincide. The ratio of earnings to book value (return on capital) therefore does not, and cannot in general, measure the true economic return directly.

In exploring this problem, this chapter will follow the structure of Chapters 6 and 7, and it will start by attempting to reconcile the accounting and economic measures of the rate of return. This reconciliation will then form the basis for an understanding of how, in practice, the accounting return on capital can be used for

---

[4] See Johnson and Kaplan (1987) for a full discussion of the historical context of the DuPont formula.

economic decision making. To keep the discussion straightforward and consistent with earlier chapters, the focus will be on the ROE rather than the ROCE, although (as has been shown above) the two measures are readily interchangeable according to whether a shareholder value or an enterprise value perspective is taken.

ROE targets

Credit Suisse Group on Thursday raised its performance targets in a move viewed by analysts as a bid to maintain its share price premium over peers, notably its Swiss banking rival UBS. The new targets reflect the planned acquisition of Donaldson, Lufkin & Jenrette and the enhanced earnings from investment banking and asset management which the US bank is expected to generate . . . Credit Suisse announced that it would target a long-term group return on equity of between 18 and 22 per cent from the previous benchmark of 'over' 15 per cent. This compares with the actual ROE of 18.2 per cent in 1999 and the 15-to-20 per cent targeted by UBS.

Source: Financial Times, Doug Cameron, 15 September 2000

This example illustrates the commonplace practice of measuring performance on the basis of return in capital (in this case, return on equity capital). Additionally, the importance of the ROE in making direct comparisons between companies within sectors is highlighted. As is typical, however, the basis of measuring the ROE goes unquestioned. It is convenient to assume that ROEs have an unambiguous economic interpretation, and that they can be compared meaningfully across companies and over time. This chapter addresses the validity of this convenient assumption.

8.2 Differences between economic return (IRR) and accounting return (ROE)

The economic rate of return over the life of an investment is the internal rate of return (IRR). As was seen in Chapter 2, the IRR is defined as the discount rate that equates the initial cost of an investment with the present value of future cash flows from the investment, implying zero net present value. The IRR is the constant, annualized rate at which the value of shareholders' invested capital grows, from the date of their initial investment to the point at which the investment is liquidated. If the IRR exceeds the cost of capital, then the investment is value creating.[5]

---

[5] There are two ways in which to consider the initial investment against which the IRR is measured. On the one hand, an investor could acquire shares in the company at some stage during the company's life. In this case, the initial investment is given by the share price, and the expected IRR will simply equal the cost of capital (i.e. the IRR multiplied by the share price will equal expected permanent earnings). This is nothing other than an equilibrium condition: if the share price did not promise an IRR equal to the cost of capital, then the share would be mis-priced. Of course, the actual IRR that the investment achieves is likely to differ from that which had originally been expected. On the other hand, an investor's investment could have been in the initial capital of the company, such that his or her value-gain equals the net present value generated by the investment, or the difference between shareholder value and the value of invested capital. If there is positive net present value (NPV), then the IRR exceeds the cost of capital. It is in this second sense that the IRR is most directly comparable with ROE. The IRR is a measure of the expected lifetime economic return on an investment, that may be compared with its cost of capital in determining the investment's value.

As was the case with asset values and earnings, economic and accounting measures of the rate of return on shareholders' invested capital are analogous but different. In particular, there are three sources of difference between the two measures, and these can be illustrated using the drinks vendor example from earlier chapters (see Table 8.1).

Table 8.1 Return on equity

	Year				
	1	2	3	4	5
Opening book value (B_t)	10 000	8 000	7 500	8 500	10 500
Net cash flow (C_{t+1})	0	1 500	3 000	4 000	7 500
Depreciation	−2 000	−2 000	−2 000	−2 000	−2 000
Earnings (E_{t+1})	−2 000	−500	1 000	2 000	5 500
Return on equity (R_{t+1})	−20.00%	−6.25%	13.33%	23.53%	52.38%
Closing book value (B_{t+1})	8 000	7 500	8 500	10 500	16 000

The cash flows to and from the shareholder are the initial £10 000 investment and the £16 000 liquidation at the end of year five, and the IRR is therefore the discount rate at which £16 000 after five years has a present value of £10 000. This rate is 9.86%. The IRR is therefore a constant rate that applies to the whole life of the investment. The first difference between the IRR and the ROE, therefore, is that the former is an average while the latter measures the rate of return for each individual accounting period. The ROE actually varies considerably from year to year in the example above. Initially it is very low but it rises rapidly, reflecting a sharp increase in earnings relative to the historic cost of book values.

The second difference between the IRR and the ROE is that the IRR is concerned purely with cash flows, namely the initial invested capital and the subsequent annual net cash flows. In contrast, the ROE is determined by reference to accounting earnings and book value. As was seen in Chapters 5, 6 and 7, the actual measures of accounting earnings and book value are subjective. The combination of these two measures in the form of a ratio serves to combine all of the complications discussed in these earlier chapters. The ROE is affected by accounting policy decisions that, in themselves, do not affect cash flows. The ROE can therefore change independently of changes in shareholder value, whereas the IRR cannot.

Finally, the third difference is that the IRR takes account of the time value of money, by means of discounting cash flows, whereas the ROE makes no such accommodation.[6]

---

[6] There is, in fact, a theoretical special case (known as economic depreciation) where the ROE takes implicit account of the time value of money. This is discussed later in this chapter.

In summary, then, the IRR and the ROE are superficially similar yet fundamentally different. While both measure the rate of return on capital, the IRR is a constant rate that is based exclusively upon cash flows and takes into account the time value of money, whereas the ROE is a variable measure that is based upon book value and earnings and that ignores the time value of money. The IRR is the 'true' (annualized) measure of economic return, but being based upon projections of the future it is not, of course, observable. As was the case with book value and accounting earnings, reported (historic) ROE has the advantage of being observable and therefore usable by analysts, but it has the disadvantage that its economic relevance is not obvious. A very simple question therefore emerges from this discussion. Can the ROE be used in practice as a measure of the IRR and, if so, how?

The first systematic attempts to answer this question were by Harcourt (1965) and Solomon (1966). Both reached conclusions that were remarkably negative. In Harcourt's case, a simulation approach tested the ROE–IRR relationship under a range of different scenarios, with different growth rates and different depreciation schedules being assumed. Harcourt concluded his study as follows

[Anyone] who compares rates of profit in different industries, or of the same industry in different countries, and draws inferences from their magnitudes as to the relative profitability of investments in different uses or countries, does so at his peril.

Solomon reached a similar conclusion.

The rate of return on investment is . . . of central importance for the financial evaluation of a company's performance . . . [but] the ratio of net income to net book assets is not a reliable measure of return on investment.

Likewise, Fisher and McGowan (1983) saw no straightforward relationship between the ROE (a one-year measure based upon historic accounting data) and the IRR (a life-cycle annualized economic rate of return)

It should be obvious that only by the merest happenstance will the accounting rate of return on a given investment, taken as the ratio of net revenue to book value in a particular year, be equal to the economic rate of return that makes the present value of the entire revenue stream equal to the initial capital cost. Indeed . . . accounting rates of return on individual investments generally vary all over the lot.

This chapter will proceed with an analysis of why these conclusions are rather *too* negative. First, a special case is examined where the ROE is actually equal to the IRR. Then, it is shown that, even when the ROE does not equal the IRR, the two measures can nevertheless be reconciled. This is shown to be the case both over the whole life of a company and also over a limited period of the company's life. It is concluded that the ROE can be used in analysts' valuation models, but that its usefulness varies according to factors such as stock market sector, corporate growth rates and variation over time in the ROE itself.

Changes in the ROE can be independent of the IRR

Vodafone AirTouch yesterday gave the first indication of how much money it expects to make from third generation mobile networks during the release of better-than-expected full-year results. Ken Hydon, finance director, said that the projected rate of return on the large capital investment required for licences and infrastructure was at least 15 per cent. Although the £6bn cost of Vodafone's new UK licence will be spread over its 20-year lifespan, most of the estimated £4bn network spending and handset subsidy will be required in the first four or five years. This implies that the company is projecting potential operating profits of about £75m above its existing performance. Vodafone described this extrapolation as 'simplistic', but the rough figures give an idea of just how profitable it imagines the new services will be.

Source: Financial Times, Dan Roberts, 31 May 2000

The relevance to valuation of the £6bn operating licence cost is limited to the cash outflow at the time that the licence was acquired. Yet the method of accounting for the cost could give rise to a whole range of different possible measures of return on capital. For example, if the licence is capitalized and then amortized evenly over 20 years, the return on capital is likely to start low and then to rise, with particularly high returns in later years. Alternatively, writing off the cost would give a hugely negative return on capital in the current year and a misleadingly high return in all future years. Given that the investment has a highly uncertain IRR and that the role of the accounting measure of return is to provide evidence that reduces this uncertainty, it is not clear that useful information arises from a cost allocation that is subjective and independent of the IRR.

8.3   The special case where the IRR equals the ROE

In attempting to understand the economic relevance of the ROE, an obvious starting point is to consider the conditions under which the ROE and the IRR are equal to one another. By understanding these conditions, it becomes possible to understand the relationship between the ROE and the IRR whenever the two differ.

Since the IRR is constant over the life of an investment, so equality between the ROE and the IRR requires that the ROE must be constant also. As will be seen, this special case requires a specific method of asset valuation that is very highly improbable in practice. It is, however, a very useful illustration. It shows the onerous conditions required for the ROE to be of unambiguous economic relevance, thereby highlighting the difficulties arising in practice when taking the ROE directly from the accounts.[7]

It was demonstrated by Hotelling, as long ago as 1925, that the ROE and the IRR are constant and equal to one another only when a specific method of asset valuation is employed (Hotelling, 1925). This method is to record the book value

---

[7] There is also a second (and final) theoretical possibility for equality between the IRR and the ROE, which is that the company can be in a steady state of growth, at a rate equal to the IRR (Kay, 1976).

of equity at the present value of future cash flows, discounted at the IRR.[8] This is illustrated in Table 8.2, using the same data as above.

Table 8.2 The special case where ROE equals IRR

	Year				
	1	2	3	4	5
Opening book value (B_t)	10 000	10 986	12 068	13 258	14 565
Closing book value (B_{t+1})	10 986	12 068	13 258	14 565	16 000
Earnings (E_{t+1})	986	1 082	1 190	1 307	1 435
Return on equity (R_{t+1})	9.86%	9.86%	9.86%	9.86%	9.86%

Book value at the start of year 1 is £10 000, which increases by the 9.86% IRR in each year until it reaches £16 000 at the end of year 5. All book values are therefore the present value equivalents of one another, using the IRR as the discount rate. Earnings are simply the difference between the book values, but since this difference is the economic gain of 9.86% each year, then the ROE must also be 9.86%. This would remain the case if cash flows were returned to shareholders during the life of the company. In this case, earnings would be the sum of the cash flow to shareholders and the gain in the book value of invested capital, and the amount of the capital gain would be lower by precisely the amount of the cash flow. In other words, the ROE would remain at 9.86%. What makes this possible is the method of asset valuation. By making book value equal to the present value of future cash flows (discounted at the IRR), it is ensured that the ROE in each period is equal to the IRR across all periods.[9]

This example appears rather abstract. In practice, of course, assets are not valued at cash flows discounted at the IRR. But this is precisely the point of the example. Because assets are not so valued, the ROE cannot be expected to equal the IRR, except by chance, in any given period. In practice, the ROE and the IRR will differ. The difficulty then arises of how they can be reconciled. If a company achieves an ROE of 25% in a given period, and its IRR is 15%, then what does the ROE of 25% mean, and how can it be interpreted? It would clearly not be sensible to forecast a dividend growth rate by taking 25% multiplied by the retention rate. This would give a highly inflated share price. Equally, it cannot be claimed that the company has made an economic return of 25% on shareholders' funds. But what, then, can be said?

---

[8] The term 'economic depreciation' is used for the difference over an accounting period between the opening and closing values of an asset whenever Hotelling depreciation is used.

[9] Notice that all three of the theoretical differences outlined above between the ROE and the IRR are reconciled by the use of Hotelling valuation. First, the ROE does not vary across periods, and its value in any given period is therefore equal to its average. Second, book values, earnings and ROEs are not determined by arbitrary accounting convention but are instead uniquely determined by expected cash flows. Third, the time value of money is implicit in the calculation of ROE, since it is incorporated in book values.

Before proceeding to address this question, it is worth noting the relationship between the current discussion and the earlier analysis of the dividend yield and PE ratio valuation models. In particular, it can now be seen that the assumption of constant dividend growth requires the additional, previously hidden, assumption that book values are equal to future cash flows discounted at the IRR. Specifically, a constant rate of dividend growth was shown to be equal to the product of a constant ROE and a constant rate of new investment. In turn, the assumption of the constant ROE implies that the ROE must be equal to the IRR. This assumption has now been shown to be unrealistic. This highlights that simple valuation models, such as the dividend growth model and the PE ratio, should be used cautiously as a means of modelling real-world complexity.

The analysis here relates also to the discussion of the price–book value ratio in Chapter 6. Specifically, if Hotelling valuation is used, then the price–book value ratio will be equal to 1 whenever the IRR is equal to the cost of capital. This is because the rate of return that the company is expected to achieve is equal to the rate of return that shareholders demand. If the IRR exceeds the cost of capital, then the price–book value ratio will exceed 1, because the discount rate at which future cash flows are converted into book value is higher than that which determines shareholder value. Moreover, the amount of the price–book value ratio has a precise meaning. Consider a $100 investment in an asset that returns $120 at the end of its one-year life, giving an IRR of 20%. If the cost of capital is (say) 10%, then the value of the investment to shareholders is $120 discounted at 10%, which is $109.09. The price–book value ratio is 1.09, which means simply that shareholders have achieved a value creation of 9% by making the investment. Alternatively stated, there is 9% of pure goodwill, or 9% net present value, relative to the amount of the investment. In general, and for an investment generating a cash flow, C, in perpetuity, the ratio of the IRR to the cost of capital is equal to the price–book value ratio, as follows:[10]

$$Price\text{-}book\ value\ ratio = \frac{P}{B} = \frac{C/k}{C/IRR} = \frac{IRR}{k}$$

8.4 The general case where the IRR is a weighted average of the ROEs

As was seen in Chapter 6, the reality of asset valuation is very far from Hotelling's special case. From the above discussion, this implies that the ROE must vary in practice, and that in general it will therefore differ from the IRR. The question now arises whether there exists any relationship between an ROE that varies and an IRR that is constant.[11]

[10] For an investment of a duration of t years, the following relationship holds: PBV ratio = $(1 + IRR)^t/(1 + k)^t$. This reduces to IRR/k for an infinite duration. The examples in this chapter include a one-year return of 20% with a 10% cost of capital (i.e. P–BV ratio = 1.2/1.1 = 1.09), and a five-year IRR of 9.86% with a cost of capital of 9% (i.e. $1.0986^5/1.09^5 = 1.04$).

[11] Though note that the IRR is itself subject to change, in that expectations of the future are always likely to be revised. While it is true that, at any given point in time, the expected IRR can be regarded as an average future rate of return, the expected IRR will itself change over time.

This question was answered by Kay (1976), who demonstrated that the IRR over a company's life is a weighted average of the ROEs in each period.[12] This is intuitively appealing. The IRR is the annualized economic rate of return over the total life of a company (or investment project), while the ROE is a measure of the return in each period of the total life. It stands to reason, therefore, that the sum of the periodic returns, suitably weighted, should in some way equate to the overall return.

Kay's solution requires book values to be discounted to present value, using the IRR as the discount rate. These present values are then used as the weights in the calculation that shows the IRR to be equal to the weighted average of the ROEs. This process is illustrated in Table 8.3, making use again of data from the earlier example.

Table 8.3 Reconciling ROE with IRR

	Year					Total
	1	2	3	4	5	
Opening book value (B_{t-1})	10 000	8 000	7 500	8 500	10 500	
Earnings (E_t)	−2 000	−500	1 000	2 000	5 500	
Return on equity (R_t)	−20.00%	−6.25%	13.33%	23.53%	52.38%	
Discount factor (at 9.86%)	0.91	0.83	0.75	0.69	0.62	
Discounted book value	9 103	6 629	5 657	5 836	6 562	
Sum of discounted book value						33 787
Book value weights	26.9%	19.6%	16.7%	17.3%	19.4%	100%
Weighted, discounted ROEs	−5.39%	−1.23%	2.23%	4.06%	10.17%	
Weighted average ROE						9.86%

The opening book values are discounted at the IRR and then summed, giving a present value of £33 787. The discounted book value for each year is then expressed as a percentage of the total. For example, the present value of the year 3 book value (£5 657) is equal to 16.7% of the aggregate present value of book values. These percentages are then used as weights in the calculation of a weighted average ROE. For example, the ROE of 13.3% in year 3 is multiplied by 16.7% to give 2.23%. When added to the equivalent numbers for the other four years, this gives an overall weighted average ROE of 9.86%, which is equal to the IRR. It might be noted that a simple average of the ROEs is 12.6%, which overstates the IRR. Only the weighted averaging mechanism proposed by Kay will allow a precise reconciliation of the ROEs with the IRR. Moreover, as long as data are used for the whole life of a company (or an investment project), then the analysis holds true regardless of the method of accounting used by a company. For example, changing the rate of depreciation would change both the book values and the earnings, and thereby also the ROEs. Yet the weighted average calculation would still give the correct IRR of 9.86%.

---

[12] See Whittington (1979) for a review and interpretation of Kay's paper.

It is not obvious why this calculation works, and some intuition behind it is called for. Suppose, for example, that a company has an option to depreciate an asset either quickly or slowly. Whatever the company decides, its cash flows will be unchanged, and so its value and its underlying IRR will also be unchanged. Clearly, however, the choice of faster depreciation will reduce earnings initially (thereby reducing ROE), whilst also reducing subsequent book values and increasing subsequent earnings (with both effects increasing the ROE beyond the first year). Faster depreciation therefore implies that the ROE is first lower, and then higher, than it would otherwise be. This is illustrated in Table 8.4, which repeats the example above except that £500 of depreciation expense is transferred from year 2 into year 1.

Table 8.4 Reconciling ROE with IRR (with change in accounting policy)

	Year					Total
	1	2	3	4	5	
Opening book value (B_{t-1})	10 000	7 500	7 500	8 500	10 500	
Earnings (E_t)	−2 500	0	1 000	2 000	5 500	
Return on equity (R_t)	−25.00%	0.00%	13.33%	23.53%	52.38%	
Discounted book value	9 103	6 215	5 657	5 836	6 562	
Sum of discounted book value						33 373
Book value weights	27.28%	18.62%	16.95%	17.49%	19.66%	100%
Weighted, discounted ROEs	−6.82%	0.00%	2.26%	4.11%	10.30%	
Weighted average ROE						9.86%

Although the change in accounting gives a different ROE in years 1 and 2, the weighted average ROE is the same and equals the IRR of 9.86%. Kay's weighting mechanism achieves this by taking into account two reconciling factors between the ROE and the IRR. First, the time value of money implies that a given ROE in the near future is worth more than the same ROE in the distant future. This is recognized by the mechanism of discounting book values to present value. Since the discounted book values are used to weight the ROEs, the weighted average ROE places more emphasis on near-term ROEs. Second, the ROE is influenced by accounting policy, which is unrelated to cash flows and therefore unrelated to shareholder value. This is important because accounting policy has a significant distorting effect on the ROE. In particular, asset write-offs will tend to lead to a low ROE in the year of the write-off, but a disproportionately high ROE in subsequent years, as is the case in the above example. The weighted averaging mechanism corrects for this because ROEs are not taken at face value but are instead expressed relative to the absolute book values on which they are earned. For example, the book value in the first year of the example above is high relative to that of the later years, because of the write-off in year 1. The weight attached to the year 1 ROE is therefore correspondingly larger than it was under the original accounting policy.[13]

---

[13] This method of calculation is analogous to that of reconciling the yield to maturity on a bond (the analogue of the IRR) with the underlying annual rates of interest (the analogues of the ROEs).

A key strength of Kay's analysis is that the ROE is characterized correctly as a *periodic* measure of performance, in contrast to the IRR, which is an *average* rate over the life of a given investment. The importance of this is explained by Vatter (1966), as follows (note that the term 'book yield' is used to mean ROE):

> The truth is that every situation is somewhat different; each year of operation of a project is different from the earlier ones; the attempt to force a given rate of return from any and all situations is not likely to succeed. The way to compare a book yield with the project plan is not to use the overall project rate of return but to set up for each year of the project that rate of return which applies to it; comparison of the rate expected for that year with the actual experience will not show large discrepancies – certainly not so large as the average-internal-project rate (IRR) would suggest.

While it is important to understand the relationship between a series of ROEs and the IRR, as has been reviewed above, the actual ROE for any given period of time should be compared with the expected ROE for that same period, and not with the IRR.

There is also an additional consideration if the ROE is being examined over a finite segment of a company's life. Kay's model has been shown to work over the whole lifetime of a company. Indeed, it is this property that ensures the model works regardless of the methods of accounting employed by the company. In practice, however, the analyst has at his or her disposal measures of the accounting rate of return over only a limited segment of a company's life. Suppose, for example, that a company has been in operation for 20 years, and that the analyst is examining the company's performance over the most recent five years. In this case, the opening book value for the analyst will be the cumulative value of shareholders' capital and retained profits over a 15 year period. This value will be an aggregation of all of the accounting valuation decisions made over the life of the company. It is not the economic value of shareholders' invested capital, and therefore not the basis against which the shareholders measure their return on capital. Similarly, if the investment is disposed of at the end of year 20, then it is the share price at that date which is relevant to shareholders. The book value will have changed also, but this change does not represent the change in the shareholders' economic position. This example stands in contrast to the example above, where the whole life of a company was analysed. In such a case, the opening and closing book values are zero, and in this sense they do represent the shareholders' economic position before and after the investment. All cash flows are recorded through the accounts, and the accounts can therefore be used to record the change in economic position. By contrast in the current example, the goodwill at the end of year 15 records the difference between the value in the accounts and the true value, while the goodwill at the end of year 20 does likewise. In attempting to relate the ROEs during the five-year period to the IRR over the period, this goodwill must therefore be taken into account.

The solution to this problem is due to Peasnell (1982) and it takes the form of a simple extension of the Kay result given above. All that is necessary is to take the opening and closing values of goodwill, and then to incorporate these into the calculation of the weighted average ROE. Peasnell's adjustment is as follows[14]

$$IRR\ adjustment = \frac{present\ value\ of\ terminal\ goodwill - current\ goodwill}{sum\ of\ present\ values\ of\ forecast\ horizon\ book\ values}$$

The denominator in this calculation is exactly the same as that already seen in Kay's model. The numerator is simply the present value of terminal goodwill (discounted at the IRR) less current goodwill. So, for example, suppose that the data for the drinks vendor example do not represent the whole of the company's life, but that instead they are data for a five-year segment only. If, in this case, the opening market value of the company was £15 000 and the market value after five years was £26 000, then opening and terminal goodwill would be £5 000 and £10 000, respectively. The five-year gain in market value of £11 000 represents an IRR of 11.63%. Using this IRR to weight book values, Kay's method (which assumes zero goodwill) estimates an IRR of 9.25% which, when adjusted as above for the growth in goodwill, is reconciled with the true IRR of 11.63%.

This analysis provides some insight into the effect of goodwill on the measurement and interpretation of the ROE. First, if the price–book value ratio is low, then the effect of the above adjustment will be small. In turn, this implies that the ROE is a better measure of the underlying IRR. In other words, the ROE is of greater economic relevance for companies (and, more generally, industries), where there is little goodwill and the price–book value ratio is low. Second, an alternative solution to the problem of goodwill arises where the present values of the opening and closing goodwill are of similar magnitude, which serves to eliminate the distortion represented by the adjustment above. Finally, the IRR estimated from accounting data will understate the true IRR to the extent that a company is increasing the present value of goodwill, and vice versa. For example, if a company invests heavily with a view to long-term value creation, then if the forecast horizon is relatively short, the estimated IRR using Kay's method will be unduly pessimistic.

8.5   How to interpret and use ROE data in practice

A fundamental problem with Kay's model (with or without goodwill) is that the only derivation of a method of weighting the ROEs requires that the data needed to calculate the IRR are already known. This makes the process akin to assuming a share price in order to determine a share price. Nevertheless, the model turns out to be extremely helpful as a practical guide in interpreting and using the ROE and ROCE.

For example, given the insight from Kay's model that the IRR is a weighted average of the ROEs, then the value of the IRR must fall below that of the highest ROE and above that of the lowest ROE. Suppose that a company has ROEs ranging from 10% to 20%, then the IRR itself must lie between these two values. An implication is that the smaller the variation in ROEs for a given company,

---

[14] See Peasnell (1982) for a formal proof.

the greater is the accuracy with which the IRR can be known, and the greater the reliance that can be placed on the company's ROE as a measure of economic performance. In the extreme case, where the ROE is constant, then the IRR is necessarily equal to the ROE.

Second, if the ROE always exceeds the cost of capital, then the IRR must also exceed the cost of capital, because it is an average of the ROEs. Positive NPV is therefore implied by a rate of return spread that is always positive.

Third, if the ROE is growing over time, then a simple average of ROEs will overstate the economic return achieved by a company. This was seen in both of the above numerical examples. In the first example, the ROE increased in each period, and the average of 12.6% exceeded the IRR of 9.86%. In the second example, the revised accounting policy caused the ROE to grow somewhat faster between years 1 and 2, with the effect that the average ROE increased to 12.8%. If Kay's weighting mechanism is used, whereby the time value of money is taken into account, then this growth in ROE caused by conservative accounting is adjusted to reflect the true economic return of 9.86%.

Finally, the correct interpretation of the ROE is dependent upon the existence of goodwill. Specifically, if there is growth in the present value of goodwill, then (other things being equal) the ROE will understate the true economic return. This effect reinforces the benefit in using ROE data over an extended period of time.

Comparing ROCEs

The bell has rung in the fight for supremacy between the three heavyweights that now top the oil industry – ExxonMobil, Royal Dutch/Shell and BP Amoco. Last week Lee Raymond, ExxonMobil's combative chairman, used an analysts' meeting in New York to make it clear that the US energy group saw itself as the dominant fighter in the oil industry's super league . . . The tough talk from Mr Raymond is no coincidence, as consolidation has sharpened the rivalry between the top tier companies. With today's publication of BP Amoco's interim results, which for the first time include earnings from Atlantic Richfield (Arco), analysts and investors will now be able to compare the three companies – which all report in US dollars – with the bulk of their recent mergers and acquisitions consolidated into a single set of accounts . . . the companies are more comparable now than at any time in their recent history (although) some technical differences remain over how each company reports its results and calculates key performance measurements, such as return on average capital employed . . . Sir John Browne, BP's chief executive . . . added that the transparency of quarterly reporting was a healthy discipline, but warned there was a danger in too much focus on short-term performance – 'It's the longer wave length trends that make the difference.'

Source: Financial Times, Robert Corzine, 8 August 2000

The return on capital employed is a particularly important measure of financial performance in the oil industry. Analysts seeking to assess an oil company's ROCE should take into account factors such as the following: differences in methods of asset valuation between companies; volatility in the ROCE (and thereby in the rate of return spread) over time; differences in growth rates; and differences in price–book value ratios. Perhaps most important, analysts should heed the advice of BP's CEO and recognize that ROCE data are best viewed over as long a time period as possible.

Summary

The main points from this chapter may be summarized as follows:

- The rate of return on shareholders' capital is of central importance to equity valuation, because it measures the efficiency with which assets are employed to generate earnings. It is the return on capital, relative to the opportunity cost of capital, that determines the value of an equity investment.

- The return on equity (ROE) and on capital employed (ROCE) are rates of return that use accounting measures of earnings and net assets. They are relevant to shareholder value and to enterprise value, respectively.

- The internal rate of return (IRR) is a true, economic measure of the rate of return achieved by an investment over its life.

- The DuPont formula shows that the ROE and ROCE are products of the profit margin (i.e. the ability of the company to convert sales revenues into earnings) and asset turnover (i.e. the efficiency of the company in using its asset base to generate sales).

- The economic relevance of the ROE and ROCE (and of the DuPont analysis) depend critically upon the measurement of net asset values and earnings in the accounts. In practice, the differences between values in the accounts and true economic values generate problems for the ROE and ROCE. There is no *simple* relationship between economic and accounting rates of return, implying that ROE and ROCE data should be treated with caution. For example, it should not be assumed that the ROE is an appropriate measure for determining growth rates in dividend yield and PE ratio models.

- The IRR is a constant rate of return over a lifespan, that is determined by cash flows and that recognizes the time value of money. The ROE (or ROCE) is a variable, periodic rate of return that is affected by accounting conventions that can change independently of economic value, and that ignores the time value of money.

- The ROE (or ROCE) is constant and equal to the IRR only in the theoretical special case where assets are valued at present value, using the IRR as the discount rate. In general, a weighted average of ROEs equals the IRR, where the weights are given by book values discounted at the IRR.

- ROE (or ROCE) data for a company are likely to be of greater economic relevance if there is little variation over time in ROE/ROCE, and also if the price–book value ratio is low.

References

Fisher, M.F. and J.J. McGowan (1983). 'On the Misuse of Accounting Rates of Return to Infer Monopoly Profits', *American Economic Review*, 73(1), 82–97.

Harcourt, G.C. (1965). 'The Accountant in a Golden Age', *Oxford Economic Papers*, 17(1), 66–80.

Hotelling, H. (1925). 'A General Mathematical Theory of Depreciation', *Journal of the American Statistical Association*, 20, 340–53.

Johnson, T. and R. Kaplan (1987). *Relevance Lost: The Rise and Fall of Management Accounting.* Boston, Mass: Harvard Business School Press.

Kay, J.A. (1976). 'Accountants, Too, Could be Happy in a Golden Age: The Accountants Rate of Profit and the Internal Rate of Return', *Oxford Economic Papers*, 28(3), 447–60.

Peasnell, K.V. (1982). 'Some Formal Connections Between Economic Values and Yields and Accounting Numbers', *Journal of Business Finance and Accounting*, Autumn, 361–81.

Solomon, E. (1966). 'Return on Investment: The Relation of Book-Yield to True Yield', in Jaedicke, R.K., Ijiri Y. and O. Nielsen (eds), *Research in Accounting Measurement*, American Accounting Association, pp. 232–44.

Vatter, W.J. (1966). 'Income Models, Book Yield, and the Rate of Return', *The Accounting Review*, 41(4), 681–98.

Whittington, G. (1979). 'On the Use of the Accounting Rate of Return in Empirical Research', *Accounting and Business Research*, Summer, 201–8.

9 Abnormal earnings valuation and EVA®[1]

Overview
- Abnormal earnings model: valuation using book value and earnings
- Ohlson's variant of the model: links between PE, price-book value and ROE ratios
- Accounting and valuation problems that the model does not avoid
- EVA – a special case of the abnormal earnings valuation model
- Empirical evidence on abnormal earnings valuation and EVA

Chapters 6, 7 and 8 reviewed the relationships that exist between share prices and, respectively, accounting measures of book value, earnings and return on equity. The analysis in these chapters revealed limitations in the data that are available for use in valuation models. For example, it was shown that there is no straightforward relationship between shareholder value and the accounting measure of book value. Likewise, accounting earnings do not measure economic earnings, and they cannot in themselves be used to determine share prices. Equally, the return on equity is a measure taken from the accounts that has only limited relevance for an equity investment's economic rate of return.

In spite of these manifest weaknesses, it is necessary to rely upon financial statement data as the basis of valuation models. Indeed, as was discussed in Chapter 5, the financial statements are our best attempt at recording economic transactions and events, and earnings are likely to be superior to cash flows as a predictor of future performance.

This chapter extends the discussion by introducing a general model of the relationships between shareholder value and financial statement data. Specifically, the model expresses the share price in terms of book value, earnings and the cost of capital. It is called the abnormal earnings valuation model. It will be shown that the model is, in fact, formally equivalent to the dividend discount model (DDM). It is a direct alternative to the DDM that makes use of accounting data rather than dividends. In the same way as the DDM, it makes no unrealistic, constraining assumptions. Book value, earnings and return on equity can all vary by any amount within the model. Any method of accounting can be used. There are, for example, no difficulties posed by accounting policies for depreciation, asset valuation, R&D, provisions or anything else. In other words, there is

---

[1] EVA is a registered trademark of Stern Stewart and Co.

always a definable, straightforward relationship between the share price and both book value and earnings. In fact, the abnormal earnings model is the *only* valuation model that holds true for any method of accounting. This gives the model a special importance.

In view of the discussion in previous chapters, it might appear that the abnormal earnings valuation model is too good to be true. Superficially, at least, it really is as good as it appears. Its obvious attractions have generated a great deal of interest in recent times. The consulting firm Stern Stewart & Co. has been the leader in bringing the model to the financial markets. The firm has christened the model Economic Value Added (EVA), and heavy publicity has enthused practitioners. In the academic world, the response has been no less enthusiastic. James Ohlson has done the same for academic research that Stern Stewart has done for practitioners. Both Stern Stewart and Ohlson are well-deserving of the credit they have received for bringing the model to a wider audience. Both have built, however, on a well-established tradition. The model appears to have been first formulated by an economist, Gabriel Preinreich, in 1938.[2] It has since been discussed in some detail by (notably) Edwards and Bell (1961) and Peasnell (1982). In short, the model is not new, but general awareness of it is.

Since the model has appeared in different places and at different times, it is unsurprising that it has come to be given different names. The main ones are economic value added (EVA), abnormal earnings, residual income, super profits, excess earnings, economic income and economic profit. Each of these names is intended to convey the same meaning, and the underlying structure of the model is precisely the same in each case. The term 'abnormal earnings' is used in this chapter, because it is consistent with the terminology of earlier chapters, and also because it is entirely general, avoiding the specific interpretation of the model imposed by the term EVA. A specific analysis of the EVA variant will be offered later in the chapter.

In spite of its obvious attractions, the abnormal earnings model is unfortunately not the 'answer' to the problems of asset valuation, earnings measurement and share price determination. Beneath the surface of the model, there remain all of the problems with accounting data that were discussed in Chapters 6, 7 and 8. It must be stated clearly that the abnormal earnings model does not make those problems go away. What the model does provide, however, is a rigorous framework for structuring information in the determination of share prices. It helps to make explicit some of the relationships and assumptions discussed in earlier chapters and, if properly understood and used, it can be a valuable tool for investment analysis.

This chapter will proceed as follows. First the abnormal earnings model will be derived and explained. Second, Ohlson's adaptation of the model will be explored. It will be shown that this adaptation parallels that which simplifies the DDM into the dividend growth model. Some useful properties of the

---

[2] Although Preinreich's article itself refers to the model as a 'well-known formula', implying that its origins are earlier even than 1938. Indeed, the importance of measuring abnormal earnings has been recognized at least as far back as Marshall's *Principles of Economics*, published in 1890.

adapted model will be analysed. The model illustrates, for example, that the price–book value ratio and the PE ratio cannot, in fact, be viewed in isolation from one another, since the value of either ratio depends in part upon the value of the other. This discussion will lead into an analysis of the weaknesses and limitations of the abnormal earnings model. Finally, the chapter will assess the specific strengths and weaknesses of the EVA approach, citing empirical evidence in support of the assessment.

9.1 Abnormal earnings model: valuation using book value and earnings

This section will show the derivation of the abnormal earnings valuation model, explaining the intuition behind it.[3] As a starting point, it was shown in Chapter 3 that shareholder value will be equal to book value whenever the return on equity is expected to equal the cost of capital. This is the situation where growth is neither value creating nor value destroying. Alternatively stated, goodwill exists whenever the return on equity is expected to differ from the cost of capital, implying that it is the expectation of abnormal earnings that generates goodwill.

It must follow that shareholder value can be expressed as a combination of book value and abnormal earnings, with the latter defined as the amount of earnings achieved at the rate of return spread.

Denoting abnormal earnings as A, we have

$$A_1 = B_0 \times (R_1 - k)$$

Since earnings are equal to book value multiplied by the return on equity (i.e. $E_1 = B_0 \times R_1$), the above expression can also be shown as follows

$$A_1 = E_1 - (B_0 \times k)$$

In words, abnormal earnings equal earnings less a cost of capital charge. If, for example, a company has a book value of $1 000 and a cost of capital of 15%, then its normal earnings would be $150. If, in practice, it achieves $180, then its abnormal earnings are $30.

Clearly, the value of abnormal earnings in any period must depend upon the method of accounting used by any given company. Chapter 6 demonstrated the multitude of possibilities for asset valuation in the accounts, and Chapters 7 and 8 discussed the implications of asset valuation for the accounting measures of earnings and return on equity. The value of abnormal earnings combines book value and earnings (and thereby ROE). It must therefore share the weaknesses that these measures have. In particular, it must be subjective, such that any given set of underlying cash flows can give rise to any number of measures of abnormal earnings. It must also be an imperfect measure of economic performance, combining past performance with a limited reflection of current performance.

---

[3] For some reason, this derivation is not promoted by Stern Stewart, even though it is the foundation of the EVA model. This is pointed out by O'Hanlon and Peasnell (1998): 'Stern Stewart neither offers a formal proof of the residual income-based valuation relationship nor directs the reader to one.'

While the argument presented above suggests that shareholder value must depend in some way upon book value and abnormal earnings, the precise form of this relationship therefore appears somewhat elusive, given the difficulties of measurement in the accounts.

Fortunately, these difficulties can be reconciled. The key to this is an understanding of the relationships between, on the one hand, the DDM and, on the other, book values and abnormal earnings. In particular, if forecasts are made for earnings and book values, then enough information is available from which to derive expected dividends. This is because a simple relationship exists between dividends, earnings and book value whenever, first, dividends are defined broadly to include all cash flows between the company and its shareholders and, second, earnings measure all changes in the book value of shareholders' funds (i.e. 'full articulation' or the 'clean surplus' relationship).[4] Specifically, the difference between the book value of shareholders' funds at the start and the end of any accounting period is the amount of earnings less the amount of dividends paid:

$$book\ value\ of\ equity_0 + earnings_1 - dividends_1 = book\ value\ of\ equity_1$$

$$B_0 + E_1 - D_1 = B_1$$

For example, suppose that a company has shareholders' funds of $1 700 at the start of a year. If earnings for the year are $200, of which $100 is paid out as dividends, then book value at the end of the year must be $1 800.

This relationship can be rearranged to show that dividends are equal to earnings for a period less the increase in book value (i.e. retained earnings) over the period

$$D_1 = E_1 - (B_1 - B_0)$$

The advantage of expressing dividends in this way is that it allows earnings and book values to be related to dividend-based valuation. We know from the DDM that shareholder value is equal to the discounted future dividend stream. Additionally, the expression above states that dividends are themselves equal to earnings less the increase in book value. If information is available about earnings and book values over the whole life of a company, then it is a simple matter to derive the company's lifetime dividends. In other words, it actually does not matter what asset valuation decisions are made *during* the company's life, because all such decisions 'come out in the wash'. Over the life of a company, book value starts and ends at zero. Between these two points in time, book values (and therefore earnings) can be whatever they like. If assets are over-valued at any point in time, such that earnings are overstated for the corresponding period of time, then this must lead to a fall in asset values and an off-setting under-statement of earnings at some future date. Over the life of a company, aggregate earnings will necessarily equal aggregate dividends, and book value changes will net to zero.

This use of lifecycle data appears to bypass the problems of asset valuation, thereby allowing book values and earnings to be used in place of dividends in

---

[4] Earnings are therefore defined to be equal to comprehensive income (see Chapter 5).

valuation. A second problem remains, however, before the abnormal earnings model can be derived. Recalling Chapter 4, the discussion of the PE ratio assumed, for convenience, that earnings were equal to cash flows. This allowed earnings to be discounted in a simple fashion. If, however, earnings do not equal cash flows, then simple discounting will give a misleading valuation. This being the case, a valuation model that employs earnings must be used with care. A good illustration of this is a growth company. If a company is growing, then the use of accruals accounting is likely to cause earnings to exceed cash flows in the early years of the company's life, due to the capitalization of fixed assets, inventory and accounts receivable. These early differences between earnings and cash flows will eventually reverse, as the assets are used up or liquidated towards the end of the company's life. Overall, the sum of earnings will equal the sum of cash flows. From a valuation perspective, however, simple discounting will give a *present value* of earnings that exceeds that of cash flows. This is simply because the earnings are greater in the near future (with a low discount rate) and smaller in the distant future (with a high discount rate). The correct valuation, of course, is based upon cash flows, such that the simple discounting of earnings will give an inflated estimate of shareholder value.

Fortunately, the use of discounted *abnormal* earnings gives a clever solution to the problem of discounting earnings. It does this by introducing asset values into the calculation. In the example above, earnings exceeded cash flows by an amount equal to the increase in assets. If, then, some adjustment can be made to earnings to compensate for the distortion caused by the change in asset values, then it will be valid to discount the adjusted earnings. In fact, abnormal earnings provide precisely the correct adjustment, and an example will now be used to illustrate why this is the case.

Table 9.1 shows accounting data for a company that, for simplicity, is assumed to have an opening book value of zero. The company spends and receives $100 in its first year, and it receives $150 in its second year. All net cash flows are paid out as dividends. There are no other transactions. To keep the example simple, it is assumed that the company has only one choice over accounting method: either it does not use accruals at all, or else it capitalizes all

Table 9.1 Present value: earnings, abnormal earnings and cash flows (cost of capital = 10%)

	Year 1	Year 2	Total
Opening book value (B_t)	0	100	
Net cash flow (C_{t+1})	0	150	
Capitalization/write-off	100	−100	
Earnings (E_{t+1})	100	50	
Discounted earnings	90.9	41.3	132.2
Abnormal earnings (A_{t+1})	100	40	140
Discounted abnormal earnings	90.9	33.1	124
Discounted cash flow	0	124	124

of its first year expenses, and then writes them off in year 2. These two options are reflected in the difference between, on the one hand, net cash flow and, on the other, earnings. In effect, the accruals accounting option is assuming that all expenses in year 1 are incurred in order to generate receipts in year 2, while the cash flow option is conservatively writing off all expenses as they are incurred.

Under accruals accounting, aggregate earnings are equal to aggregate cash flows, but because earnings are recognized earlier than cash flows, their discounted value is greater ($132.2 as opposed to $124). The discounting of earnings therefore overstates present value by $8.20. In contrast, discounted abnormal earnings are equal to $124, and they are therefore able to adjust correctly for the error of $8.20. This is achieved by the cost of capital charge. The error in the discounted earnings method arises because $100 of earnings is recognized in year 1 instead of in year 2. The present value of $100 in year 1 is $90.9 (equal to $100/1.1) and in year 2 is $82.7 (equal to $100/(1.1)^2), with the difference being $8.20. This error is equivalent to $9.01 in year 1 cash flows, or $10 in year 2 cash flows. In other words, if the cash flows in year 2 are reduced by $10, then this will have the effect of reducing the present value by $8.20, thereby offsetting the valuation error. This is, in fact, what the abnormal earnings calculation is doing. The cost of capital charge in year 2 is $10. This is precisely the correct amount because it is calculated by reference to the amount of earnings that was recognized early. The effect of recognizing $100 earnings in excess of cash flows in year 1 is to increase the book value at the beginning of year 2. In turn, this book value incurs a $10 charge in year 2, which reduces the present value by $8.20. In other words, the sum of $100 in year 1 and $(10) in year 2 has the same present value as $100 in year 2. This can be demonstrated easily. At a 10% discount rate, $100 in year 1 is worth $110 in year 2, and $110 less $10 is equal to $100. In summary, if earnings differ from cash flows, then the book value will change. If this change in book value is interpreted as the source of error in the present value calculation, then making a cost of capital charge against the book value will offset the error. If earnings are adjusted for this cost of capital charge, then they can be discounted without error.

Another way to view this is to recognize that, in effect, the model makes no distinction between revenue expenditure and capital expenditure, such that accruals accounting has no impact on valuation. Accruals can distort the underlying reality that, from a shareholders' perspective, an investment return is required from the moment cash is invested until the moment it is returned by the company. If a company invests cash in buying an asset, then the capitalization of the cash outflow results in a balance sheet asset being created, with expenditure effectively deferred from the current income statement into future years. This belies the reality that the investment in the asset is a cash outflow, and that a return must be made on it. For example, if a company buys a truck and depreciates it over a ten-year life, then the income statement understates the effective cost to shareholders. The shareholders want not only to recover their cash investment in the truck, but also to earn an annual return on that investment. If the cost of capital is charged against the book value of the truck, then this problem is resolved. Suppose that the truck costs $10 000, and the cost of capital is 10%.

If the truck is written-off in the year of purchase, such that accruals are not used and the cash outflow is treated as revenue expenditure, then the accounts reflect correctly the timing of the shareholders' investment. If, in contrast, the truck is capitalized, then an additional charge of $1 000 is made in the accounts for the following year. This reflects that, with a 10% cost of capital, shareholders are indifferent between a cash outflow of $10 000 in year 1 and $11 000 in year 2. If, therefore, accruals accounting allows capital expenditure to be deferred until future years, then the abnormal earnings model ensures consistency with revenue expenditure by, in effect, charging interest until the time at which the expenditure is recognized. It does not matter whether shareholders' money is expensed (for example on salaries or materials) or capitalized (for example on equipment or inventory). Either way a cash outflow has been made in expectation of cash inflow, and the cost to shareholders is the same.

Abnormal earnings and value creation

Competition for investor favour among the 'Three Sisters' in the oil industry super league is hotting up. Shell yesterday signalled that it does not see the competition as a two-way battle between Exxon and BP Amoco. It calculated its return on capital employed – the most closely watched indicator of financial efficiency in the integrated oil sector – at an 'industry leading' 16 per cent. Investors will be watching closely to see whether Shell will be able to boost its capital budget – and fund future growth – in a way that does not erode a position that was achieved in large measure by imposing a strict capital diet.

Source: Financial Times, Robert Corzine, 4 August 2000

The abnormal earnings model makes it explicit that value creation depends both on maximizing profit and minimizing capital employed. Shell has achieved a high ROCE through tight control of its capital. In order to grow, however, growth in capital expenditure is required; and in order to achieve growth in value creation, this new capital expenditure must generate a positive rate of return spread. Alternatively stated, achieving faster growth in shareholder value than in book value requires the expectation of positive abnormal earnings on new investment.

This discussion has shown that shareholder value can be expressed in terms of book value and earnings, without direct reference to dividends. Between them, lifecycle book value and earnings can be used to derive lifecycle dividends, and thereby shareholder value. If shareholder value exceeds book value, then future abnormal earnings must exist. When discounted to present value, these abnormal earnings will be precisely equal to the value of goodwill. This must be the case because the method of calculating abnormal earnings reconciles their present value to the opening book value and the underlying dividend payments. In short, the value of a company can be expressed as follows

shareholder value
= current book value + present value of future abnormal earnings

$$P_0 = B_0 + \frac{A_1}{(1+k)} + \frac{A_2}{(1+k)^2} + \ldots + \frac{A_N}{(1+k)^N}$$

Or, in summary form

$$P_0 = B_0 + \sum_{t=1}^{\infty} \frac{A_t}{(1 + k)^t}$$

The intuition behind this model has been outlined above. It is also helpful, however, to see a proof of the derivation of the model, demonstrating that it is formally equivalent to the DDM. This proof is provided in the Appendix.

In the numerical example just given, the opening book value was zero, such that shareholder value was equal simply to the discounted value of abnormal earnings. The example can now be extended by the introduction of a positive opening book value. This will illustrate that the abnormal earnings model assumes, in effect, that the return on equity comprises a normal and an abnormal element. Suppose, for example, that the book value started at $1 000 and earned a normal return of 10% each year. Adding to this the abnormal return from the example above gives us Table 9.2.

Table 9.2 Combining book value with abnormal earnings

	Year 1	Year 2	Total
Opening book value (B_t)	1 000	1 100	
Cash flow – normal	100	100	
Cash flow – abnormal	0	150	
Total net cash flow (C_{t+1})	100	250	
Capitalization/write-off	100	−100	
Normal earnings	100	110	
Abnormal earnings (A_{t+1})	100	40	
Total earnings (E_{t+1})	200	150	
Discounted abnormal earnings	90.9	33.1	124
Discounted cash flow/dividends (includes repayment at end of year 2 of original capital investment)	91	1 033	1 124
Shareholder value (= opening book value + discounted abnormal earnings)	1 124		

This example simply adds a $1 000 book value with a constant ROE to the previous example. In both years, cash flows and earnings are $100 higher and book value is $1 000 higher. Shareholder value can be calculated in one of two ways. It is either the discounted value of dividends, or else it is the opening book value (which generates a normal rate of return) plus the discounted value of abnormal earnings. Notice that the shareholder value would be equal to the book value only if a normal return was made. The abnormal earnings model effectively takes a normal return on equity as a starting point, and is therefore able to derive shareholder value by adding book value to the present value of abnormal earnings.

A numerical illustration will help to reinforce this discussion, and the drinks vendor example from Chapter 5 is therefore reproduced in Table 9.3.

Table 9.3 Abnormal earnings valuation

	Year 1	Year 2	Year 3	Year 4	Year 5
Opening book value (B_t)	10 000	8 000	7 500	8 500	10 500
Sales	2 400	4 800	7 200	8 800	14 400
Cost of sales	(900)	(1 800)	(2 700)	(3 300)	(5 400)
Admin costs	(1 500)	(1 500)	(1 500)	(1 500)	(1 500)
Net cash flow (C_{t+1})	–	1 500	3 000	4 000	7 500
Depreciation	(2 000)	(2 000)	(2 000)	(2 000)	(2 000)
Earnings (E_{t+1})	(2 000)	(500)	1 000	2 000	5 500
Return on equity (R_{t+1})	−20.00%	−6.25%	13.33%	23.53%	52.38%
Closing book value (B_{t+1})	8 000	7 500	8 500	10 500	16 000
Normal earnings	900	720	675	765	945
Abnormal earnings (A_{t+1})	(2 900)	(1 220)	325	1 235	4 555
Discount factor	0.92	0.84	0.77	0.71	0.65
Discounted abnormal earnings	(2 661)	(1 027)	251	875	2 960
Present value abnormal earnings	399				
Shareholder value (= opening book value + discounted abnormal earnings)	10 399				
Shareholder value (= discounted dividends)	10 399				

As discussed earlier, this example contains only two cash flows to shareholders. There is a £10 000 outflow at the beginning of year 1, and a £16 000 inflow when the company ceases trading at the end of year 5. Shareholder value is equal to the discounted value of the cash inflow, which is £10 399, as shown in the final row of Table 9.3. The table illustrates that this same valuation is attainable by adding the opening book value, £10 000, to the present value of abnormal earnings, £399. Indeed, the present value of abnormal earnings is simply the net present value of the investment. It reflects the economic return over the life of the investment relative to the shareholders' required rate of return.[5]

A key feature of the abnormal earnings valuation model is that it holds true regardless of the method of accounting employed by a company. As long as data are available for the whole life of the company, and as long as the clean surplus relationship holds, then book value and earnings data allow the underlying dividends to be valued. In this context, asset valuation and earnings measurement do not matter. To illustrate this, a simple change can be made to the depreciation policy in the example above, allowing the asset to be written-off at a faster rate in year 1 than in year 2. This is shown in Table 9.4.

The change in depreciation policy changes the accounting measures of earnings and return on equity in the first two years. While the underlying economics

---

[5] Hence the use of the term 'economic value added'.

Table 9.4 Abnormal earnings valuation with a change in accounting policy

	Year 1	Year 2	Year 3	Year 4	Year 5
Opening book value (B_t)	10 000	7 500	7 500	8 500	10 500
Net cash flow (C_{t+1})	–	1 500	3 000	4 000	7 500
Depreciation	(2 500)	(1 500)	(2 000)	(2 000)	(2 000)
Earnings (E_{t+1})	(2 500)	–	1 000	2 000	5 500
Return on equity (R_{t+1})	−25.00%	0.00%	13.33%	23.53%	52.38%
Closing book value (B_{t+1})	7 500	7 500	8 500	10 500	16 000
Abnormal earnings (A_{t+1})	(3 400)	(675)	325	1 235	4 555
Discounted abnormal earnings	(3 119)	(568)	251	875	2 960
Shareholder value (= opening book value + discounted abnormal earnings)	10 399				
Shareholder value (= discounted dividends)	10 399				

of the company are unaltered, a reliance on accounting measures alone would give investors a different impression of the company. In particular, the change in accounting policy makes the performance appear to be worse in the first year, but dramatically improved in the second. This illusory difference is consistent with the analysis in Chapters 6, 7 and 8 of the difficulty in deriving economic meaning from accounting measures of book value, earnings and return on equity.

Notice, however, that the shareholder value derived by the abnormal earnings valuation model is not 'fooled' by the change in accounting policy, and it still gives the correct answer. For example, the new depreciation policy gives a value of £(2 500) for earnings in year 1 and £7 500 for book value at the beginning of year 2, as opposed to £(2 000) and £8 000, respectively. The difference in earnings has a present value of £(458.72). This difference is compensated for, however, by the cost of capital charge in the following year. Under the original policy, the book value at the beginning of year 2 is greater by £500, and the capital charge is therefore also greater by £45. Additionally, the depreciation is greater by £500, due to the later recognition with the original policy. In total, abnormal earnings are lower by £545 for the original policy which, discounted from year 2 to present value, is exactly equal to the £(458.72) present value of the difference arising in year 1.

9.2 Ohlson's variant of the model: links between PE, price–book value and ROE ratios

This chapter has so far demonstrated the theoretical validity of the abnormal earnings model. It now remains to explore the usefulness of the model in practice, viewed from the perspective of the valuation task faced by analysts.

As has been seen, the abnormal earnings valuation model has two components, which are current book value and the present value of future abnormal earnings. The book value component is readily available, and the challenge for valuation is therefore the forecasting and discounting of abnormal earnings. This problem is very similar to that posed by the DDM, because it requires estimation of highly uncertain future business performance. In Chapter 2 it was shown that the problem can be made tractable by making assumptions about the relationship between current and future performance. In particular, it was shown that the assumption of constant growth in dividends allowed the derivation of the DGM that, in turn, allowed *current* dividends to be used to estimate the current share price. Much the same approach can be used with abnormal earnings, although possibly to greater effect. It was argued in Chapter 3 that the value of dividend growth cannot be fully understood without consideration of its underlying determinants, notably the rate of return spread. This makes abnormal earnings a natural focus, because they arise whenever the rate of return spread differs from zero. In estimating the relationship between current and future abnormal earnings, the analyst must therefore consider directly the competitive environment in which the company operates, and the likely extent and duration of the company's ability to make abnormal returns. In contrast to dividend-based valuation, the analysis is therefore more likely to be grounded in the economic fundamentals of the company. The strength of the abnormal earnings valuation model is that it addresses these determinants of value creation directly, while maintaining a valuation framework consistent with the DDM.

If a relationship can be assumed between current and future abnormal earnings, then currently available information on book value and on abnormal earnings can be used to estimate the share price. While such a relationship could take one of many different forms, Ohlson (1995) has proposed a particularly important model. Ohlson's model makes the underlying assumption that, in a competitive economic environment, abnormal earnings are likely to be temporary. If, for example, a company enjoys a positive rate of return spread, then this is likely to attract competition, forcing returns to fall towards the cost of capital. Specifically, Ohlson proposes a 'persistence parameter' that measures the sustainability of abnormal earnings. If a company can continue to achieve abnormal earnings for a prolonged period, then these earnings are said to be relatively persistent. Ohlson's persistence parameter is denoted as ω and defined as the relationship between abnormal earnings in two consecutive years, as follows[6]

$$A_{t+1} = \omega A_t$$

To illustrate, suppose that a company has a book value of $1 000, an expected ROE in the current year of 15%, a cost of capital of 10% and a persistence parameter of 80%. The company is expected to generate abnormal earnings of $50 in the current year and, using the model above, $40 in the following year.

------

[6] This is actually a simplified version of Ohlson's model. This simplification does not compromise the insights of the model. See Rees (1995) for an excellent introduction to the full Ohlson model, and Walker (1997) for a more advanced review.

Ohlson imposes two assumptions on the model which are, first, that the value of the persistence parameter lies between 0 and 1 and, second, that any given persistence parameter is constant over time. Taken together, these assumptions ensure that, over time, abnormal earnings become gradually closer and closer to 0. The higher the persistence in abnormal earnings, the longer it takes for the return on equity and the cost of capital to converge; but it is not possible within the model for the two to diverge and for the rate of return spread to grow.

The assumption of a constant persistence parameter allows the use of current abnormal earnings to predict future abnormal earnings, and thereby current share price. For every $1 of abnormal earnings that a company expects to achieve in the current year, it is expected to earn (according the equation above) ω in the following year, ω^2 in the year after that year, and then ω^3, and so on. In total, every dollar earned in the most recent year therefore has a present value equal to a perpetuity cash flow that starts at ω and grows at a rate of $(\omega - 1)$ each year.[7] This present value may be termed the price-abnormal earnings (PA) ratio because, similarly to the PE ratio, it is the multiple that converts current abnormal earnings into shareholder value. The method of valuing this perpetuity is the same as that employed in the DGM, where ω and $\omega - 1$ are the analogues of dividends (D) and dividend growth (g), respectively. The present value of $1 of abnormal earnings is therefore calculated as follows:

$$\textit{present value of \$1 of current abnormal earnings} = \textit{PA ratio} = \frac{\omega}{k + 1 - \omega}$$

Using this expression, the abnormal earnings valuation model can now be presented as follows

$$P_0 = B_0 + \left(\frac{\omega}{k + 1 - \omega}\right)A_0$$

As abnormal earnings persistence increases, so the numerator in the PA multiple rises and the denominator falls, with both effects increasing the value of abnormal earnings. For a given shareholder value, the persistence of abnormal earnings therefore determines the 'split' of value between book value and discounted abnormal earnings.

This expression can be used to illustrate the inter-relationship between the PE, price–book value and PA ratios. Consider the extreme cases where the value of the persistence parameter, ω, is either 0 or 1. If it equals 0, then the PA ratio is also 0, and price equals book value. This is simply because zero persistence implies that, whatever the level of abnormal earnings in the most recent period, expected future abnormal earnings are equal to 0. In other words, the rate of return spread remains constant and equal to 0. The company might be expected to grow, but the growth is not expected to create or to destroy value for shareholders. This is the case of windfall gains. If, as discussed in Chapter 7, earnings are entirely transitory, then they affect future earnings only indirectly through

---

[7] For example, if abnormal earnings are $50 and ω equals 0.8, the abnormal earnings grow at the negative rate of (20)%, equal to $\omega - 1$.

a change in book value. In Ohlson's model in this case, the expected return on equity is equal to the cost of capital and the PE ratio is at its normal level.

At the other extreme, the value of the persistence parameter is 1, and the PA ratio becomes equal to 1 over the cost of capital. The company is able to sustain a constant return on equity that differs from the cost of capital, and abnormal earnings are constant in perpetuity. This requires, in fact, that all earnings are either paid out as dividends or re-invested at a return equal to the cost of capital. Otherwise, the retention of earnings would allow growth in abnormal earnings, causing the persistence parameter to exceed 1. In turn, and as will be recalled from Chapter 4, this assumption of constant abnormal earnings in perpetuity implies that there is a constant PE ratio, equal to 1 over the cost of capital.[8] The share price can therefore be expressed in terms of just current earnings and the cost of capital, or alternatively in terms of current book value, current abnormal earnings and the cost of capital. The proof of this is very straightforward, and it is now presented to support the discussion. If the persistence parameter equals 1, then we have the following[9]

$$P_0 = B_0 + \frac{1}{k}A_1$$

Given the definition of abnormal earnings, this can be re-stated as follows

$$P_0 = B_0 + \frac{E_1 - B_0 k}{k} = \frac{B_0 k + E_1 - B_0 k}{k} = \frac{E_1}{k}$$

To illustrate, suppose that a company is started with capital of $10 000, a cost of capital of 10% and an expected constant return on equity of 20%. Annual earnings are $2 000 and abnormal earnings are a constant $1 000. The share price is $20 000. This can be determined as either earnings over the cost of capital ($2 000/0.1) or book value ($10 000) plus abnormal earnings divided by the cost of capital ($1 000/0.1). The PE ratio equals the PA ratio, because both earnings and abnormal earnings are constant in perpetuity, allowing both to be capitalized at the cost of capital.

This discussion has shown that, within Ohlson's model, when the persistence parameter on abnormal earnings is either 0 or 1, price equals either book value or earnings divided by the cost of capital, respectively. In other words, the persistence of abnormal earnings determines the relative importance of book value and earnings in valuation. This is best seen, in fact, when the persistence parameter lies somewhere between 0 and 1, such that neither the price–book value ratio nor the price–earnings ratio can be interpreted independently of one another. Table 9.5 illustrates the range of possibilities. It uses the insights of the abnormal earnings valuation model to summarize the relationships between the PE and price–book value ratios.

---

[8] Notice that the assumption of zero growth in abnormal earnings ensures that the PE ratio cannot exceed its normal level. This is the same case that was explored in Chapter 3, where the rate of return spread was constant and positive and the retention ratio was 0.

[9] Note that, since abnormal earnings are constant, A_0 equals A_1.

Table 9.5 Joint behaviour of PE and price–book value ratios

	P–BV ratio > 1	P–BV ratio = 1	P–BV ratio < 1
PE ratio above normal	Expected positive abnormal earnings, though current earnings below sustainable level and expected to grow.	Earnings transitorily below normal level. Otherwise, zero abnormal earnings expected.	Expected negative abnormal earnings, though current earnings below sustainable level and expected to grow.
Normal PE ratio	Constant, positive abnormal earnings.	Zero rate of return spread (zero abnormal earnings).	Constant, negative abnormal earnings.
PE ratio below normal	Expected positive abnormal earnings, though current earnings above sustainable level and expected to fall.	Earnings transitorily above normal level. Otherwise, zero abnormal earnings expected.	Expected negative abnormal earnings, though current earnings above sustainable level and expected to fall.

To illustrate, a PE ratio above its normal level suggests that current earnings are transitorily low with respect to their sustainable trend. In itself, though, the PE ratio cannot reveal whether or not a company is creating value for its shareholders. As Table 9.5 shows, this additional information is available from a joint evaluation with the price–book value ratio. If the price–book value ratio exceeds 1, then the return on equity is expected to exceed the cost of capital. Combined with a PE ratio above normal, this suggests that earnings growth is expected to be value creating. Conversely, if the price–book value ratio is less than 1, then a higher-than-normal PE ratio suggests that earnings are expected to recover, but that their sustainable level is below that required to create shareholder value.

Interpreting PE and price–book value ratios

Martin Kohlhaussen (of Commerzbank) . . . balked at the €800m Banco Santander Central Hispano wanted for CC Bank, its German consumer credit unit . . . CC Bank has been growing fast. But €800m – 25 times historic earnings and 7 times book value – looked rich . . . (meanwhile) Commerzbank has lagged behind the European banking sector by 40 per cent in the last five years. At least, trading barely above book value, it is hard to imagine the shares going much lower.

Source: Financial Times, Lex Column, 24 October 2000

A sales price of €800m for CC Bank corresponds to a PE ratio well in excess of a normal level and a price–book value ratio well above 1. If the price is to be justified, then not only are future abnormal earnings expected to be positive, but current earnings must be very significantly below their sustainable level. In the event, Commerzbank took the view that the price was not justified by the fundamentals. Commerzbank might, however, take the opposite view of its own share price. Its price–book value ratio of approximately 1 implies that the market does not expect the company to generate abnormal earnings. If Commerzbank values its assets at market values, then this is no cause for concern. If, however, net assets are stated conservatively, then the accounting policies alone should lead to positive abnormal earnings being reported in the future, and the expectation of zero abnormal earnings would therefore equate to the company having lost shareholder value.

Consider also the following example:

The strength of the housing market helped buoy results of Bellway, one of the top 10 house-builders (in the UK) . . . pre-tax profit rose 31 per cent to £89.1m on turnover 26 per cent higher at £634m in the year to July 31 . . . Earnings per share rose 32 per cent to 55.4p . . . Bellway said its net asset value was 289p per share, a 17 per cent increase on a year ago and a mere 12p above the level at which its shares closed yesterday . . . Charterhouse Securities has upgraded its forecast for Bellway's pre-tax profit this year to £99m for earnings of 61.8p. This represents a prospective multiple of only 4.5.

Source: Financial Times, 18 October 2000

A normal PE ratio of 4.5 would imply a cost of capital of 22%. This is rather high, suggesting that Bellway is trading at a PE ratio below normal. Meanwhile, its price–book value ratio is only marginally above 1. Taken together, this evidence suggests that the market does not believe Bellway's current earnings performance to be sustainable. This would be consistent with the housing market nearing the top of its economic cycle.

9.3 Accounting and valuation problems that the model does not avoid

Valuation using the abnormal earnings model appears to be straightforward. Since the current book value is readily available, all that is required is to explain the difference between shareholder value and book value, and this can be done by forecasting and discounting abnormal earnings. Unfortunately, however, this dramatically over-simplifies the valuation problem. It does so because it seems to imply that book value and abnormal earnings are independent of one another. In practice, we cannot just take book value as given and try to explain goodwill independently, because the value of goodwill is itself dependent upon that of book value (and vice versa). Indeed, and as explained above, it is precisely this inter-dependence that allows the abnormal earnings model to 'work'.

This inter-dependence is of very considerable practical importance. The value of a company depends entirely upon the present value of the cash flows that it generates. The book value, by contrast, depends upon the asset valuations determined by the accountant. For a given pattern of cash flows, and therefore a given shareholder value, the book values at any point in time can be whatever they like. Any change in accounting policy that changes book value does not lead to a change in shareholder value, but only to a change in the present value of abnormal earnings. In other words, the value of the company is in no way determined by the book value of the assets.[10] It depends only upon cash flows, and the value

---

[10] This is explained by Bierman (1996), who states simply that 'the equity value is not a function of book value'.

of these cash flows can (in principle) be divided in any way whatsoever between book value and discounted abnormal earnings. While the sum of these two parts must add to shareholder value, their relative size depends upon accounting conventions, such as conservatism and accruals. In short, the expression of shareholder value in terms of book value and abnormal earnings can be misleading.

A different way to look at this problem is to remember that the abnormal earnings model is formally equivalent to the DDM. This being the case, the requirements of the model to forecast book values and earnings are no different, in fact, from the requirement to forecast dividends. The model is valid because knowledge of future book values and earnings is equivalent to knowledge of future dividends. Or, alternatively, the models are formally equivalent because they are based upon precisely the same information. This being the case, it is difficult to argue that one model is necessarily superior to the other. Again, the benefit of splitting value into its book value and abnormal earnings components is somewhat illusory.

If, in spite of this, the abnormal earnings approach does actually have incremental benefits to the DDM, then this is not because it somehow contains more information. It does not. Any benefit must therefore arise in the way in which the information is presented and in the effect that this has upon the user's understanding of valuation. There must, in fact, be something that is neither arbitrary nor illusory about treating book value and abnormal earnings separately from one another.

An apparently obvious attraction in a model such as Ohlson's is the economic intuition behind the notion of a persistence parameter. Such a parameter could equally be defined for dividends, of course (it would simply be 1 plus the growth rate), but Ohlson's parameter has the benefit of being linked to the ROE, and thereby to both the underlying economics of the company and to the structure of the company's accounting data. There are, however, two significant problems in using Ohlson's persistence parameter, each of which is fairly subtle and not immediately apparent.

The first problem is that Ohlson's persistence parameter does not escape the issue of forecasting dividends. While the abnormal earnings model might appear to be independent of dividends, in fact it is not. This is because (as was seen in Chapter 3) a company's rate of new investments affects its value. If any direct relationship is assumed between current earnings and future earnings, then it must contain a further assumption about dividends, whether hidden or otherwise. As was indicated above, the assumption of a constant persistence parameter in Ohlson's model actually forces one of only two possible assumptions about future dividends: either that all earnings are paid out as dividends, or that re-invested earnings generate a return equal to the cost of capital. These two assumptions are familiar from the discussion in Chapters 2, 3 and 4. They are the very assumptions that render dividend policy irrelevant.[11]

While it may have seemed innocuous to assume that abnormal earnings are related across years by means of a persistence parameter, it now becomes clear

---

[11] See Lundholm (1995) and Bierman (1996) for an expanded discussion.

that such an assumption is highly restrictive. The assumption of dividend irrelevance is equivalent to the assumption that *all* new investment projects undertaken by a company will have zero net present value. If we add to this the assumption implied in the persistence parameter that existing capital will generate a return that declines at a predictable rate, then we are left concluding that the analyst's valuation task is remarkably straightforward. All he or she needs to do, the model contends, is take an unadjusted measure of book value and abnormal earnings, and then estimate a persistence parameter. If only it could be that simple! The model denies the very real problem that analysts face in forecasting non-zero net present value. Additionally, it precludes the possibility that dividends can be used to signal value (which, as discussed in Chapter 2, is an important justification for the dividend growth model).

In addition to this issue of the incremental investment associated with dividend policy, there is a second fundamental problem with Ohlson's model. This concerns the return on equity earned on existing assets. The simple assumption that the ROE will decline over time towards the cost of capital is, indeed, simple. It would be so even if the accounting-based measure of ROE had a reliable economic significance, but it is especially so given the practical problems with the ROE discussed in Chapter 8. When looking at the abnormal earnings model, we see a series of ROEs, continuing indefinitely from the current year on. At first sight, it is tempting to think that the values ROE_1 and ROE_3 (for example) must somehow be related to one another. After all, they are the same variable, just in different time periods, and we are reassured by the knowledge that the mechanics of the abnormal earnings model ensure their economic relevance.

Chapter 8 has shown, however, that the economic relationship between ROEs is very far from straightforward. It is not possible to simply extrapolate the current ROE to give future ROEs, yet this is precisely what the persistence parameter requires. In other words, the persistence parameter attributes economic relevance to a variable that might, in practice, be highly distorted. It is true, of course, that if the analyst understands the extent of this distortion, then he or she can impute the correct persistence parameter. But this just means that the abnormal earnings model is in no way a solution to the practical problems of measuring and forecasting accounting information. Before the analyst can extrapolate existing accounting data, he or she must understand its relationship to the underlying economic fundamentals of the company. In short, he or she must appreciate the difficulties outlined in earlier chapters.

This can be seen by reviewing the analyst's task in forecasting ROE. First, he or she must forecast earnings. This requires a forecast of operating cash flows and accruals (and also of dividend policy and capital expenditure). Since the accruals are merely allocations of cash flows between time periods, as reflected in changes in the balance sheet, then the critical component of forecasted earnings is forecasted cash flows. Indeed, the abnormal earnings model explicitly 'corrects' accruals in order to reveal the underlying cash flows. Assumptions such as the rate of depreciation turn out to be irrelevant to the valuation. Second, the analyst must forecast the balance sheet. This does not, however, require any more information than has already been used in forecasting earnings. Third, the analyst can derive future

ROEs by simply dividing the forecasts for earnings by those for book values. The ROEs are therefore secondary calculations, and while their value in each period will depend in part upon the forecasting of accruals, it is the forecast of future cash flows that really determines their economic significance. This must, of course, be the case because value depends upon cash flows. It is misleading to think that we are forecasting earnings, book values and ROEs when, in reality, we are using a model that forces these variables to be consistent with our underlying assumptions about cash flows and dividends.

The very strengths of the abnormal earnings valuation model are therefore also its weaknesses. If the model allows any method whatsoever of asset valuation and earnings measurement, then the model simply ignores the very real practical problems faced by analysts in interpreting financial statement data. This is a serious issue, although one which proponents of the model tend to gloss over. The discussion of book value and earnings in Chapters 5–8 focused on the difficulty of measuring *periodic* performance. The abnormal earnings model is, however, silent on this measurement issue. Indeed, the model 'works' precisely because it renders irrelevant the issue of periodic asset valuation and earnings measurement. While the interaction between book value and abnormal earnings ensures the equivalence of the abnormal earnings model with the dividend discount model, it also deprives book value and earnings of any underlying economic meaning within the model. This is not very helpful. The analyst must, in practice, use a periodic measure of performance as a means of extrapolating future performance, and the accounts must provide such a measure.

A related problem with the abnormal earnings model is that of measuring terminal value. In just the same way that dividend-based valuation must, in practice, use an estimate of terminal value at the end of a forecast horizon, so too must the abnormal earnings model. An added difficulty, however, is that the formal equivalence of the two models relies upon book value and earnings data being available for the whole life of an investment. If, in practice, the available data are truncated, then shareholder value is no longer precisely defined by the sum of book value and discounted abnormal earnings. Instead, there will be an error term, equal to the value of goodwill at the end of the forecast horizon. This error term arises because the limited book value data cannot be used to estimate total lifetime dividends. This may or may not turn out to be serious. If the forecast horizon is long, then there will be only a small present value of goodwill. If, as is likely, the forecast horizon is fairly short, with goodwill a significant component of terminal value, then the estimation error from an abnormal earnings model could turn out to be large. This is another manifestation of the (now familiar) difficulty posed by asset valuation in the accounts.

To summarize the discussion so far, it has been argued that the abnormal earnings model uses the same data as the DDM, except in a different format. The use of abnormal earnings does not escape the need to forecast dividends any more than the forecasting of dividends escapes the need to forecast earnings. Moreover, the forecasting of abnormal earnings is not straightforward, because it relies upon the use of existing accounting information. The abnormal earnings model does not, in fact, offer any guidance on how book values and earnings

Table 9.6 Abnormal earnings valuation

	Year 1	Year 2	Year 3	Year 4	Year 5
Opening book value (B_t)					
Operating cash flow (C_{t+1})	2 800	2 600	3 400	3 200	3 500
Depreciation	(1 600)	(1 680)	(1 944)	(1 855)	(1 884)
Earnings (E_{t+1})	1 200	920	1 456	1 345	1 616
Capital expenditure	−2 000	−3 000	−1 500	−2 000	−1 500
Dividends	600	460	728	672	808
Closing book value (B_{t+1})	10 600	11 060	11 788	12 460	13 268
Terminal value (end year 5)					16 158
Return on equity (R_{t+1})	12.0%	8.7%	13.2%	11.4%	13.0%
Abnormal earnings (A_{t+1})	200	(140)	350	166	370
Discounted abnormal earnings	182	(116)	263	113	230
Discounted dividends	545	380	547	459	502

Opening book value	10 000
+ discounted abnormal earnings	672
+ discounted goodwill, end year 5	1 795
Shareholder value	12 467
Discounted dividends	2 433
+ discounted terminal value	10 033
Shareholder value	12 467

should be measured, and it is therefore difficult to implement. This is illustrated in Table 9.6, which shows a valuation based upon a five-year forecast and an estimate of terminal value at the end of the forecast horizon. The company is assumed to have an opening book value of $10 000, which is comprised of $8 000 in depreciable assets and $2 000 in cash. The assets are incremented each year by capital expenditure, and depreciation is charged at 20% each year on the book value of the depreciable assets. The example assumes some fluctuation in annual operating cash flows. A 50% dividend payout ratio is assumed. The terminal value is based upon an assumption that year 5 dividends will grow at a constant rate of 5%, which is consistent with an ongoing ROE of 10%. On the basis of this terminal value, the company has an internal rate of return of 13%.

This simple example illustrates a number of points. First, the forecasts for book value are affected directly by the forecasts for dividends, because of the need to forecast retentions. This affects the valuation if, as is likely, the economic return on retained earnings differs from the cost of capital. Second, the ROE varies in each year. In year 5 it happens to be precisely equal to the IRR, although in year 3 it is marginally greater, and in years 1, 2 and 4 it is lower, falling as low as 8.7%. If the analyst happened to have data for just the first two years, then it is likely that an ROE significantly below the IRR would be assumed. There is therefore no simple sense in which a persistence parameter can be applied to these data.

Third, abnormal earnings are variable across years, and they even become negative in year 2. This illustrates that abnormal earnings must be viewed over a period of a number of years, and not in isolation. Indeed, this is complicated by the existence of goodwill, whereby the distribution of abnormal earnings between the forecast horizon and the terminal value is affected by the method of asset valuation used at the end of year 5.[12] Fourth, shareholder value can be derived in one of two ways. Either discounted dividends can be added to terminal value, or else opening book value can be added to discounted abnormal earnings and discounted terminal goodwill. The approach taken is just the same as that which was recommended for dividend-based valuation, namely the use of a forecast horizon and a terminal value. Finally, while the abnormal earnings and the DDMs may have the same data requirements, the abnormal earnings model has the benefit that the data are structured in the form of accounting information. This is no small advantage, because it allows analysts' earnings forecasts and companies' financial statements to play a more direct role in equity valuation.

9.4 EVA – a special case of the abnormal earnings valuation model

The discussion so far has focused on the general abnormal earnings model, with respect to which EVA is a special case. This section will now focus on the EVA model.

The difference between the EVA model and the general abnormal earnings model is that the former imposes a specific method of accounting, whereas the latter does not. This is important because of its implications for the measurement of periodic economic performance. Different methods of accounting give different periodic measures of book value and earnings. Abnormal earnings can therefore differ across periods according to the method of accounting used, even though the sum of the present values of abnormal earnings will remain the same. Within the EVA model, a series of adjustments are made to reported financial statement data, with the aim of generating a superior measure of abnormal earnings. For it to be possible to generate a superior measure in this way, the method of accounting underpinning EVA must give greater economic meaning to annual book values and earnings than would otherwise be the case. In short, the EVA model must generate a measure of return on equity that can be more meaningfully compared with the cost of capital, giving a superior measure of value-added during a period of time. This possibility is of considerable practical importance, of course, because historic performance is used as a basis from which to forecast

---

[12] Goodwill at the end of year 5 is $2 890 (equal to terminal value of $16 158 less book value of $13 268). If book valuation had been, say, higher, then abnormal earnings during year 5 would have been higher, with the discounted value of goodwill correspondingly lower. Likewise, abnormal earnings in years 1–4 could also have been 'traded off' against terminal value.

future performance, and forecasts for the near future feed directly into estimates of terminal value.

Stern Stewart do not disclose fully the precise adjustments made to financial statement data in generating EVA. This is an understandable protection of a proprietary process. There is, however, plenty of guidance in Stern Stewart's published literature (e.g. Stewart, 1991), and a reading of this literature gives a fairly comprehensive view of the nature, purpose and effects of the various adjustments. Additionally, an excellent (and independent) review can be found in O'Hanlon and Peasnell (1998).[13]

Perhaps the most important of Stern Stewart's adjustments concerns the undoing of accounting conservatism, not least because there is typically a very considerable degree of conservatism in financial statements. In particular, and of increasing practical importance, intangible assets such as R&D, training, advertising, software development and the like, are rarely recognized in practice. These expenditures share a defining characteristic of capital expenditure on tangible assets, namely that they are incurred with a view to generating cash flow benefits in future years. They differ, however, in that their value is more subjective and uncertain. In Stern Stewart's view, the similarity is more important than the difference, and intangible assets should be capitalized and amortized, in precisely the same way as tangible assets. This is likely to give a more sensible measure of abnormal earnings, because it shifts the book value of shareholders' invested capital closer to a 'true' measure of how much has been invested in expectation of a future return. Consider, for example, an R&D expenditure that does not start to pay off until ten years after it is made. If this expenditure is capitalized in the balance sheet rather than written-off, and if an associated cost of capital is charged in the income statement, then a better picture of the company's economic performance is given. An asset is shown because economic benefits have yet to be realized, and a cost of capital is charged because an annual return is demanded on the shareholders' funds that are tied up. Also, the asset can be written-off against its income stream from year 10 onwards, with the annual EVA matching revenues and costs and giving a measure of whether or not value is being created for shareholders.[14]

It is important to recognize, however, that this method of calculating EVA does not attempt to capture economic earnings. Conceptually, it differs from 'traditional' accruals accounting only in so far as, first, there is a greater emphasis on matching in preference to conservatism and, second, a cost of capital is charged. The critical difference between EVA and economic earnings can be illustrated using Stern Stewart's own metric, Market Value Added (MVA). The term MVA is

---

[13] O'Hanlon and Peasnell suggest that Stern Stewart's adjustments fall into three broad categories: the undoing of accounting conservatism; the discouragement of earnings management; and the immunization of performance measurement against past accounting 'errors'.

[14] There are plenty of further examples that could be used. To take an important one, purchased goodwill should be held on the balance sheet to the extent that its value is not impaired, since this best reflects shareholders' invested capital. Purchased goodwill should not be revalued upwards, since this would anticipate future EVA.

used to mean goodwill in the special case where abnormal earnings are defined using the EVA model. In other words, MVA is the sum of the present values of EVA for a given company. Since EVA is calculated using capitalized costs, with book value intended to measure invested capital, whereas MVA includes all future cash flows, the two measures are fundamentally different. EVA does not measure changes in MVA, in much the same way that accounting earnings for a period do not measure changes in goodwill (see Chapter 7). Both EVA and accounting earnings are historic measures that record realized performance. Neither is a model of economic earnings, where book value would record the present value of all expected future cash flows. In this sense, EVA is not really a measure of economic value-added at all. In fact, this is probably a good thing, because EVA is attempting to measure economic performance in the period in which it occurred, rather than anticipating future performance. This is more useful to analysts, since they are using historic performance measures to, first, understand the accuracy of forecasts for the period and, second, to extrapolate this performance into future periods. The EVA model sensibly does not confuse the value of invested capital (measured by book value) with the returns made on this capital (measured by EVA). In so doing, the model does not measure economic earnings. If a value-creating investment decision is made in the current period, then this is unlikely to be reflected until the EVA of future periods is measured. Value can therefore be created, as measured by MVA, but EVA will not capture it.

A second, and more fundamental issue concerning EVA is whether or not, as presumed above, meaningful and reliable measurement of invested capital and annual performance can really be achieved by means of simple adjustments to reported financial statement data. In fact, there are many reasons to suppose that it cannot. Despite protestations to the contrary, EVA appears to introduce even more subjectivity into accounting than would normally be the case. Deciding what should be capitalized as an intangible asset and what should not is far from straightforward; and having capitalized, the problem remains of the time period and the methodology to be used for amortization. Other areas of subjectivity in the accounts remain, also, such as inventory valuation and revenue recognition. Stern Stewart make some attempt to reduce earnings management by means of eliminating general provisions, but the effect of this on the informativeness of earnings measurement is unclear. Indeed, taking this and other factors into account, O'Hanlon and Peasnell (1998) conclude their review of the EVA adjustments with the following statement:

> The various Stern Stewart accounting adjustments . . . are essentially *ad hoc* in character. It is unclear whether they fit together . . . even after the 'tailoring' process, positive EVA will not necessarily signal superior management performance, nor will negative EVA indicate that value has been destroyed.

Ultimately, empirical data must be used to test whether or not the EVA method of accounting yields superior measures of periodic economic performance. Some research has been done on this subject, and it is reported in the next section of this chapter.

EVA in practice

Tate & Lyle, the sweeteners group . . . yesterday gave the stock market a pleasant surprise when it reported better than expected figures for the 12 months to September 25. Pre-tax profits were up 35 per cent to £223m. The shares jumped 27p to 427p . . . Part of the profit improvement was put down to the application of EVA (economic value added) performance measures which had motivated managers to maximise returns. Simon Gifford, finance director, said the process has also improved the balance sheet far more than anticipated. The introduction of EVA had also convinced the group to make more disposals of non-core assets or even core assets that did not make target returns.

Source: *Financial Times*, Observer Column, 5 November 2000

Tate & Lyle's use of EVA enabled a better focus on value creation, not least in helping to identify whether invested capital was failing to achieve a positive rate of return spread. Since the company's in-house financial statements (i.e. management accounts) do not need to conform to financial reporting standards, they can incorporate policies on asset valuation and profit recognition that maximize their economic relevance. In principle, the in-house numbers could be disclosed to investors, although this is rarely done in practice and investors have to rely on making their own adjustments to reported data.

9.5 Empirical evidence on abnormal earnings valuation and EVA

In any valuation model, the problem of terminal value is likely to be considerable. This is simply because the future is uncertain, and reliable forecasts can be made for a limited period only. The importance of the terminal value calculation appears, at first sight, to be much greater for dividend-based valuation than for the abnormal earnings model, suggesting that the latter has an advantage. For example, Bernard (1995) compared, over a four-year forecast period, book value and expected earnings with expected dividends. He found that the variation in share price across companies was much more readily explained using book value and earnings rather than dividends, suggesting that the estimation of terminal value is more problematic for a dividend-based model.[15] Unfortunately, results such as these can be misleading. As was discussed earlier in the chapter, the information required to estimate either an abnormal earnings model or a dividend-based model is actually the same. The only way that an abnormal earnings model can be superior to any other approach is if it provides a more effective basis with which to understand and to extrapolate economic performance. This has been tested directly in a number of ways, and the conclusions are generally rather discouraging.

Dechow, Hutton and Sloan (1999) tested explicitly the persistence parameter in Ohlson's model, with the aim of demonstrating that the economic insights of

---

[15] The R-squared of the book value/earnings model was 68%, while that of the dividends model was only 29%.

the model allow a better understanding of valuation. They found weak evidence in support of the assumptions behind the persistence parameter. In particular, abnormal earnings decline over time, and this rate of decline varies according to three factors: first, the quality of earnings (i.e. higher quality earnings are more likely to behave predictably); second, the dividend payout ratio (i.e. higher retention suggests greater value-creation opportunities); and, third, industry (i.e. the economics of different industries vary). Dechow, Hutton and Sloan were not, however, successful in attempting to use Ohlson's model to explain share price behaviour.

Biddle, Bowen and Wallace (1997) address the question of whether or not EVA 'beats earnings'. They test the relationships between share prices and each of earnings, EVA, abnormal earnings and cash flow from operations. On balance, and across a range of tests, they find that changes in share prices and absolute levels of share prices are both marginally better explained by earnings than by the other variables, including EVA. When the measures are used in combination with one another, then each contributes marginally to a better understanding of the share price, although each also contains mostly common information.[16]

While the empirical evidence is somewhat limited at this point in time, its conclusions can best be regarded as somewhat ambivalent. Certainly, there is as yet little evidence to suggest that abnormal earnings in general, or EVA in particular, are a significant improvement on more 'traditional' valuation models.

Summary

The main points from this chapter may be summarized as follows:

- The abnormal earnings valuation model expresses the share price in terms of book value, earnings and the cost of capital. The model is formally equivalent to the DDM, but it uses accounting data rather than dividends. It is entirely general, and it holds true for any and all accounting policies adopted by a company. It is the *only* accounting-based valuation model that does not make any constraining assumptions. This gives the model a unique importance.

- The possibility of expressing the share price in terms of financial statement data arises because of the relationship that exists between book value, earnings and dividends. In each year of a company's life, dividends are equal to earnings less the increase in book value. Over the whole life of a company, aggregate earnings are equal to aggregate dividends, and the net change in book value is 0. If annual book values and earnings are known, then dividends are therefore derivable, such that the abnormal earnings model can be derived from the DDM.

- The model expresses shareholder value as the sum of current book value plus the present value of future abnormal earnings. The model therefore incorporates

---

[16] A possible bias against EVA exists in this test. EVA data published by Stern Stewart use the same accounting adjustments across all companies, whereas a better measure of EVA would be tailored to the specific characteristics of different industries.

a formal expression for goodwill, and it recognizes that shareholder value differs from book value to the extent that the expected rate of return spread differs from 0.

● The abnormal earnings model provides a framework for interpreting the PE and price–book value ratios relative to one another. The model demonstrates that the analysis of either ratio in isolation can be misleading, since their values are co-dependent.

● The abnormal earnings model has two main benefits. First, it utilizes financial statement data consistently with valuation theory, thereby allowing direct links between financial statements, analysts' earnings forecasts and shareholder value. Second, it focuses attention on the rate of return spread, and thereby on the determinants of value creation.

● There are, however, several drawbacks with the model. Book values and abnormal earnings are not independent of one another, but are instead affected jointly by a company's accounting methods. An implication is that annual abnormal earnings (or EVAs) cannot be viewed in isolation, but only in the context of long-run data. Also, the model does not escape the need to forecast dividends or terminal values, and it does not resolve issues of the usefulness of financial statement data in forecasting and valuing financial performance. In short, while the abnormal earnings model contributes to an understanding of the valuation relationships between financial statements and shareholder value, it does not in itself resolve the difficulties of using financial statements to measure economic performance.

References

Bernard, V.L. (1995). 'The Feltham-Ohlson Framework: Implications for Empiricists', *Contemporary Accounting Research*, 11(2), 773–47.

Biddle, G.C., R.M. Bowen and J.S. Wallace (1997). 'Does EVA Beat Earnings? Evidence on Associations with Stock Returns and Firm Values', *Journal of Accounting and Economics*, 24, 301–36.

Bierman, H. (1996). 'Accounting and Equity Valuation', Working paper, Cornell and Cambridge Universities.

Dechow, P.M., A.P. Hutton and R.G. Sloan (1999). 'An Empirical Assessment of the Residual Income Valuation Model', *Journal of Accounting and Economics*, 26, 1–34.

Edwards, E.O. and P.W. Bell (1961). *The Theory and Measurement of Business Income*. Berkeley: California University Press.

Edwards, J.S.S., J.A. Kay and C.P. Mayer (1987). *The Economic Analysis of Accounting Profitability*. Oxford: Oxford University Press.

Feltham, G.A. and J.A. Ohlson (1995). 'Valuation and Clean Surplus Accounting for Operating and Financial Activities', *Contemporary Accounting Research*, 11(2), 689–731.

Lundholm, R.L. (1995). 'A Tutorial on the Ohlson and Feltham/Ohlson Models: Answers to Some Frequently Asked Questions', *Contemporary Accounting Research*, 11(2), 749–61.

Marshall, A. (1890). *Principles of Economics*. London: Macmillan.

O'Hanlon, J. and K. Peasnell (1998). 'Wall Street's Contribution to Management Accounting: The Stern Stewart EVA Financial Management System', *Management Accounting Research*, 9, 421–44.

Ohlson, J.A. (1995). 'Earnings, Book Value and Dividends in Equity Valuation', *Contemporary Accounting Research*, 11(2), 661–87.

Peasnell, K.V. (1982). 'Some Formal Connections Between Economic Values and Yields and Accounting Numbers', *Journal of Business Finance and Accounting*, Autumn, 361–81.

Preinreich, G.A.D. (1938). 'Annual Survey of Economic Theory: The Theory of Depreciation', *Econometrica*, July, 219–41.

Rees, W.P. (1995). *Financial Analysis* (2nd edn). Hemel Hempstead: Prentice Hall International.

Stewart, G.B. (1991). *The Quest for Value*. New York: HarperCollins.

Walker, M. (1997). 'Clean Surplus Accounting Models and Market Based Accounting Research: A Review', *Accounting and Business Research*, 27(4), 341–55.

Appendix — Derivation of the abnormal earnings valuation model

The DDM expresses a company's shareholder value in terms of lifetime dividends, as follows

$$P_t = \frac{D_{t+1}}{(1+k)} + \frac{D_{t+2}}{(1+k)^2} + \frac{D_{t+3}}{(1+k)^3} + \cdots + \frac{D_{t+N}}{(1+k)^N}$$

In order to express shareholder value in terms of book value and earnings, it is first necessary to assume the clean surplus relationship, whereby all gains and losses in shareholders' funds pass through the income statement

$$B_t + E_{t+1} - D_{t+1} = B_{t+1}$$

Rearranging

$$D_{t+1} = E_{t+1} + (B_t - B_{t+1})$$

The next stage is to define abnormal earnings, as follows

$$A_{t+1} = E_{t+1} - B_t k$$

Earnings are therefore equal to abnormal earnings plus the cost of capital charge. The above expression for dividends can therefore be re-written as follows

$$D_{t+1} = A_{t+1} + B_t k + (B_t - B_{t+1})$$

Rearranging and inserting into the dividend discount model gives the following

$$P_t = \frac{A_{t+1} + B_t(1+k) - B_{t+1}}{(1+k)} + \frac{A_{t+2} + B_{t+1}(1+k) - B_{t+2}}{(1+k)^2} + \frac{A_{t+3} + B_{t+2}(1+k) - B_{t+3}}{(1+k)^3} + \cdots$$

This expression simplifies very easily by cancelling terms on the right-hand side, leading to the following

$$P_t = B_t + \sum_{\tau=1}^{\infty} \frac{A_\tau}{(1+k)^\tau}$$

The Feltham and Ohlson (1995) model

This chapter has shown that the abnormal earnings model is valid regardless of the method of asset valuation used in the accounts. The expression of shareholder value as a split between book value (generating 'normal' earnings) and goodwill (the present value of abnormal earnings) is therefore somewhat tautological. The same is not true, however, for Ohlson's (1995) adaptation of the model, since abnormal earnings are competed away to 0, and the implicit assumption is therefore made that the book value of shareholders' equity equates to the capitalized value of normal earnings (i.e. book value has a simple economic meaning and is said to be 'unbiased', as was assumed in Chapters 2–4).

In practice, of course, book values are unlikely to be unbiased, and the assumptions of the Ohlson model are therefore unlikely to hold. This is recognized by Feltham and Ohlson (1995), who extend Ohlson's model to allow for the conservative valuation of operating assets. The Feltham and Ohlson analysis is rather tortuous and esoteric and it will not be repeated here. Nevertheless, there are some useful insights to be gained. A simplified version of the Feltham and Ohlson valuation model is as follows (where oa denotes operating assets):

$$P_t = B_t + \alpha_1 A_t + \alpha_2 oa_t$$

The parameter α_1 depends, as in the Ohlson model, on the persistence of abnormal earnings. The parameter α_2, meanwhile, depends jointly on the persistence of abnormal earnings, the degree of conservatism in the accounts and the rate of growth of operating assets. In the special case where book value is unbiased, the parameter α_2 equals 0 and the model reduces to the Ohlson model. In the general case where operating assets are valued conservatively, abnormal earnings have two components. The first is 'genuine' abnormal earnings, in the sense of economic gains exceeding the cost of capital, and the second is 'artificial' abnormal earnings, which are achieved simply because book value is understated by conservative accounting.

Feltham and Ohlson's model shows that, in the presence of the artificial abnormal earnings created by conservative accounting, abnormal earnings no longer decline at a constant rate towards 0 (as in the Ohlson model). Instead, they include a constant term that equals the artificial abnormal earnings and that is determined by the extent of asset valuation bias. The greater the goodwill, the greater the care required in interpreting the pattern of abnormal earnings over time.

The Edwards, Kay and Mayer (1987) model

A final model worth exploring is that of Edwards, Kay and Mayer (EKM, 1987). The EKM model can be seen as a development and synthesis of both the Kay/Peasnell model (see Chapter 8) and the abnormal earnings model. EKM start by questioning the relevance of the IRR to equity investment decisions. The IRR concerns cash flows over the life of a business, whereas investors (and accounting systems) focus only on performance over a limited segment of this life. EKM define their own measure of the single-period accounting rate of return, denoted ARR, which is the rate of return that discounts cash flows, including the terminal book value of capital employed, back to the initial book value of capital.

The ARR depends for its valuation-relevance upon the valuation of opening and closing capital employed. The insight of the EKM model comes from its valuation of assets at 'deprival value', or 'value-to-the-business'. If a firm is deprived of an asset, then its loss will be equal to the lower of replacement cost (RC) or economic value (EV) and, if the latter, will be the higher of value in current use (PV) or net realizable value (NRV). Expressed formally, this valuation rule is

$$\min\{RC_t,\ EV_t\} \text{ where } EV_t = \max\{PV_t,\ NRV_t\}$$

EKM demonstrate that this valuation rule implies economic relevance for the periodic ARR. This is an intellectual breakthrough, given the difficulties with ROE described in this chapter.

As a first step, the abnormal earnings model is expanded to separate the expected abnormal earnings of period 1 from that of subsequent periods

$$P_0 = B_0 + (A_1)(1 + k)^{-1} + \sum_{\tau=2}^{\infty}(A_\tau)(1 + k)^{-\tau}$$

Next, the value of discounted abnormal earnings starting in period 2 (the third term on the right-hand side of the equation above) is expressed in terms of the expected price and book value at the end of period 1

$$P_1 = B_1 + \sum_{\tau=2}^{\infty}(A_\tau)(1 + k)^{-\tau-1}$$

$$\sum_{\tau=2}^{\infty}(A_\tau)(1 + k)^{-\tau} = (P_1 - B_1)(1 + k)^{-1}$$

Combining this equation with the earlier equation for price gives the value of current accounting goodwill (price less book value) as the sum of the discounted abnormal earnings for the period and the value of expected goodwill after the end of period 1

$$P_0 - B_0 = \frac{A_t}{(1 + k)} + \frac{P_1 - B_1}{(1 + k)}$$

Finally, by decomposing abnormal earnings into the ARR and the cost of capital, we have:

$$P_0 - B_0 = \frac{B_0(ARR_1 - k)}{(1 + k)} + \frac{P_1 - B_1}{(1 + k)}$$

This equation can now be used to interpret the accounting rate of return. Deprival valuation implies that the second term on the right-hand side of the equation is non-negative, since book value would be written down to economic value as a minimum. This being the case, if current book value is positive and if, for example, the expected ARR exceeds the cost of capital, then book value must be at replacement cost. This is because a positive right-hand side to the equation implies positive goodwill, consistent with economic value exceeding asset valuations at replacement cost. The use of deprival valuation therefore leads to the single period accounting rate of return recording value creation unambiguously.

While this analysis suggests economic relevance for the accounting rate of return, it is important to recall that the model depends upon a specific method of asset valuation. A practical objection to this is that deprival values are not available to investors. More fundamentally, the conceptual difficulties in reporting deprival values compound the specific problems of all three of its underlying valuation bases. While the model makes the implicit assumption that the estimation of its asset values is feasible, the reality is that this estimation is similarly problematic to that of the share price itself.[17]

---

[17] Though note that asset valuations can be estimated on the basis of the *private* information of company management, whereas share prices rely on *public* information alone. Potentially, therefore, the application of EKM model could extend the information set upon which stock market prices are based.

Cash flow models – from shareholder value analysis to CFROI

Overview
- Discounted cash flow (DCF) model
- Price–cash flow (PCF) and enterprise value–cash flow (EVCF) ratios
- Shareholder value analysis (SVA)
- Cash recovery rate (CRR) and cash flow return on investment (CFROI)
- The real options approach to valuation

One of the key strengths of the abnormal earnings model is its direct relationship to an underlying DDM. In other words, its validity rests upon its capacity to adjust financial statement data in order to ensure consistency with a cash-flow-based valuation model. In a sense, this is an indirect way of saying that accounting data can be misleading, and that investors should have an eye on underlying cash flow data.

This chapter considers cash flow valuation models directly. First, a simple discounted cash flow (DCF) model is presented, and the relationships between this model and the DDM are explained. Ratios between cash flows and both enterprise value and shareholder value are then introduced and interpreted.

Three specific types of cash flow model are then reviewed. The first is shareholder value analysis (SVA). This model was created by Alfred Rappaport, whose book can claim to have initiated the popularity of the term 'shareholder value', giving it a central role in the language of financial markets.[1] In effect, the SVA model is a refinement of the DCF model. It retains the same framework and assumptions, but also attempts to model the relationships between the key determinants of shareholder value, thereby enhancing the usefulness of the cash flow approach.

The second model can be referred to by either of two names, which are the cash recovery rate (CRR) or the cash flow return on investment (CFROI). This approach uses financial statement data to approximate the internal rate of return on a company's existing assets. It is, in effect, an alternative to the return on equity (or return on capital employed), though based upon different assumptions.

Finally, the chapter concludes with an introduction to real options, which is a relatively recent and novel approach to valuation. The real options framework

---

[1] Rappaport's book was first published in 1986, and then revised in 1998. See reference at the end of the chapter.

can be particularly useful in estimating the value of investments that have highly uncertain future payoffs, such as R&D, oil exploration or (more generally) technology-based companies.

10.1 Discounted cash flow model

Corporate managers commonly use discounted cash flow (DCF) models in the evaluation of individual investment projects. It is also fairly common to find DCF models applied to a company as a whole, with the company being viewed simply as a collection of investment projects. In this respect, the DCF and DDM valuation models appear to be very similar frameworks for discounting future cash flow.

The DDM is a shareholder value model because it deals only with the net cash flows to the shareholder, calculated after the deduction of interest payments. In contrast, the DCF model is used to estimate enterprise value. It takes cash flow before interest payments, which is a measure of cash flow that represents the return to both shareholders *and* debtholders. Since each model takes cash flow belonging to different claimants, so too each requires a different cost of capital. For the DDM, the appropriate cost of capital is simply that of the shareholders (the cost of equity), whereas for the DCF the cost of capital must also reflect the claims of the debtholders. The appropriate measure is a weighted average of the cost of equity and the cost of debt. This is commonly known as the WACC (weighted average cost of capital). As an illustration, consider the following example shown in Table 10.1, where a company is expected to earn its cost of capital.

The company is financed by $400 000 equity and $600 000 debt, at a cost of 20% and 10%, respectively. As Table 10.1 shows, this implies that the WACC

Table 10.1 DCF vs. DDM valuation models – constant, normal return

		Cost of capital	Capital structure	Weighted cost of capital
1 *Calculation of the WACC*	Equity	20%	40%	8%
	Debt	10%	60%	6%
				14%
2 *Valuation data ($'000)*		1	2	3 ...
Capital structure	Equity	400	400	400 ...
	Debt	600	600	600 ...
	Total	1 000	1 000	1 000 ...
Operating cash flow		140	140	140 ...
Interest		60	60	60 ...
Cash flow available for shareholders		80	80	80 ...
Dividends		80	80	80 ...
Retained cash flow		0	0	0 ...

for the company as a whole is 14% (equal to (20% × 40%) + (10% × 60%)). The company is non-value creating, and it is therefore expected to achieve a return equal to its cost of capital, such that an investment of $1 000 000 generates a $140 000 operating cash flow in the first year.[2] The interest payment is $60 000 ($60 000 × 10%), leaving $80 000 available for shareholders. The whole of this $80 000 is paid as dividends, such that there is no retention of net cash flow and the capital structure remains unchanged. In the second and all subsequent years in perpetuity, the same pattern is repeated. There is therefore a perpetuity net cash flow of $140 000, a perpetuity dividend stream of $80 000, and a perpetuity interest payment of $60 000.

In this example, the enterprise value can be derived in one of two ways. First, the dividend and interest streams can be capitalized at their respective costs to give a value for each of equity and debt, and these two values can be added together. For equity, the DDM is, in effect, being used in its simple dividend yield form. The value of equity is simply dividends divided by the cost of equity capital ($80 000/20% = $400 000). Likewise, the market value of the debt is $600 000.

The second way to derive enterprise value is to discount the operating cash flow at the WACC, thereby valuing equity and debt jointly. It can be seen that this gives the same answer, because a perpetuity cash flow of $140 000 is worth $1 000 000 with a 14% cost of capital. In this example, it is therefore theoretically equivalent to use the DCF model with discounting at the WACC, or else a sum-of-the-parts valuation, with shareholder value estimated using the DDM.

The same conclusion can be reached if the company earns an abnormal return. Suppose, for example, that the company earns a perpetuity cash flow of 28%, double the previous level of 14%. In this case, the annual interest payment remains at $60 000, while the annual dividend increases to $220 000. The value of debt remains at $600 000 and shareholder value increases to $1 100 000 (equal to $220 000/20%), giving an enterprise value of $1 700 000. The same value is attainable by the DCF method, although this requires that the correct WACC is used, which in turn requires the correct measurement of capital structure.

There are two possible measures of capital structure. The first is based on the balance sheet, whereby the value of equity is equal to the book value of net assets. The second is based upon market values, whereby the value of equity is equal to the discounted value of future dividends. As was discussed in Chapters 5 and 6, a difference will arise between these two measures whenever (as in the example above) a company is expected to earn an abnormal return on book value.

It is the capital structure based upon market prices that is the correct one to use, because this reflects correctly the economic value of the investment made in the company. Shareholders do not expect to earn 20% on the original $600 000 investment in the company, but rather upon the $1 100 000 that their investment is now worth. Accordingly, the WACC must change to reflect the greater relative stake of shareholders in the overall economic value of the firm. Another way to view this is to recognize that abnormal returns benefit the shareholders and not the debtholders, since the interest payments are fixed and residual gains

---

[2] Investing cash flows and taxes are both implicitly assumed to equal zero in this example.

Table 10.2 DCF vs. DDM valuation models – constant, abnormal return

		Cost	Capital structure	Weighted cost
Calculation of the WACC	Equity	20%	64.7%	12.9%
	Debt	10%	35.3%	3.5%
				16.5%
$'000		1	2	3 . . .
Opening capital structure	Equity	1 100	1 100	1 100 . . .
	Debt	600	600	600 . . .
	Total	1 700	1 700	1 700 . . .
Operating cash flow		280	280	280 . . .
Interest		60	60	60 . . .
Cash flow available for shareholders		220	220	220 . . .
Dividends		220	220	220 . . .
Retained cash flow		0	0	0 . . .

belong to the shareholders. The capital structure based upon market values takes this into account, whereas a book value measure does not.

Table 10.2 shows the correct measurement of capital structure and the WACC, using market prices. In contrast to the earlier example, the WACC is now 16.5% which, when applied to the cash flow of $280 000, gives the correct enterprise value of $1 700 000. If the book-value-based WACC of 14% had been used, then the enterprise value would have been overstated.

The DCF model is used very commonly. Indeed, while sharing the same theoretical foundations as the DDM, it can be regarded as superior in so far as it separates more effectively the operating and financing decisions of a company. It values the whole of a company's operation, irrespective of how it is financed, rather than focusing on the equity-financed portion. This allows companies with different capital structures to be more readily compared with one another. For example, market capitalization can be a misleading measure of the relative size of two companies if their respective levels of debt differ. It is also more meaningful to compare variables such as sales with enterprise value rather than with shareholder value, because sales are generated by total capital employed and are independent of capital structure.[3] Finally, the separation of operations from finances is also helpful if individual business units within a group are valued separately, in a sum-of-the-parts valuation.

---

[3] The ratio of sales to enterprise value is being used increasingly commonly by analysts. One reason for its use is that it captures the scale of a company's operation relative to its value, thereby offering a crude benchmark of relative valuation that is (almost entirely) independent of a company's method of accounting. This benchmark has become especially important for internet companies, where profits are often negative but where growth in sales and market share is seen as fundametal to future value creation (see the discussion below on real options). It is important to recognize, however, that sales alone cannot be a measure of value, because operating costs and capital employed are ignored. At best, therefore, the sales-enterprise value ratio is a rough guide, and it is not a valuation model in its own right.

The DCF approach does, however, require more careful use than the DDM. For example, if the rate of return spread is not constant over time then the WACC must vary also. The working definition of cash flow must also be selected carefully, especially when operating cash flow is either re-invested or simply retained in the form of cash.[4]

Consider, for example, the case of a variable rate of return spread. Table 10.3 reports identical data to that above, except that the company achieves double its normal return in the first year, followed by a normal return in all subsequent years.

Table 10.3 DCF vs. DDM – the problem of abnormal returns ($'000)

	Year 1	Year 2	Year 3 ...
Operating cash flow	280	140	140 ...
Interest	60	60	60 ...
Net cash flow	220	80	80 ...
Dividends	220	80	80 ...
Retained cash flow	0	0	0 ...
Shareholder value – DDM (correct)	$517		
– DCF, constant WACC (incorrect)	$479		

The one-off gain of $140 000 in year 1 feeds directly into increased dividends. Its present value to shareholders is therefore equal to $117 000, which is $140 000 discounted at the 20% cost of equity. The underlying annual dividend stream of $80 000 has a present value of $400 000, such that shareholder value in total is $517 000. Added to the value of debt, this gives an enterprise value of $1 117 000. In turn, these market values imply a WACC of 14.6%. But when all operating cash flows are discounted at this WACC, an enterprise value of $1 079 000 results.

Why the difference? The reason is that the use of a constant WACC assumes implicitly that the cash flows generated in each period are attributable to shareholders and debtholders in the same proportion as the capital structure. This is equivalent to assuming that interest payments and earnings must either be constant over time or else that both grow at the same rate. If there is variation in the proportionate returns to shareholders, then the WACC must be adjusted each year to take this into account. In the example above, the correct enterprise value is given by discounting cash flows from year 2 onwards at 14%. This gives an enterprise value at the end of year 1 which, when added to operating cash flow in year 1, should be discounted to present value at 14.6%. In general, if a DCF model is used to estimate enterprise value, then the valuation of a variable return on capital employed requires that the WACC is itself variable. If, however, interest payments are deducted from enterprise cash flow to give cash flow to shareholders,

---

[4] There are also additional difficulties with the WACC, notably in adjusting for taxation, inflation and currency.

Table 10.4 DCF vs. DDM valuation model – the effect of retained cash flows ($'000)

	Year 1	Year 2
Opening capital	1 000	1 100
Operating cash flow	100	110
Dividends	0	210
Closing capital	1 100	1 000
PV closing capital		826.4
PV net cash flows	90.9	90.9
PV DCF	1 008.3	
PV dividends	173.6	
PV DDM	1 000	

then debt and equity can be valued separately and the problem of adjusting the WACC is addressed directly.[5]

A second problem with using a DCF model can arise whenever cash flow is retained by a company and re-invested. A common criticism of the DDM is that it values only the cash flow distributed to shareholders, in contrast to the DCF model, which is perceived to value the cash flow generated by the company's operations. The DCF model therefore appears more useful because it focuses on the sources of value creation, rather than on the subsequent distribution. In reality, however, this view is somewhat misleading, and the models are much closer to one another than is typically acknowledged. To illustrate this, consider the two-period example (Table 10.4), where the ROE in each period is 10% and where net cash flow is retained at the end of the first year and paid out at the end of the second. For simplicity, the example assumes that there is no debt and that the rate of return spread is 0 (i.e. the cost of equity is equal to the ROE of 10%).[6]

Cash flow of $100 000 is earned in year 1, representing a 10% return. This is re-invested, causing the book value to increase to $1 100 000 at the start of year 2. A 10% return is earned again in year 2, generating cash flows of $110 000. Cumulative net cash flows are then paid as dividends, such that shareholders receive $210 000 at the end of year 2. If this $210 000 is added to the book value of $1 000 000 at the end of year 2, then the total present value is $1 000 000, consistent with no value being created.

The present value estimated by discounting operating cash flow is $1 008 300 rather than $1 000 000. This is because the implicit assumption is made that the $100 000 year 1 cash flow is made available to shareholders, whereas in fact it is re-invested. If $100 000 is discounted at the year 1 discount rate, then it is implicitly assumed to be worth $110 000 at the end of year 2, when in fact only

---

[5] It should be noted that a change in capital structure will itself lead to a change in shareholders' required return. For example, an increase in shareholder value relative to debt will decrease gearing, which itself might be expected to decrease the cost of equity.

[6] If the ROE is constant then it must equal the IRR (see Chapter 8). In turn, since the company is non-value-creating, the IRR must equal the cost of capital. All are equal to 10%.

$100 000 is actually available to shareholders. And it is this $10 000 difference that, when discounted to present value, is the $8.30 difference between the DCF and the DDM valuations. If, therefore, cash flow is re-invested, discounting cash flow from operations will lead to an over-valuation of the company.[7] To allow for this, the DCF method requires the use of free cash flow, which is operating cash flows net of investing cash flows, as defined in Chapter 5. It is therefore the net cash flow between the company and its providers of finance that is being valued, regardless of whether a DCF or a DDM approach is adopted. The only difference between the two models is that the DCF model incorporates the value of debt rather than just that of equity. In neither case is the value created by a company's operations somehow disentangled from the sources of finance. This is much the same conclusion that was reached in the analysis of the abnormal earnings model in Chapter 9. The measurement of shareholder value in terms of book value and earnings required embedded assumptions about dividend policy. Likewise, forecasts of net operating and investing cash flows imply forecasts of cash flows between a company and its providers of finance.

10.2 Price–cash flow (PCF) and enterprise value–cash flow (EVCF) ratios

This discussion of the DDM–DCF relationship can be extended to consider ratios between corporate value and current-period cash flow. Specifically, the derivation of the dividend yield from the DDM (see Chapter 2) is paralleled by the expression of the DCF in the simplified form of a cash flow ratio.

The above discussion highlights, however, that such a ratio must be based upon an appropriate definition of cash flow. It is common, for example, to find ratios of share price to cash flow (PCF ratios), which typically use operating cash flow, net of investment in working capital but before fixed capital investment. Yet there are two flaws with a measure of this type. The first is that the numerator and denominator do not correspond, since operating cash flows are not generated by shareholders' funds alone. The relationship of operating cash flow to share price depends in part upon capital structure, and higher levels of debt lead to a misleading decrease in the ratio. The second problem, which is similar to the first and similar also to the problems with EBITDA (see Chapter 5), is that fixed capital expenditures are arbitrarily ignored. Other things being equal, a capital-intensive company will have a misleadingly low PCF ratio.

Addressing both of these problems leads to the enterprise value–cash flow (EVCF) ratio. The use of enterprise value resolves the issue of capital structure, since the aggregate cash flows generated by a company are attributable to the sum of equity and debt investment. Meanwhile, the use of free cash flow takes into account fixed capital expenditure, and it is therefore a comprehensive measure of the cash flow returns to the providers of finance.

As with the dividend yield, however, the EVCF ratio is based upon a measure

---

[7] Another way to say this is that a DCF model based upon operating cash flow alone will over-value growing companies.

of the distribution of cash flows and it does not attempt to capture the sources of value creation. There is therefore a less straightforward economic interpretation of the EVCF ratio than of the PE ratio (or, indeed, of the equivalent ratio of enterprise value to NOPAT). This is because a simple growth rate assumption is less likely to hold for free cash flows than for earnings. In turn, this exposes a weakness common to all simple valuation ratios, namely that a valid growth rate is essential for the ratio to have a straightforward interpretation.

In practice, therefore, the EVCF ratio is likely to be of secondary importance. Yet it can also have an important role: this is so because of the objectivity and underlying importance of cash flows.[8] Since earnings are subjective, and since value depends ultimately on a company's ability to generate cash flow, the EVCF ratio is a potentially useful validator of earnings quality.

10.3 Shareholder value analysis (SVA)

While the EVCF ratio attempts to make the DCF model operational by making simplifying assumptions, an alternative approach is to impose some structure on the model. This is the route taken by Rappaport (1998) in his shareholder value model.[9] Rappaport builds a model that is grounded on different types of management decision, concerning operations, investment and financing. These decisions determine the 'value drivers' of the company. Specifically, operating decisions affect the level of sales growth and the operating profit margin (and associated taxes). Investment decisions affect the growth in fixed and working capital expenditure, and financing decisions affect the cost of capital. In turn, the value drivers are themselves the determinants of DCFs and, thereby, of shareholder value.

The shareholder value model has three distinctively strong features. The first is the explicit linkage between managerial decisions and valuation, which give operational meaning to the model. Second is the all-inclusive nature of the model, whereby the effects of different types of decision can all be evaluated against the common criterion of shareholder value maximization. For example, it becomes straightforward to assess the relative economic merits of decisions as diverse as capital expenditure, cost saving, revenue growth or changes in capital structure. It is also straightforward to disaggregate the total shareholder value of a company into the standalone values of its business units. Third, and finally, the validity of the model's forecasting assumptions can be reality-tested against the company's own historic performance, and also against the realizations and expectations of benchmark companies.

The framework of Rappaport's model is as shown in Figure 10.1.[10]

This framework is used to structure the data in a DCF model, as is demonstrated in the numerical example in Table 10.5.

---

[8] One aspect of the importance of cash flow is the need to recover outlays as quickly as possible. In this respect, the EVCF ratio can be viewed as a form of payback ratio, since it captures the number of years of current free cash flow required to justify the enterprise value.

[9] Rappaport co-founded the Alcar Group Inc., which offers software services based around the shareholder value model.

[10] See Chapter 4 of Rappaport (1998) for both the diagram and the numerical example used here.

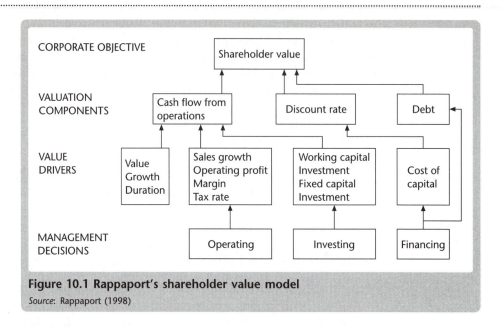

CORPORATE OBJECTIVE

VALUATION COMPONENTS

VALUE DRIVERS

MANAGEMENT DECISIONS

Figure 10.1 Rappaport's shareholder value model
Source: Rappaport (1998)

Table 10.5 Shareholder value analysis

Value driver assumptions

Sales growth rate	10.5%
Operating profit margin	8.0%
Tax rate	35.0%
Incremental fixed capital investment rate	24.0%
Incremental working capital investment Rate	18.9%
Weighted average cost of capital	10.0%[11]
Forecast horizon	5 Years

Data ($'000)	0	1	2	3	4	5	Terminal value
Sales	100.00	110.50	122.10	134.92	149.09	164.74	
Operating profit		8.84	9.77	10.79	11.93	13.18	13.18
Tax		3.09	3.42	3.78	4.17	4.61	4.61
Fixed capital investment		2.52	2.78	3.08	3.40	3.76	
Working capital investment		1.98	2.19	2.42	2.68	2.96	
Cash flow		1.24	1.37	1.52	1.68	1.85	8.57
							85.67
Discounted cash flow		1.13	1.13	1.14	1.14	1.15	53.19
Enterprise value	58.89						
less market value of debt	10.00						
Shareholder value	**48.89**						

Source: Rappaport (1998)

---

[11] The example makes the simplifying assumption of a constant WACC.

Shareholder value is $48 890, which is equal to enterprise value minus debt. In turn, enterprise value is comprised of the value of a company during a forecast period and the terminal value thereafter. In this example, the present value of cash flow during the forecast period is $5 700, and the company's terminal value of $85 670 has a present value of $53 190, giving an enterprise value of $58 890 (see below for the calculation of terminal value).

There are two possible rationales for splitting the overall valuation into a forecast period and a terminal value. The first is that the forecast period is measured to include all years in which the company is creating (or, indeed, losing) shareholder value, whereas the terminal value is based upon the assumption of normal returns. Alternatively, a second rationale is that the forecast period extends as far as is reasonably possible, given available information, and that terminal value therefore makes the plausible (but untestable) assumption of normal returns. Either way, the first value driver in the model is termed 'value growth duration' because it reflects the period over which the rate of return spread is expected to differ from zero.

The shareholder value model is a structure within which financial statement data can be used to extrapolate financial performance. The dynamics of the model rely heavily on the second value driver, which is the sales growth rate. The assumption that is made for this growth rate will depend upon recorded performance in previous income statements, adjusted for the analyst's judgement of future market conditions. The assumed level of future sales is critical, because it feeds directly, by means of additional value drivers, into a comprehensive financial forecast. The expected operating profit margin and tax rate, which are themselves extrapolated from the financial statements, are applied to the forecasted sales. Likewise, the assumed level of investment required for fixed and working capital is also extrapolated.[12] It is assumed that additional investment is driven by the change in sales, because a larger scale of operation requires a proportionately larger amount of fixed and working capital. Similar to the forecasts for the income statement, these forecasts of capital requirements will be based upon an historic analysis of the financial statements, but will be adjusted in the light of expected changes in fixed asset productivity, working capital efficiency and so on.

Notice that the terminal value calculation is based upon the continuation in perpetuity of the after-tax operating profit in year 5, with the assumption that there will not be any further requirement for capital investment. This is equivalent to assuming that the annual depreciation charge is equal to the annual need for replacement fixed capital expenditure, and that working capital does not change. In other words, the business is assumed to be in a no-growth state. This is a convenient assumption because it allows the business to be valued as a perpetuity cash flow, which is in turn consistent with the business being non-value creating beyond the forecast horizon. As was demonstrated in Chapter 3, it does not matter whether or not the business actually grows beyond the forecast period, because

---

[12] The forecast for operating profit margin is calculated after depreciation, and the forecast for fixed capital expenditure is also a net amount after depreciation. Operating profit therefore overstates cash inflow by precisely the same amount that investment expenditure understates cash outflow, with there being no effect on the calculation of overall net cash flow. This method gives a more meaningful measure of the operating profit margin, consistent with the discussion in Chapter 5.

the assumption of a zero rate of return spread means that growth does not affect its terminal value. The actual terminal value above is $85 670, which equals profit after tax ($13 180 less $4 610) divided by the 10% cost of capital. This $85 670 is the terminal value at the end of year 5 which, when discounted back to the current time, has a present value of $53 190.[13]

The example presented here makes simple assumptions, using the value drivers in a rather naïve way. One of the strengths of this model, however, is that it can accommodate any degree of complexity. For example, rather than imposing a top–down assumption of a sales growth rate, a bottom–up forecast can be created using any level of product and market data that is available. Likewise, working capital data (for example) can be projected at the same level of detail, building in assumptions about efficiency gains from growth, from improved supply chain management, and so forth. In turn, these bottom-up forecasts can be used to work backwards to overall growth rates in sales and in working capital, and then these overall rates can be reality-tested against the past experiences of the company and its industry peer group. In this way, by highlighting the relationships between the underlying value drivers, the shareholder value model exposes the underlying assumptions behind a valuation.

Shareholder value analysis in practice

BP Amoco, the UK-based oil group, yesterday unveiled a shift in emphasis towards organic growth after years of cost-cutting and acquisitions. Sir John Browne, chief executive, said: 'We have moved from a phase of rationalisation to a phase of expansion' . . . For BP Amoco, the need to push top-line growth was perhaps more pressing than for its competitors because it is more advanced in cutting costs and integrating acquisitions. One analyst said: 'BP is the first to break the mould in stepping up its spending. It wants to prove that there is still growth potential' . . . However, Alan MacDonald, an analyst at UBS Warburg, said: 'The shift in emphasis for BP perhaps appears more dramatic because they have had such a strong focus on cost cutting in the past two years, at times at the expense of growth' . . . Sir John said BP Amoco would use its strong global position to boost growth, but that the group would continue to focus on taking cost out of its operations and using capital efficiently.

Source: Financial Times, Thorold Barker, 12 July 2000

In aiming to maximize shareholder value, BP has at least three strategic alternatives. These are the creation of value through acquisitions, through cost-cutting and rationalization, or through capital expenditure and organic growth. On the face of it, these alternatives are difficult to compare, yet their relative merits can (in principle) be assessed straightforwardly within a shareholder value model. The first and third alternatives concern operating, investing and financing decisions and thereby affect all value drivers, while the second alternative is more straightforwardly focused on operating value drivers (though presumably also with an impact on working capital investment, in particular). In all three cases the strategic decisions can be taken against the common benchmark of shareholder value.

---

[13] There are alternative, theoretically equivalent ways in which to calculate the terminal value. For example, the assumption of a zero rate of return spread implies a normal PE ratio. For a 10% cost of capital, the normal PE equals 10, and it can be seen that simply multiplying the year 5 profit after tax by 10 gives the terminal value.

10.4 Cash recovery rates (CRR) and cash flow return on investment (CFROI)

A quite different approach to using cash flow data arises by focusing on the estimation of the internal rate of return. In Chapter 8, it was shown that the accounting measure of return on equity is of limited use in this estimation. There is, however, an alternative approach to deriving an estimated IRR from financial statement data. This approach originated under the name 'cash recovery rate' (CRR), and its early proponents included Ijiri (1978), Salamon (1982) and Stark (1987). In recent years, the practitioner-oriented work of Madden (1999) has brought the approach into the financial markets mainstream, under the name 'cash flow return on investment' (CFROI®).[14] This section will review the underlying logic and merits of the CRR, and it will then explore the specific strengths and weaknesses of the CFROI model.

Any attempt to estimate the IRR using financial statement data runs into the fundamental problem that the IRR necessarily requires some forecast of the future. A financial statement-based estimate of the IRR equates the cost of the shareholders' investment in a company, as represented by the book value of the company's assets, with the cash flow stream that the assets generate. For any company at any given point in time, therefore, the estimation of the IRR requires a forecast of the expected life of the company's assets and the cash flow generated in each year of this life. The accounts in themselves are historic, of course, and therefore able to provide only limited input to these forecasts. Moreover, the accounts report an aggregation of a company's activities. While any company may be regarded as comprising a series of different investment projects, each at different stages of their lives, with different capital investments and cash flow payoffs, the accounts report only the aggregate asset value and aggregate cash flow at any given point in time. This presents a practical problem in forecasting cash flow in that the IRRs of individual projects cannot be estimated directly.

Of necessity, both the CRR and the CFROI models make simplifying assumptions that deal with this fundamental forecasting problem. The simplest set of assumptions can be illustrated with an example. Suppose that a company has a gross book value of assets of $1 000, an annual depreciation charge of $250 and a cash flow for the year of $400. It seems reasonable to assume that the company's assets have a life of four years, since the gross book value is four times the depreciation charge. If the gross book value is taken as the amount of invested capital, and if the cash flow is assumed to continue at its current level over the four-year life of the assets, then the company's IRR is estimated to be 22%. This is shown in Table 10.6.

The CRR is simply the ratio between the cash flow during year 1 and the gross book value of assets at the beginning of year 1. Since the book value represents the cash invested by shareholders in the business, and since the cash flows are annual returns, the CRR can be regarded as a cash-based return on investment.

If expected cash flow is constant, then there is a simple relationship between the IRR and the CRR. In particular, the CRR is equal to the reciprocal of the present value of an annuity payable over the life of the assets. From the example

---

[14] CFROI® is a registered trademark of Holt Value Associates, LP.

Table 10.6 Estimating the IRR on existing assets

	Year 0	Year 1	Year 2	Year 3	Year 4
Cash flows		400	400	400	400
Gross book value of assets	1 000				
IRR	22%				
CRR	40%				

above, with a discount rate of 22%, the present value of $1 every year for four years is $2.49.[15] The reciprocal of 2.49 is 40%, which is the CRR. This leads to a simple way of estimating the expected IRR from the existing assets of the company. As above, take the ratio of cash flow to the gross book value of assets.[16] This is the CRR. Then calculate the average life of the company's assets by dividing the gross book value of tangible fixed assets by the annual depreciation charge. Finally, derive the IRR as the discount rate that equates the CRR with the reciprocal of an asset-life annuity.

The CRR can be considered analogous to the ROE in that both are single period measures of the rate of return. In view of the limitations of accounting information, neither the CRR nor the ROE can be regarded as reliable methods for estimating the IRR. The CRR does have an advantage over the ROE, however, in that it attempts explicitly to take into account future cash flow, making it conceptually closer to the IRR. Moreover, it relies on cash flow data and is not subject to the distortions caused by depreciation. To the extent that it is less reliant on accounting practice, it can be compared more easily between companies and across borders.

Necessarily, however, the CRR makes strong assumptions. Some of these can be dealt with by extending the simple model presented so far. It is not, in fact, necessary to assume that the cash flow recoveries from an investment are constant over time. For example, any given investment might have a high payoff in early years, followed by a diminishing payoff in later years. This can be dealt with by assuming a relationship between annual cash flow, analogous to the persistence parameter in the abnormal earnings model. Likewise, a growth rate can be assumed

---

[15] An annuity is an annual payment for a limited period, whereas a perpetuity is an infinite annual payment. The value of an annuity can be calculated as the difference between the present values of a perpetuity that starts now and one that starts at the end of the annuity. For example, $1 in perpetuity with a 22% discount rate has a present value of $4.54, while the same perpetuity starting four years from now has a present value of $2.05. The difference of $2.49 is the value of a four year annuity.

[16] The definition of the appropriate measures of book value and cash flow depends upon whether one takes an enterprise value or a shareholder value perspective. If the latter, then book value should be the gross book value of fixed assets (i.e. net book value with cumulative depreciation and amortization added back), plus working capital (current assets less current liabilities, less the book value of debt). Cash flow should be measured consistently, and it would therefore be operating cash flow (i.e. operating profit with depreciation and amortization added back, and after any change in working capital) less interest and tax. Financing cash flow and capital expenditure can be ignored on the basis that they do not form part of the IRR calculation for the beginning-of-year asset base. If an enterprise value perspective is chosen, then assets should not be stated net of debt, and cash flow should be stated before interest and tax.

if a company increases its level of investment over time, and the simple relationship above between the CRR and the IRR can be adjusted accordingly. Salamon (1985) derives a general model of the relationship between the CRR and the IRR, which incorporates both a time profile of cash recoveries and a growth rate.[17]

Although the CRR model can be modified to allow a variable future cash flow pattern, the underlying problem remains of the difficulty of forecasting. This problem is very much the same as that for the abnormal earnings valuation model. It was seen in Chapter 9 that a practical obstacle to the estimation of the persistence parameter is the need for book value, earnings and ROE to be 'economically meaningful' measures, with their current values being informative of their future values. Likewise, the PE ratio is not straightforward to interpret when there is no simple relationship between current earnings and sustainable earnings. So too, the CRR methodology is dependent upon the assumptions implicit in the financial statements, and it does not escape the important influence of accruals. For example, the calculation of CRR assumes that the gross book value of net assets represents shareholders' invested capital. This will be distorted to the extent that the company has invested in intangible fixed assets, such as R&D, advertising and the like, because these are not reflected in gross book value. Related to this, the assumption that asset life can be calculated by reference to tangible fixed assets ignores that the life of an investment project might, in fact, be better represented by the life of a patent, or the goodwill generated by a marketing campaign. It also ignores that the company is comprised of a range of different investment projects, each with different assets, and that the future asset life might not be well represented by the current rate of depreciation. In general, the CRR methodology actually requires the implicit assumption that the company's investment projects are all alike, and that the total cash flow of any given year therefore includes amounts relating to assets of all ages.[18] If there is actually a variety of investment projects, and if the method of accounting does not capture shareholders' invested capital and, further, if the annual cash flow is volatile, then there is no simple relationship between the CRR and the IRR.

The CRR can be viewed as an alternative to measures such as the ROE. The CRR brings its own particular insights, makes its own assumptions and is subject to its own set of measurement problems. On a theoretical level, it is neither a better nor a worse approach than the other valuation models already reviewed. Its usefulness depends, as with other models, upon the data available and it can usefully be calculated in addition to other measures to see whether or not consistent results emerge.[19]

---

[17] Salamon's model is as follows. CRR $= v[(1 + v)^n - w^n][(1 + r)^n(1 + r - w)]/[(1 + v)^n - 1][1 + v - w]$ $[(1 + r)^n - w^n]$, where v is the rate of growth, w is a cash recovery profile parameter (e.g. $w = 1$ if cash flows are constant), n is the asset life and r is the IRR.

[18] Note the inclusion in the CRR calculation of the gross book values of all assets, irrespective of whether they are new or nearing retirement. This requires an assumption that the associated cash flows have the same degree of maturity, which is satisfied by assuming that all investment projects are homogeneous.

[19] A major limitation of the CRR model is that the future profile of cash flow is difficult to predict, and yet the model requires some assumption to be made about them in order to estimate the IRR from the CRR. In this respect some fairly reassuring empirical evidence comes from Griner and Stark

This discussion can be reinforced and extended by considering the CFROI approach. A worked example will be presented, showing the derivation of the annual CFROI measure and making explicit the close relationship between the CRR and the CFROI (including the assumptions made by each).

Following closely the principles of the CRR approach, the CFROI model uses cash flow data to estimate a company's internal rate of return. Additionally, the CFROI model takes a lead from Miller and Modigliani (1961) by dividing the total value of a company into two parts, an amount generated by existing assets and an amount due to investments that have not yet been made. So, for example, a company might have net assets of $20 000, with a present value of $30 000. Additionally, it might have the opportunity to invest in *future* projects with a positive NPV of (say) $10 000. The total value of the company would therefore be $40 000. In principle, this separation of current and future assets has a number of benefits. It allows a distinction between the current performance of the existing business and the expected performance of the future business. A CFROI is an expected IRR for an existing set of assets at a given point in time. There is therefore an annual CFROI measure for each year of a company's life, relating a specific asset base with a cash flow stream expected over the life of these assets. If calculated over a number of years, the CFROI measure is able, in principle, to identify trends in the underlying economics of the business. If, for example, the CFROI diminishes over time, then the company's rate of return spread is declining with its incremental investments, suggesting a declining potential to create value for shareholders. This is very similar in principle to the persistence parameter embedded in the abnormal earnings valuation model, and the trend in the CFROI over time has obvious implications for forecasts of business performance, and thereby for valuation. The trend in the CFROI can be viewed alongside the rate of growth of a company's assets, highlighting whether or not growth is value creating and thereby in the best interests of shareholders.

This reasoning suggests that the CFROI trend can be viewed alongside the amount of a company's goodwill. This is the approach taken in the DualGrade® scorecard system of Holt Value Associates[20]. Companies are ranked in two ways. The first rank is based upon their expected near-term CFROIs, and the second upon the value of their goodwill as a percentage of their total market value. If a company is ranked highly on the latter measure but not on the former, then this suggests that it might be over-valued, because the returns achieved on existing assets appear inconsistent with the expected returns from future assets.

A worked example of the CFROI methodology will allow an analysis of the strengths and weaknesses of the approach. This example is taken from Madden (1999), which is the most comprehensive reference for the CFROI approach (see Table 10.7).

(1991), who show that a ranking of firms based upon estimated IRRs is not very sensitive to the assumptions made about the cash recovery profile. In other words, while the absolute estimate of the IRR might not be reliable, this is compensated for by the CRR being relatively informative about the relative economic returns from different companies. This is reassuring because relative valuation is arguably the primary function of investment analysis.

[20] DualGrade® is a registered trademark of Holt Value Associates, LP.

Table 10.7 CFROI – Valuation data ($'000)

		Year									
		1	2	3	4	5	6	7	8	9	10
Operating cash flow											
Project number (IRR)											
1 (20%)			42.0	42.0	42.0						
2 (20%)				46.2	46.2	46.2					
3 (20%)					50.8	50.8	50.8				
4 (20%)						55.9	55.9	55.9			
5 (17%)							57.2	57.2	57.2		
6 (15%)								59.1	59.1	59.1	
7 (12%)									58.8	58.8	58.8
Gross operating cash flow		0.0	42.0	88.2	139.0	152.9	163.9	172.2	175.1	117.9	58.8
Investing cash flow											
Working capital	New	−20.0	−22.0	−24.2	−26.6	−28.9	−31.0	−32.9	0.0	0.0	0.0
	Release				20.0	22.0	24.2	26.6	28.9	31.0	32.9
	Net Change	−20.0	−22.0	−24.2	−6.6	−6.9	−6.8	−6.3	28.9	31.0	32.9
Capital expenditure		−80.0	−88.0	−96.8	−106.5	−115.5	−124.2	−131.6	0.0	0.0	0.0
Gross investing cash flow		−100.0	−110.0	−121.0	−133.1	−144.4	−155.2	−164.5	0.0	0.0	
Net investing cash flow		−100.0	−110.0	−121.0	−113.1	−122.4	−131.0	−137.9	28.9	31.0	32.9
Total net cash flow		−100.0	−68.0	−32.8	25.9	30.5	32.9	34.3	204.0	148.9	91.7
Balance sheet (extract)											
Working capital		20.0	42.0	66.2	72.8	79.7	86.5	92.8	63.9	32.9	0.0
Gross book value		80.0	168.0	264.8	291.3	318.8	346.2	371.3	255.8	131.6	0.0
Total		100.0	210.0	331.0	364.1	398.5	432.7	464.1	319.7	164.5	0.0
% assets non-depreciating		20.0%	20.0%	20.0%	20.0%	20.0%	20.0%	20.0%	20.0%	20.0%	0.0%

Source: Madden (1999)

The example shows a company with a ten-year life. The company starts a new investment project in each of its first seven years. Each project has an initial investment in both depreciating fixed assets (which are assumed to have zero residual value) and working capital (which is assumed to be recoverable on completion of the project). Also, each project generates operating cash flows for three years, starting one year after the project is initiated. This information allows an IRR to be calculated for each project. For example, the first project has an investment of $100 000 in year 1, followed by cash inflows of $42 000 for three years, and a recovery of $20 000 working capital at the end of the third year, giving an IRR of 20%. In fact, the IRR is 20% for the first four projects, but it then declines gradually to 12% by the time of the final project. In each year of the company's life, total cash flow is comprised of operating and investing cash flows. In year 4, for example, projects 1, 2 and 3 contribute operating cash flow of $139 000 in total, while the completion of project 1 releases working capital of $20 000, and the start of project 4 requires an investing cash flow of $133 100 ($106 500 in fixed assets and $26 600 in working capital). Overall, the cash flow for year 4 is therefore $25 900, and this is assumed to be distributed to shareholders. These activities are recorded on the balance sheet. For year 4, the balance sheet includes a gross book value of depreciating assets of $291,300 and working capital of $72,800, with both figures being the sum of expenditures for projects 2, 3 and 4.

Having presented the underlying data for the CFROI example, the next stage is to show the methodology behind calculating the CFROI itself. This will be done by taking year 4 as an example. Consider first Table 10.8, which shows how the

Table 10.8 Separate valuation of existing assets and future investments

$'000				Year				
DCF valuation		4	5	6	7	8	9	10
Net cash flow		25.9	30.5	32.9	34.3	204.0	148.9	91.7
Present value		23.5	25.2	24.7	23.4	126.7	84.1	47.1
Shareholder value	354.7							
Valuation of existing assets								
Operating cash flow		139.0	97.0	50.8				
Working capital release		20.0	22.0	24.2				
Total net cash flow		159.0	119.0	75.0				
Present value		144.5	98.3	56.3				
Total PV existing assets	299.2							
Value of future investment								
Investing cash flow		−133.1	−144.4	−155.2	−164.5	0.0	0.0	0.0
Operating cash flow			55.9	113.1	172.2	175.1	117.9	58.8
Working capital release						26.6	28.9	31.0	32.9
Total net cash flow		−133.1	−88.5	−42.1	34.3	204.0	148.9	91.7
Present value		−121.0	−73.1	−31.6	23.4	126.7	84.1	47.1
Net PV future investment	55.4							
Existing plus future value	354.7							

Source: Madden (1999)

shareholder value of the company in year 4 can be broken down into the present value of existing assets and the NPV of future investments yet to be made.[21]

As was the case with the CRR model, the CFROI approach takes the existing assets as its starting point, and attempts to estimate the internal rate of return that the company is expected to achieve on these assets. The actual calculation of annual CFROIs requires four data inputs, which are gross book value, expected cash flow, expected asset life, and the value of working capital recoverable at the end of the expected life. Just as in the earlier example, the CFROI approach operationalizes these data requirements by making the simplifying assumptions that cash flow is constant and that gross book values measure the initial investment. Additionally, the working capital at the beginning of year 4 is assumed to be released at the end of year 6. These data give a CFROI of 20%, as shown in Table 10.9.

Table 10.9 Calculating CFROI for year 4

	Year 4	Year 5	Year 6
Operating cash flow	139.0	139.0	139.0
Working capital release			66.2
Gross book value of assets	331.0		
CFROI (i.e. IRR)	20%		

Source: Madden (1999)

At this level the CRR and CFROI methods are barely distinguishable, with the exception that the CFROI method attempts to identify recoverable working capital. The practical distinction between the two methods lies in the specific measurement criteria for assets and cash flow under the CFROI approach. These adjustments are directly analogous to those made by Stern Stewart in deriving the EVA model. In both cases adjustments are made to underlying financial statement data in order to reduce ambiguity in the economic interpretation of a given valuation model. Some of the CFROI adjustments are reviewed in Madden (1999), although (as with EVA) a comprehensive analysis of these adjustments is not publicly available.[22]

---

[21] Notice that the whole of the value of future investment is subsumed within a company's current goodwill, and that goodwill is additionally comprised of the future value-added from existing assets.

[22] Some comment on these adjustments can be made. First, the estimation of asset life sensibly excludes non-depreciating assets from gross book value. Second, in calculating CFROI, gross book value includes purchased goodwill, capitalized leases and a general inflation adjustment. Third, the measure of 'cash flow' is taken from the income statement rather than the cash flow statement (Madden, 1999, p.108). This endorses the discussion in Chapter 5 of the role of accruals in smoothing cash flows and in enhancing the predictability of sustainable cash flow, but it also reinforces the argument above that the CFROI approach does not escape the difficulties of accruals accounting. Finally, non-depreciating assets are estimated to be recoverable at the end of the life of tangible assets. See Madden (1999) for further details on the calculation of CFROI. As a final comment, it is worth noting that incorporating the recovery of non-depreciating assets is more problematic than it might at first appear. It ignores holding gains or losses on these assets. Also, the relevant data are difficult to extract from the accounts. At any given point in time, non-depreciating assets are being invested in new projects while they are also being retired from competed projects. Stark (1987) shows that aggregate reported gross book values therefore understate invested capital while operating cash flow understates actual recoveries. A distorted estimate of IRR is the result.

A final comment on the CRR/CFROI methodologies concerns their implicit treatment of future cash flow, and the implications of this for the calculation of the IRR. In the example above for year 4 of the company's life, the calculated CFROI happened to be precisely equal to the true IRR. This was because the assumptions of the model held, notably in that the company comprised homogeneous investment projects, each with the same cash flow profile and the same 20% internal rate of return. In later years, however, there is some degree of variability between the projects. The effect that this has on the CFROI is as shown in Table 10.10.

Table 10.10 Annual CFROIs

				Year				
2	3	4	5	6	7	8	9	10
20.0%	20.0%	20.0%	20.0%	18.9%	17.2%	14.6%	13.5%	12%

Source: Madden (1999)

From year 5 onwards, the company starts to invest in projects with an IRR lower than 20%. Since the CFROI methodology extrapolates historic performance, however, it does not pick up this effect straight away. Rather, there is a time lag, with the gradual decline in the CFROI responding after a delay to the actual decline in the project IRRs. Only in year 10, where the assumption of homogeneous underlying investments is satisfied once more, do the CFROI and the actual IRR return to equality.

In concluding this discussion, a balanced summary of the CRR/CFROI approach is provided by Madden (1999):

CFROIs should not be calculated in an unquestioned belief that they are always useful. For a business entity having a large portfolio of ongoing projects, CFROIs provide useful indications of average ROIs earned on the portfolio of projects. Due to the varied NCR (net cash receipt) patterns over time for specific projects, all cross-sectional measures based on project data at a point in time will give readouts across time that differ from the real, achieved ROI on the specific projects. However, monitoring trends in CFROI can identify firms which may be investing in distinctly higher or lower project ROIs compared to the firm's average, or CFROI, level.

In other words, the CRR/CFROI approach is not able to predict an uncertain future any more than alternative valuation models. Its method of extrapolating performance into the future requires the underlying assumption that a company comprises homogeneous investment projects. If, in practice, this assumption does not hold, then there will be error in estimating the IRR but, in common with other valuation models, the approach is nevertheless able to generate useful information for investors.

This is a simple illustration of the CFROI being used as a measure of value creation. It is pointed out, correctly, that growth in earnings per share does not necessarily equate with growth in shareholder value added. Equally, however, CFROI should be viewed as but one of a number of possible indicators of value creation.

10.5 The real options approach to valuation[23]

In concluding this chapter, a relatively recent development in valuation theory will be discussed. This is the real options approach, which is based upon applying the insights of financial option pricing to real investment decisions, and thereby to corporate values. The distinctive strength of the real options approach is its recognition that there is value in having the opportunity (but not the obligation) to exploit an uncertain future. For example, a mining company may have untapped reserves that, at current market prices, cannot be extracted profitably. A DCF model would report negative present value, and the reserves would therefore be attributed a value of 0. There is always the possibility, however, that mineral prices will increase, and therefore the possibility that extraction might eventually prove worthwhile. This being the case, there is presumably value in the mining company's *option* to extract minerals when (and only when) it is profitable to do so. The reserves are not worthless, and an inherent weakness in DCF models is therefore suggested by the calculation of a negative present value.

The real options approach attempts to value options of the type just described. It does so by first recognizing a direct analogy between financial options and options to invest in 'real' commercial projects. This recognition allows commonly used financial option pricing models to be used in corporate valuations. Specifically, the celebrated Black–Scholes formula (Black and Scholes, 1973) underpins the approach. This formula shows that the value of an option is a function of six variables.[24]

---

[23] Excellent practitioner introductions to real options can be found in Copeland and Keenan (1998, a and b) and Leslie and Michaels (1997). A more advanced treatment is available in Dixit and Pindyck (1994).

[24] Specifically, the Black-Scholes option pricing model (adjusted for dividends) is the following: $Se^{-\delta t} \times \{N(d_1)\} - Xe^{-rt} \times \{N(d_2)\}$, where $d_1 = \{\ln(S/X) + (r - \delta + \sigma^2/2)t\}/\sigma \times \sqrt{t}$ and $d_2 = d_1 - \sigma \times \sqrt{t}$, and where S = stock price, X = exercise price, δ = dividends, r = risk-free rate of interest, t = time to expiry, and $N(d)$ = cumulative normal distribution function. The application of financial options pricing to real assets originates in Brennan and Schwartz (1985) and McDonald and Siegel (1986).

To illustrate this, consider a call option on a share, which allows the purchaser to buy the share in the future at a price that is agreed when the option itself is purchased. The six variables that determine the value of the option are as follows. First is the current share price, which equals the discounted value of future dividends. This is analogous to the present value of the cash flow from a real investment. Second is the exercise price, which is the agreed price at which the option-holder can purchase the share. For example, if the share price rises above the exercise price, then the option is said to be 'in-the-money', because it can be exercised profitably. The real-world analogy to the exercise price is the present value of all the future (irreversible) investment expenditures that are required to generate the investment's cash flow. For the mining company, the exercise price would be the present value of the fixed cost of preparing the mine for production.[25] The third variable is uncertainty, which is fundamental to the insights of the real options approach. Specifically, uncertainty for a financial option is the standard deviation ('variability') of the share price return. The greater the volatility, the more valuable the option, because wider fluctuations in the share price make the possible spread between the share price and the exercise price greater. Of great importance here is the fact that the option-holder has a one-way bet. He or she 'wins' if the share price exceeds the exercise price, but does not lose if the opposite happens. This is directly analogous to real investments, since the company has the opportunity but not the obligation to undertake any given investment. Indeed, the analogy is complete if the company has an exclusive right to invest, rather than just an opportunity. This was the case in the mining example, since ownership of the reserve gave the company an exclusive (and therefore valuable) extraction right. The fourth option pricing variable is time to expiry. In the case of a financial option, the holder will have a limited time during which exercise can take place. If the option is never in the money it will never be exercised. Clearly, the longer the time to expiry, the greater the chance that the option will be in-the-money, making value depend positively upon unexpired time. In real investments, the time-opportunity to invest is likely to be longer than for financial assets, and in some cases it can reasonably be assumed to be infinite. The fifth variable is dividends foregone during the period when the option is held. If the holder chooses not to exercise before a company pays dividends, then this income stream is foregone, representing a lost opportunity. Similarly, holding on to a real option can have an ongoing cost, in the form of foregone production (and hence foregone profits). Additionally, there might be ongoing costs of keeping the option alive (e.g. holding mineral reserves might imply maintenance costs), or in the form of losing business to competitors (e.g. withholding extraction may allow another company to satisfy market demand). Finally, the sixth variable is the risk-free interest rate, which matters because the present value of the exercise price falls as the interest rate rises, making the option more valuable.

---

[25] The ongoing costs of mineral extraction would be netted off the cash flows to give net cash flow per tonne mined, which would be the basis of the present value of cash flow (the first variable above).

The real options approach is a general valuation methodology, embracing not only discounted cash flows but also the value of options that would otherwise be ignored by a DCF model. In this sense, the DCF is a theoretically consistent sub-set of the real options model. For the real options approach to give a different valuation from a DCF model, three necessary conditions must hold. First, there must be uncertainty surrounding the underlying cash flow stream, and the greater the uncertainty the greater the usefulness of the model. Second, the company must have the right, but not the obligation, to make future investments that generate a future cash flow stream. It is this opportunity to invest in the future, should (uncertain) conditions turn out to be favourable, that distinguishes an option from any other form of investment. For example, if a company incurs capital expenditure with uncertain future returns, then unless there is the opportunity to make sequential investments that are *conditional* upon the favourable resolution of uncertainty, then the company does not hold any form of option, but has instead just made a one-off 'bet'. Finally, the investments made by the company must be irreversible (or 'sunk'), meaning that there cannot be any re-sale or recovery of cost once incurred.

These three conditions hold for a number of different types of real option, and the approach is therefore more general than it might at first appear. One type of option is simply that of deferring an investment. This was the option held by the mining company, which was able to defer investment until (and if) it became profitable. Another example of a deferral option would be where a company owns a patent that is not yet (but that may become) commercially exploitable. A second type of real option is a learning option, whereby a company can invest in order to reduce uncertainty. For example, the underlying uncertainty for the development of a drug might be whether or not the drug will be successful in clinical trials. One way to reduce this uncertainty is through further investment in research and development. This investment might appear unprofitable on a present value basis, but it gives the company the option of further investment to bring the drug to market if, and only if, it appears likely that the drug will be a commercial success. Finally, a third type of real option is a growth option, which takes the form of follow-up investments. For example, the concept of 'first-mover advantage' can be viewed as a real option. The first entrant in a market is likely to be best placed to invest in response to changing market conditions. The high valuations of some technology stocks (and especially internet, or 'dot.com' stocks) is rationalizable in this way. The first-movers, and those with greatest brand-awareness, have made past investments that set them up well to make future, sequential investments, should market conditions be favourable. Since there is a high degree of uncertainty about the future cash flow stream attributable to the markets in which technology-based companies operate, it is possible that future returns might be extremely favourable, implying that there is considerable value in holding an option to exploit them.

Table 10.11 presents a few examples of real options, explaining each of the variables relevant to their values.[26]

---

[26] The table excludes the risk-free rate of interest and the lost income stream, which are common to all options.

Table 10.11 Examples of real options

	Mineral reserve	Pharmaceutical	Mobile phone operating license
Cash flows	Market price for minerals	Revenue from drug sales	Revenue from phone users
Exercise price	Cost of making reserves accessible	R&D to bring drug to market	Future software/network development costs
Uncertainty	Market price for minerals	Success/failure of clinical trials	Demand for mobile communication, especially internet-related
Time to expiry	For practical purposes, can be assumed to be infinite	Patent life	Length of license

The real options approach offers a number of insights. Primarily, of course, the approach recognizes that holding an option in an uncertain world can, in itself, be valuable. Specifically, there is value in having an option (as opposed to a full commitment) to exploit an opportunity once uncertainty about it has been resolved. This is not recognized by the DCF approach, because of its underlying assumption that uncertainty reduces present value. The DCF model discounts expected (average) returns, meaning that future gains and losses are treated equally. If there is a wide range of possible outcomes, then the investment is considered risky and a high discount rate is applied to it, giving a low present value. In contrast, the real options approach recognizes that future gains and losses need not necessarily be treated equally, because a company might have the opportunity to exploit future investments that are profitable but to avoid those that are not. This leads to the insightful (though at first sight counter-intuitive) conclusion that uncertainty can be a good thing. As long as a company holds a real option to exploit a given market, then the greater is the uncertainty about that market, the greater is the potential value of the company's opportunity to choose to enter the market.

An example of this insight about uncertainty concerns the use of the share-holder value model. It might be the case that the model calculates a decline in shareholder value if aggressive sales growth is pursued. The model might ignore, however, that this sales growth allows the company to acquire a number of real options, for example by giving it strategically exploitable market positions, or by accelerating its product development and making it better positioned to respond to changing market conditions. In general, the real options approach confirms our natural instinct that there is value in being strategically well-placed to respond to an unpredictable future.

The valuation of real options does not, of course, come without its practical constraints. Apart from the underlying complexity of the model itself, the data requirements are high. In particular, while it is insightful to understand that uncertainty can be a source of value, it is another matter entirely to actually measure the amount of this value. In this respect, the model shares an intrinsic weakness of all valuation models, which is that historic data alone must be used to predict the future. This is especially problematic, of course, when uncertainty is high. For example, the inherently uncertain future impact of new technology, whether in the form of pharmaceutical research, genetic engineering or the internet, is both the reason why real options in these areas are valuable, as well as being the reason why they are difficult to value. If a technology is genuinely new, then there is no basis for estimating the volatility of growth in its future income stream.[27] In this respect, there is something self-defeating about attempting to value uncertainty. This said, though, the real options approach does at least offer a formal analytical framework within which to test a range of possible assumptions, and with which to assess stock market valuations. In this respect it offers considerable utility and insight, especially into strategic investment decisions and into the importance of managerial flexibility.

Real options in practice

Sony, the consumer electronics and entertainment giant, recently opened Metreon, an innovative entertainment and retail complex in San Francisco. Sony calls it an 'urban entertainment destination' . . . Sony faced what is in many ways a typical strategic investment decision when it had to decide whether and when to move forward with Metreon, and how many centres to build initially. A standard DCF analysis would include projections for revenues and costs for different possible locations . . . This is not sufficient. Strategically, the decision of how many Metreons to build initially cannot be analysed effectively without considering the way in which different decisions affect the company as time passes and uncertainty is resolved . . . (for example) What is the shutdown cost if the concept proves unsuccessful in the marketplace? How much will be learnt from the first locations that will help decide how aggressively to expand? Where to expand? How should later Metreons differ from the initial ones? What are the costs of delay given that consumer tastes may shift and competitors may beat them to market with a substitute in some target cities? . . . All of these questions involve issues of how initial strategic choices affect future decisions as uncertainty about the market, demand and costs of Sony's offering, and competitive responses play out. This is exactly the domain of real option analysis.

Source: Financial Times, Robert Gertner and Andrew Rosenfield, 25 October 1999

This example illustrates that real options can comprise an essential component of a company's goodwill. The strategic decisions that Sony faces at the time of its initial investment have a direct impact on its opportunity to create value in future years, and thereby a direct impact on the present value of the company. Of course, the practical difficulties of valuing real options should not be understated but, even in the absence of formal attempts at quantification, the mindset of real options analysis can help investors place a subjective evaluation on a company's uncertain future opportunities.

---

[27] The real options approach has been most successful in natural resource industries (oil and other commodities), where there is rich time-series data on the market prices of the option's underlying real assets. It is in these industries where real options are most directly analogous to financial options.

Summary

The main points from this chapter may be summarized as follows:

- DCF models can be used to estimate enterprise value by means of discounting free cash flow at the weighted average cost of capital.

- The shareholder value model provides structure to a DCF analysis. It models the underlying value drivers in relation to one another, making explicit the assumptions under-pinning a given valuation.

- The enterprise value–cash flow (EVCF) ratio is a highly simplified form of the DCF model. It should be used in preference to alternative cash flow ratios but is likely to be of secondary importance as a valuation model.

- The CRR/CFROI models estimate the IRR from financial statement data, based primarily upon the gross book value of net assets, cash flows in the current period, and a forecast of asset life. The approach has three main benefits. First, it views business performance in the context of the specific assets that are in place to generate that performance. Second, while anchored in financial statement data, it takes a forward-looking perspective. Third, the framework is based upon cash flow and IRRs, and is thereby consistent with valuation theory, generating data that are directly comparable across industries, across borders and over time. Against these weaknesses are the strong assumptions made by the approach, notably that accruals-based gross book values and depreciation rates provide a sensible foundation, and that current cash flows are sustainable.

- Real options provide a framework for valuation when there is a high degree of uncertainty, and where a company has the right (but not the obligation) to make future investments contingent upon the favourable resolution of uncertainty.

References

Black, F. and M. Scholes (1973). 'The Pricing of Options and Corporate Liabilities', *Journal of Political Economy*, 81(3), 637–54.

Brennan, M.J. and E.S. Schwartz (1985). 'Evaluating Natural Resource Investments', *Journal of Business*, 58(2), 135–57.

Copeland, T.E. and P.T. Keenan (1998a). 'How Much is Flexibility Worth?', *The McKinsey Quarterly*, 2, 38–49.

Copeland, T.E. and P.T. Keenan (1998b). 'Making real options real', *The McKinsey Quarterly*, 3, 128–141.

Dixit, A.K. and R.S. Pindyck (1994). *Investment under Uncertainty*. Princeton, NJ: Princeton University Press.

Griner, E.H. and A.W. Stark (1991). 'On the Properties of Measurement Error in Cash-Recovery-Rate-Based Estimates of Economic Performance', *Journal of Accounting and Public Policy*, 10(3), 207–23.

Ijiri, Y. (1978). 'Cash-flow Accounting and its Structure', *Journal of Accounting, Auditing and Finance*, Summer, 331–48.

Leslie, K.J. and M.P. Michaels (1997). 'The real power of real options', *The McKinsey Quarterly*, 3, 4–22.

Madden, B.J. (1999). *CFROI Valuation: a Total System Approach to Valuing the Firm.* Oxford: Butterworth-Heinemann.

McDonald, R. and D. Siegel (1986). 'The Value of Waiting to Invest', *Quarterly Journal of Economics*, 101(4), 707–27.

Miller, M. and F. Modigliani (1961). 'Dividend Policy, Growth, and the Valuation of Shares', *Journal of Business*, 34(4), 411–33.

Rappaport, A. (1998). *Creating shareholder value: a guide for managers and investors* (2nd edn). New York: Free Press.

Salamon, G.L. (1982). 'Cash Recovery Rates and Measures of Firm Profitability', *Accounting Review*, April, 292–302.

Salamon, G.L. (1985). 'Accounting Rates of Return', *American Economic Review*, 75(3), 495–504.

Stark, A.W. (1987). 'On the Observability of the Cash Recovery Rate', *Journal of Business, Finance and Accounting*, 14(4), 99–108.

11 Summary and review

The essential problem of valuation is the uncertainty of the future. If there were no uncertainty, then valuation would be simple. There would be no need for multiple methods of valuation, since there would be no difficulty in forecasting future business performance correctly. The only requirements for a valuation model would be to include all relevant cash flows and to take into account the time value of money. Shareholder value would be measured using the dividend discount model (DDM), while the discounted cash flow (DCF) model would measure enterprise value. All other valuation models would be redundant.

In practice, of course, the future is highly uncertain. This uncertainty is fundamental to financial markets, since it is the source of differences in opinion between buyers and sellers. It leads to considerable problems with the DDM and the DCF valuation models, however, because it deprives these models of essential data. In effect, they become theoretical statements of how much a company ought to be worth, rather than practical models that can be used to derive actual valuations. For example, the DDM values the dividend stream over the whole of the future life of a company. If analysts can only generate reliable dividend forecasts for a short time horizon, then the model cannot be applied. In this case, it becomes necessary to make simplifying assumptions that allow for the lack of knowledge of future dividends.

As was seen in Chapter 2, a possible approach to making the DDM operational is to re-state it in the form of a two-stage model. The first stage uses available dividend forecasts to estimate the sub-set of a company's total value that is attributable to the forecast period. The second stage then employs a simplifying assumption about future dividends to derive an estimate of the company's terminal value, which is the ongoing value beyond the forecast period. The simplifying assumption is likely to be that of a constant future dividend growth rate, coupled with a constant discount rate at which these dividends are converted to present value. In most cases in practice, the forecast horizon will be short, and the value of a company will be comprised mostly of the highly uncertain terminal value. This means that the dividend growth assumptions underlying terminal value are of considerable importance.

In the extreme case, a valuation can be based on a dividend forecast for the current year only, coupled with an assumed constant dividend growth and constant cost of capital. This is the basis of the dividend growth model (DGM, also known as Gordon's growth model). The DGM states that the rate of return that shareholders expect from an equity investment equals the dividend yield (the income component) plus the constant dividend growth rate (the capital gain component).

The DGM is useful because it is a practical means of implementing the DDM. It is also a helpful starting point in interpreting the stock market valuation of one company relative to another. Additionally, it highlights the theoretical relationships between the cost of capital, the income stream from an equity investment and the rate of growth in the capital value of the investment. For example, it can be used to demonstrate that growth is value-creating only if the return on new investment exceeds the cost of capital. On the other hand, the usefulness of the DGM is limited because its assumption of a constant rate of dividend growth hides a multitude of difficulties. Estimating this growth rate is highly problematic, not least because income and growth in the DGM are not independent of one another. For example, if a company pays a lower dividend in the coming year, then (other things being equal) its future dividend growth rate will be higher. In order to forecast the rate of growth of current dividends, the analyst must understand, first, how much of the company's current return on capital is paid out in dividends and, second, what the company's prospects are for future return on capital and, thereby, for future dividend growth. In short, the implementation of the DGM (or of any other dividend-based valuation model) requires forecasting the rate at which a company is expected to earn a return on capital, since it is this return that determines the company's capacity to pay dividends.

Indeed, the expected return on capital (or, more strictly, the rate of return spread between the return on capital and its cost) is necessarily of central importance to all valuation models. For example, it is the basis of a PE ratio that exceeds its 'normal' level (see Chapter 4), or a positive economic value added (EVA, see Chapter 9), or a cash flow return on investment (CFROI) in excess of the internal rate of return (IRR, see Chapter 10). Models such as EVA or CFROI can explicitly incorporate an assumption of a declining rate of return spread (sometimes termed a 'fade' rate). Chapter 4 also showed that such an assumption can drive the expected behaviour of the PE ratio over time. For example, the PE ratio can be expected to decline if a company's competitive advantage is eroded.

The common need of all valuation models to forecast the return on capital is the reason why financial statement data are important to valuation. The only practical way to forecast an uncertain future is to use information about the past. After all, the future itself is unobservable. The financial statements are important because they record the amount of capital invested by shareholders and other suppliers of finance, and they attempt to capture the economic return made on this capital. They are the primary means by which achieved economic performance is measured, and they are therefore the logical base from which to forecast future economic performance.

This role for financial statements has two implications for valuation models. First, the usefulness of the DDM and the DCF valuation models is limited in that neither is structured in terms of financial statement data. In contrast, a valuation model that expresses value in terms of financial statement variables, such as earnings and return on capital, is better able to link historic measures of financial performance to the forecasts embedded in valuations. A demand for financial-statement-based valuation models therefore arises. Second, since the financial statements provide imperfect measures of economic performance, they must be used with care in valuation. For example, if the financial statements overstate the 'true' return on capital, then it is possible that the forecasts will be artificially inflated also. More generally, if valuation models are grounded on assumptions about the economic relevance of financial statement data, then it is important to understand the extent to which these assumptions actually hold. For example, a valuation model might make the seemingly innocuous assumption of a constant return on capital over time, yet implicit in this are very strong, further assumptions about the method of asset valuation used in a company's accounts. The effective use of valuation models therefore requires an understanding of the fundamentals of the financial statements.

These two implications of financial statements for valuation models are at the heart of this book. Chapters 2, 3, 4, 9 and 10 focus on the derivation of alternative valuation models, while Chapters 5, 6, 7 and 8 review the practical difficulties in measuring economic performance in the financial statements. A key differentiating feature of the book is that it brings both of these fundamental subject areas into explicit focus. It is insufficient to consider valuation models without reference to the financial statements. To do this is to overlook fundamental reasons why multiple valuation models exist in the first place. Equally, a review of the financial statements is of limited use if there is no direct link to valuation models, since it is through this link that financial statements are useful to investors.

As was demonstrated in Chapter 9, the most general financial statement-based valuation model is the abnormal earnings model. A company achieves abnormal earnings whenever its return on capital exceeds its cost of capital. The abnormal earnings model shows the value of a company to be equal to the balance sheet value of its net assets plus the present value of its future abnormal earnings. A key feature of the approach, therefore, is a formal definition of the value of goodwill. The abnormal earnings model is actually a re-statement of the DDM (when measuring shareholder value) and the DCF model (when measuring enterprise value), and it therefore shares both the strengths and the weaknesses of these models. In particular, a key strength is that there are no constraining assumptions about underlying financial statement data. It does not matter, for example, whether expenditure is classified in the financial statements as an asset or an expense and, if the former, whether depreciation is charged over a long or a short period. This is because the structure of the model ensures that it is always the underlying cash flows that are being valued. This said, however, a fundamental weakness of the model is that it can be misleading when used over short periods of time. While abnormal earnings and value creation are synonymous over the long run, the abnormal earnings of any given period are determined as much by accounting policies as by true economic gain. It is insufficient, therefore, to forecast abnormal earnings for only one or two years hence. This is much the same problem that was encountered with the DDM and DCF models, namely that requisite forecast data are unlikely to be available.

In the absence of forecast data, one or more assumptions are needed that allow the extrapolation of currently available data, in the same way that the assumption of constant dividend growth allows the derivation of the DGM from the DDM. One such assumption, proposed by Ohlson, is that abnormal earnings decline gradually to 0. As discussed in Chapter 9, Ohslon's model enables a range of insights into the relationships between the balance sheet value of assets, earnings, abnormal earnings and the return on capital. In particular, the model can be shown to incorporate both the PE ratio and the price–book value ratio. For example, if a company has a high price–book value ratio combined with a low PE ratio, then this indicates that positive abnormal earnings are expected, but that the current level of earnings cannot be maintained.

A problem that Ohlson's model highlights rather than solves, however, is the need to measure reliably whether or not a company that reports positive abnormal earnings is genuinely creating value. At one level, this problem appears tractable, because the model has an intuitively sensible focus on whether, and for how long, a company is able to achieve a positive rate of return spread. What is not avoided, however, is the need for the financial statements to provide a meaningful measure of the return on capital in the first place. There would be little point in applying the economic intuition of a declining rate of return spread to a subjectively determined and unreliable measure of the return on capital. More generally, any forecast of abnormal earnings is likely to be better informed and more meaningful if the financial statements provide sensible historic measures of abnormal earnings.

As discussed in Chapter 5, the economic relevance of the financial statements is governed by the effectiveness of accruals in adjusting cash flow data. The accruals adjustments are intended to serve two purposes. First, they generate a balance sheet that records existing assets and liabilities, and that therefore measures shareholders' net worth. Second, they provide a measure of profit that is, in principle, a better indicator than net cash flow of a company's sustainable economic performance. There are, however, many practical difficulties in measuring economic performance in the financial statements. A manifestation of these difficulties is the existence of creative accounting schemes, which are introduced in Chapter 5. These schemes can be viewed as a sub-set of more fundamental measurement issues in the financial statements, which are the subject of Chapters 6, 7 and 8.

In the ideal world, the balance sheet would record the economic investment made by shareholders, and the income statement would measure the economic gain made on this investment in each consecutive period of time. The actual market value of the company would exceed the balance sheet value by the amount of 'pure' goodwill, which represents the return that the company is expected to achieve above its cost of capital. The income statement would then record the company's actual achievement over time in realizing the value of this goodwill. The economic value added (EVA) model makes adjustments to financial statements data in an attempt to capture this ideal measurement system.

In principle, the selection of appropriate methods of asset valuation can enable economically meaningful aggregate values for net assets. One example is replacement cost, which is the basis of Tobin's q and which allows a straightforward interpretation of the price–book value ratio (see Chapter 6). Another example is deprival value, which is shown by Edwards, Kay and Mayer to allow an economic interpretation of the accounting return on capital (see Chapter 9). In practice, however, there is a reluctance to depart from the historic cost valuation base, because of the subjectivity that this introduces. Indeed, the accounting principle of conservatism goes further still, and it requires typically that assets without verifiable market values (notably intangibles) are excluded from the balance sheet altogether. This can lead to high price–book value ratios that defy simple interpretation. Aggregate net asset values in such cases are unlikely to provide useful information to analysts. The focus must instead be on extracting information from individual components of the balance sheet. For example, even when total assets are under-valued, working capital ratios such as inventory turnover and debt turnover can still be informative.

An important reason to be concerned about the balance sheet is that the method of asset valuation affects directly the measurement of both earnings and the return on capital. For example, if the balance sheet incorporates increases in the market values of assets, then earnings (defined as comprehensive income) will record economic gains correctly in the periods when they actually occur. This allows a better understanding of economic performance. A qualification, however, is that comprehensive income measures historic economic performance regardless of whether this is predictive of future performance. Analysts must therefore adjust comprehensive income in order to exclude performance that is not sustainable. Their adjusted measure is termed 'normalized' earnings, and it might typically exclude exceptional items, goodwill amortization and so on. Finally, analysts' earnings forecasts must adjust normalized earnings further to account for information about the future that cannot, in principle, be derived from the historic financial statements themselves.

An understanding of the derivation of both asset values and earnings is important in interpreting the accounting return on capital. In general, there is likely to be a weak relationship between the return on either equity capital or total capital (ROE or ROCE) and the expected economic return on the company's investments (i.e. the internal rate of return, IRR). This distortion is minimized to the extent that a company's price–book value ratio is low and its return on capital is stable over a prolonged period. The economic relevance of the accounting return on capital therefore varies across industries. In all cases it is better viewed over the long term rather than as a single period measure.

While it is clearly of central importance to measure the return on capital, the difficulty of doing so should not be under-estimated. This highlights the interdependence of valuation models and financial statements. On the one hand, valuation models offer formal frameworks for understanding the determinants of a company's value. Yet the implementation of these models requires an understanding of the intrinsic strengths and weaknesses of financial statement data. On the other hand, the financial statements are a system for measuring economic performance, and they provide the foundation on which valuations are based. Yet they are insufficient, in themselves, as a means of valuing companies. In short, valuation models and financial statements are inextricably linked.

Index

Note: Page numbers in *italics* refer to Figures; those in **bold** refer to Tables